Family Mourning After War and Disaster in Twentieth-Century Britain

Family Mourning After War and Disaster in Twentieth-Century Britain

ANN-MARIE FOSTER

OXFORD
UNIVERSITY PRESS

OXFORD
UNIVERSITY PRESS

Great Clarendon Street, Oxford, OX2 6DP,
United Kingdom

Oxford University Press is a department of the University of Oxford. It furthers the University's objective of excellence in research, scholarship, and education by publishing worldwide. Oxford is a registered trade mark of Oxford University Press in the UK and in certain other countries

Published in the United States of America by Oxford University Press
198 Madison Avenue, New York, NY 10016, United States of America

British Library Cataloguing in Publication Data
Data available

Library of Congress Control Number: 2024934380

ISBN 9780192872005

DOI: 10.1093/9780191968129.001.0001

Printed and bound in the UK by
Clays Ltd, Elcograf S.p.A.

Acknowledgements

This monograph started life as a doctoral thesis—my thanks first and foremost therefore go to my supervisory team, James McConnel and Jenny Macleod. Thank you for your insight, encouragement, and willingness to sit in railway carriages while talking through ideas. My thanks especially go to James, who not only helped shape thoughts, but also impressed upon me the importance of regular writing practice—it is safe to say that without these lessons this book would not be in existence. My very deep thanks go to Helen McCartney and Ann-Marie Einhaus, who offered practical advice and intellectual encouragement post-PhD. Ann-Marie in particular has been a constant mentor and reassuring presence from the very start of this research journey, gently suggesting improvements and, in the final stages of this work, providing the time and support to work on the final draft of this monograph, which I am eternally grateful for. Thanks are also due to James Koranyi, who patiently encouraged some of my first attempts at explaining family memorialization. I am very grateful to the anonymous reviewers who offered such detailed and thoughtful feedback on the draft manuscript, and to Hannah Doyle, Stephanie Ireland, Jo Spillane, and Cathryn Steele at OUP, and Vasuki Ravichandran at Straive, who helped see this through draft stage and into print.

I am also grateful for the financial support which allowed this research. The AHRC Heritage Consortium generously supported the original thesis work this book is based on. L'Historial de la Grande Guerre provided a generous scholarship which greatly helped at an important point in the writing process. The Society for the Study of Labour History funded the majority of the research about Welsh mining disasters, and the Royal Historical Society generously funded writing time. My thanks to Queen's University Belfast, who funded the transition period of this work from thesis to book, and Northumbria University, who paid the licence fees for various texts. The images in this book were kindly supported by a Publications Grant from the Paul Mellon Centre for Studies in British Art.

Excerpts from the following have been reproduced courtesy of Brunel University London Archives and Special Collections: J. H. Armitage, 'Twenty Three Years or The Late Way of Life and Living by "The Exile"'; Lottie Barker,

'My Life as I Remember It'; Miss M. Collisson, 'Memories of a Country Rectory'; Jean Nettleton, 'Autobiographical Letter'. My thanks to the Trustees of the Mass Observation Archive, University of Sussex for allowing me to use excerpts from the 1937 Mantelpiece Directive and the 2014 Autumn Directive. Thank you to editors who have allowed material to be re-adapted from publications in *Twentieth Century British History* and *Public History Review*. The images in this book are provided courtesy of the John Johnson Collection at the Bodleian Library, Imperial War Museums, National Museums Wales, and Beamish Museum.

While working on this project a wide variety of people helped me. My deep thanks to Harry Taylor, who encouraged this research and shared his collection. Special thanks to the archivists and curators at all of the research sites listed in this book—it would not exist without your help and deep knowledge of your collections. Several colleagues read drafts of this work, and my thanks go to Alison Bailey, Yassin Brunger, Eli Davies, Livi Dee, Lara Green, Andrea Hetherington, Tom Hulme, Laura King, Harry Taylor, and Keira Williams for reading early versions of various chapters. Very special thanks go to Rowan Thompson for reading multiple chapters several times, providing much needed critical friendship and strong coffee. Hanna Smyth alerted me to several important collections which I am very thankful for, and Tommy Stephens has been a wonderful trove of knowledge about pertinent war literature. Leonie Hannan helped me access institutional support at a key moment, and Chris Kempshall answered a variety of awkward questions about the nitty gritty of publishing. My thanks also go to Alison Garden for being a fantastic writing partner, and to Irena Fliter and Livi Dee for providing writing support and encouragement. They, along with Natalie Calder, Anna Liesching, Susie Deedigan, and Síobhra Aiken were part of invaluable writing groups that got me through the final stages of this manuscript. The research for this book would not have been possible without the help of my friends, who have all been very patient with me. Thank you to Rachel, Rich, Ellen, and Evan and Sarah for letting me stay on your couches throughout my research time in London. Enthusiastic thanks to Bonnie for providing snacks, and to Caitlin for cheering me on. Rachel was so supportive she created ephemera for me, which I can see from my desk.

As befits a book on the subject of family, I wish to offer my deep thanks to mine. My parents, David and Sandra, have been keen supporters and encouraged a love of learning from a young age—to them I owe an enormous debt of gratitude. My sister, Rose, provided accommodation and snacks for all of the South Wales based research. My little brother, Ethan, and recently niece Lily, have provided a welcome distraction from work. My mum very kindly proof-read multiple chapters of the manuscript, as did my father-in-law, John. Any mistakes of course remain my own. Over the course of writing this book I gained a whole new family, the Larkins, who have proved themselves to be wonderful in-laws. My spouse, Eddy, has provided practical and emotional support, encouraged distractions in the form of A.C. and Bob, but, most importantly, has made writing about family all the more meaningful. Sadly, and almost inevitably with a project this long, while I gained new family during the writing of this book, some also passed away. I write with mementoes of them surrounding me, a praxis of domestic memorialization and the power of objects in family commemoration.

Contents

List of Figures

Supported by a Publications Grant from the Paul Mellon Centre for Studies in British Art.

Introduction

In 1909, days after the West Stanley colliery disaster killed 168 workers, the parents of one of the men, Thomas Anderson, carefully selected the verses for his In Memoriam card.[1] A decade later, E. Newman sent a photograph of his son, who died in the First World War, to the newly-formed Imperial War Museum following a public call for photographs of the deceased.[2] Awarded during the same war, a widow kept her husband's citation for a Military Cross in her bedroom until the 1970s.[3] In the late 1990s, Blodwen Bryan, the last surviving widow of the Gresford mining disaster which shook North Wales in 1934, said, 'you never forget them, never. It's sixty-two years since it happened and it's as fresh today as it was then.' Gesturing to the door, she told an interviewer 'there's a good likeness of my husband in the other room...a very good likeness. Many a one would've taken it down and put it away somewhere.'[4] Bryan did not. Two decades later, a woman placed a photograph of her Uncle Alfred, who died in the First World War, on her mantelpiece, to publicly honour his memory during the centenary.[5]

Across the twentieth century families occupied multiple spaces of grief. This book is concerned with those who died in war or disaster, in Britain, across the first four decades of the twentieth century and their memorial legacy. There were a number of similarities between the dead of these groups. The most striking was the roles taken over by local and national governments: officials took over control of bodies and the state assumed bureaucratic roles, both of which would traditionally have been the family's responsibility. This had a particular effect on the ways that families mourned: their choice and expression of grief through memorial material took on enhanced meanings, as it allowed the families of the dead to redress the power balance created through their loss of postmortem autonomy. Although the ways that these families were bereaved took place in different circumstances, the ways that

1 Beamish Museum, 2006-58.13. 2 Imperial War Museums, EN1/1/PHO/027(10).

3 Durham Light Infantry Collection, 4090.

4 Blodwen Bryan, quoted in Beverley Tinson, *The Gresford Letters: Aftermath of a Disaster* (Gwespyr, 2009), 51–2.

5 Mass Observation, Autumn 2014, A3434.

families grieved were recognizable to one another. They drew on common memorial practices, augmented and altered to take on special meaning after sudden death. How this nuance was internally articulated inside and outside of the family created powerful memory cultures, which grew apart as the century continued.

For the vast majority of British society there was little change in domestic memorial practices across the first four decades of the twentieth century. War and disaster brought with them community-based opportunities for mourning, from local memorials to special church services, and it is through public acts of remembrance at local war memorials and national memorial days that understandings of war memorialization have been built.[6] These remembrance acts were primarily shaped by politicians, civil servants, and local elites.[7] Ordinary families could attend, and were in some cases honoured at these events, but they did not shape these commemorations. In spite of these external sites, domestic memorialization remained the primary way that the families of the dead mourned their loved ones. It was through commemoration in the home, through memorial ephemera, and through discussion with friends and family that people remembered war and disaster dead.

Running alongside family commemoration in domestic spaces were the delicate effects of the state. Family mourning was subtly influenced through the bureaucracy of death, state involvement in domestic war memorialization, and, tacitly, through national memory institutions. Officialdom dictated to the bereaved in multi-varied ways separate to mass memorial days, which subtly altered the possibilities of mourning in the early twentieth century. These state-sponsored forms of family memorialization prompted a split in memory cultures between the war and disaster dead. The First World War was freighted with tragedy and pathos from the 1930s; however, the tragedy of mining disasters was not emphasized in collective national memory until the end of the twentieth century. What this meant for families was that

[6] Alex King, *Memorials of the Great War in Britain* (London, 1998); Adrian Gregory, *The Silence of Memory* (London, 1994); Mark Connelly, *The Great War Memory and Ritual: Commemoration in the City and East London 1916–1939* (London, 2002); Jenny Macleod, '"By Scottish hands, with Scottish money, on Scottish soil": The Scottish National War Memorial and National Identity', *Journal of British Studies* 49:1 (2010), 73–96; Catherine Moriarty, 'Narrative and the Absent Body: Mechanisms of Meaning in First World War Memorials' (Unpublished PhD, University of Sussex, 1995); Denise Coss, 'First World War Memorials, Commemoration and Community in North East England, 1918–1939' (Unpublished PhD, Durham University, 2012).

[7] Nick Mansfield, 'Class Conflict and Village War Memorials, 1914–24', *Rural History* 6:1 (1995), 67–87; Ken Inglis, 'The Homecoming: The War Memorial Movement in Cambridge, England', *Journal of Contemporary History* 27:4 (1992), 589–92; J. Bartlett and K. M. Ellis, 'Remembering the Dead in Northop: First World War Memorials in a Welsh Parish', *Journal of Contemporary History* 34:2 (1999), 233–4.

nationally mediated long-term memories developed alongside generational family memories in rather different ways. Families of the war dead were given a national platform to proclaim their individual loss, both at the immediate end of the First World War and again during the centenary, whereas the families of the disaster dead only had this opportunity in the 2000s, when the internet allowed the sharing of family history on a global platform.

Death Practices in the Early Twentieth Century

Cultural historians have long tussled with what the First World War meant for death rituals practiced by individuals and society. One way of trying to pinpoint this is through comparing family memorialization after other mass death events. Reading the effects of war and disaster in tandem allows for a deeper understanding of memorial afterlives. Moments of difference, as well as those of similarity, subtly mark the overlapping spheres that the families of those who died suddenly and violently had the unfortunate privilege of occupying.

The study of historical British death practices is generally steered by discussions of funerary customs in the long nineteenth century. Broadly speaking, the traditional argument is that a Victorian 'celebration of death' gave way to silence following the First World War. Material culture was a key indicator of mourning in these accounts, which suggest that elaborate and expensive Victorian funeral pageantry had given way to muted mourning by the interwar period, when families ceased to commission excessive funerals and memorial paraphernalia.[8] Yet these arguments are only true for a slim, privileged, section of society, as scholars who have written about this are themselves aware.[9]

When we turn to studies about working-class death cultures during the long nineteenth and early twentieth centuries, this idea of war as a point of rupture is complicated. Here, material objects, languages of grief, and a certain level of pragmatism characterize these experiences of death. Julie-Marie Strange's study of working-class expressions grief in the long nineteenth

[8] James Stevens Curl, *The Victorian Celebration of Death* (Newton Abbot, 1972), pp. xiii, 13–17. Also see Philippe Ariès, *The Hour of Our Death* (London, 1981), 559; David Cannadine, 'War and Death, Grief and Mourning in Modern Britain', in Joachim Whaley (ed.), *Mirrors of Mortality: Social Studies in the History of Death* (London, 1981), 230; Pat Jalland, *Death in War and Peace: Loss and Grief in England 1914–1970* (Oxford, 2012), 8.

[9] Cannadine, 'War and Death', 241; Jalland, *Death in War and Peace*, 9, 83–99.

century argues that death cultures were rich, and in some cases hidden, as families sought to subdue their expression of loss while the demands of everyday life and work continued.[10] In her work on Lancashire, Elizabeth Roberts argues that working-class attitudes to death were stable from the late 1800s to the 1940s, when they became increasingly medicalized and private. Her research found that early twentieth-century working-class families were highly familiar with death, grieving their loved ones, but also able to speak about the dead with an element of pragmatism and acceptance of their loss.[11]

These studies of working-class cultures point to a stability of death practices in the interwar period. Scholars of the First World War have supported this interpretation, such as Jay Winter, who shows that cultural practices were heavily influenced by past forms of commemoration, arguing that the supposed 'rupture' which accompanied the war was not as dramatic or sustained as has been argued.[12] Studies with a narrower focus, such as Glennys Howarth's work on funerals, rebuffs the claim that the war had a large effect on the wider landscape of death. Howarth argues that it was only after the Second World War, with its high loss of life on the Home Front, that any permanent effect on the ways in which Britons mourned could be detected.[13]

The role of material culture in linking nineteenth and twentieth century death practices has been emphasized by a number of scholars. Laura King's research into working-class family mourning after child loss in the early twentieth century has emphasized the role of everyday objects, which took on commemorative meaning after death. King argues that the war prompted families to ask how to 'keep alive' the dead, noting that the interwar years brought with them increasingly personalized and private memorial forms, which focused on the life of the deceased, rather than their death.[14] This echoes Strange's work, who suggests that working-class families before 1914 would create grief objects, such as a lock of hair taken from the deceased.[15] The role of personal items in upper-class Victorian families has also been

[10] Julie-Marie Strange, *Death, Grief and Poverty in Britain, 1870–1914* (Cambridge, 2005), 23, 206–12.

[11] Elizabeth Roberts, 'The Lancashire Way of Death', in Ralph Houlbrooke (ed.), *Death, Ritual, and Bereavement* (London, 1989), 206–7.

[12] Jay Winter, *Sites of Memory, Sites of Mourning* (Cambridge, 2014 edn), 3–5. Also see Gregory, *The Silence of Memory*, 169; Stefan Goebel, *The Great War and Medieval Memory: War, Remembrance, and Medievalism in Britain and Germany, 1914–1940* (Cambridge, 2007), 28–9.

[13] Glennys Howarth, 'Professionalising the Funeral Industry in England, 1700–1960', in Peter C. Jupp and Glennys Howarth (eds.), *The Changing Face of Death: Historical Accounts of Death and Disposal* (Houndmills, 1997), 126–7; Strange, *Death, Grief and Poverty in Britain*, 263.

[14] Laura King, 'Remembering Deceased Children in Family Life: The School Case of Poor Harold (1920–31), *History Workshop Journal* 93:1 (2022), 228.

[15] Strange, *Death, Grief and Poverty*, 213.

emphasized by Jalland, who points to portraits and mourning jewellery as important markers of loss.[16] Linking peace and wartime traditions, Michael Roper's work draws attention to the working-class death practice of taking a piece of the deceased's clothing as a type of memorial continuity in the First World War.[17]

Work on individuals affected by grief in wartime has highlighted the liminal space that many of the bereaved operated in. As Carol Acton argues for the First World War, British and North American individuals were subjected to propaganda and social policing which reinforced death in a way that supported the war's aims.[18] This resulted in a split between private and public memorial forms, the latter of which curtailed the forms of mourning available to the bereaved, focusing grief 'with abstractions of honour and pride'.[19] Joy Damousi's work similarly shows the bereaved occupied a complex public space, arguing that relatives of the war dead in Australia attempted to claim legitimacy for their loss through political agitation, social networks, and identifying themselves in relation to their bereaved status.[20] This book runs alongside Damousi and Acton's arenas of grief, and points towards acts of domestic remembrance as a site of family resistance which worked both in tandem with and against state-imposed memorial narratives.

One of this book's main contentions is that families who lost loved ones in the First World War both drew on everyday memorial practices and were influenced by forms of memorialization they saw after sudden death events such as mining disasters. Families who lost a loved one in a disaster or during the First World War drew heavily on peacetime memorial forms, but added extra embellishments to their memorial practices. Mining families were part of local communities, and had to find ways of expressing their loss in a way that linked their dead to their community and everyday family memorial practices. Similarly, in wartime the majority of soldiers, servicemen, and servicewomen were, to their families, known in their civilian guise. Helen McCartney's groundbreaking study of the Liverpool Territorials emphasized that soldiers largely remained civilians in uniform throughout the war.[21]

16 Pat Jalland, *Death in the Victorian Family* (Oxford, 1996), 288, 291, 295.

17 Michael Roper, *The Secret Battle: Emotional Survival in the Great War* (Manchester, 2009), 207.

18 Carol Acton, *Grief in Wartime: Private Pain, Public Discourse* (Houndmills, 2007), 1–2; T. G. Ashplant, Graham Dawson, and Michael Roper, *The Politics of War Memory and Commemoration* (London, 2000), 8–9.

19 Acton, *Grief in Wartime*, 5.

20 Joy Damousi, *The Labour of Loss: Mourning, Memory and Wartime Bereavement in Australia* (Cambridge, 1999), 1–2.

21 Helen McCartney, *Citizen Soldiers: The Liverpool Territorials in the First World War* (Cambridge, 2005), 8.

While the state added elements to family memorialization practices, citizen soldiers were remembered by their families as individuals first, and in their military role second. There is no doubt that the war influenced how some families remembered the dead, but these family remembrances were limited and only focused on individual wartime deaths, whereas cultural practices of death within the home remained static up until the 1930s. While families may have engaged with local and national memorials built to honour the dead, their domestic memorialization practices remained bound by wider sociocultural tradition.

This is not to say that there were not broader shifts to British death practices taking place in the interwar period, which accelerated towards the end of the 1930s. Throughout this period there were gradual changes to British death practices surrounding disposal of the corpse which meant that by the Second World War the landscape of death cultures was rather different to that of the First. During the 1920s health bodies began to encourage the use of oft-despised public mortuaries as a resting place for the dead before burial.[22] From the late 1930s chapels of rest became increasingly common, which held the body before it could be buried. From the 1930s the number of hospital deaths steadily rose, but it was not until the mid-1960s that more people died in a hospital than at home.[23] This gradual removal of death from the home, be it at the moment of dying or through the care of the body, meant that family relationships with death were increasingly mediated through contact with professionals and institutions. This shift came earlier to the families of those whose loved one died in war or disaster—for them, there was little choice over where the bodies of their dead were stored.

Family mourning after the Second World War took place in a substantially different emotional landscape to that of the interwar period. As with the First World War there were still the same practical issues for the state to deal with, such as the regulation of the body, and paperwork associated with death, but these occurred alongside different expectations of how families should navigate these issues. Lucy Noakes has highlighted that domestic memorialization still took place, but it was completely hidden from public view.[24] Although families still mourned their loss, they were expected to behave in a way which limited their public expressions of grief. While traditional outlets, such as the In Memoriam column, were still used as a subtle signal of the continuity of

[22] Howarth, 'Professionalising the Funeral Industry', 130.

[23] Jalland, *Death in War and Peace*, 185.

[24] Lucy Noakes, *Dying for the Nation: Death, Grief and Bereavement in Second World War Britain* (Manchester, 2020), 222; Acton, *Grief in Wartime*, 6.

grief, the outpouring of memorial ephemera was reduced, and mass mourning took place in an altered space, with increased distance between the body of the deceased and the family and different emotional expectations. Local authorities and the national government had learned through the mass burial of men who died in war and disaster how to approach the dead of the Second World War.

Improvements in mining safety meant that there were decidedly fewer disasters in the postwar period than in the earlier part of the decade. While people waiting at the pithead had always been featured in the media, public coverage of the disasters now included newsreels broadcast across the country, which clearly showed the faces of women waiting at the pit, an exposure of their loss that took on new meanings with the advent of film making.[25] For the unfortunate families whose loved ones died in disasters such as Cresswell (1950) and Easington (1951), some of the personal aspects of mourning, particularly surrounding newspapers, continued, albeit influenced by other forms of commemoration and new societal attitudes to death. The tragedy of Aberfan, in which 116 children and twenty-eight adults died in 1966 when a colliery spoil tip slid into the village below, changed how people reacted to mining deaths, casting a pall over the way deaths caused by mining were understood.

The families who mourned their war and disaster dead in the Edwardian and interwar periods did so in a gradually changing landscape of death. For families who lost their loved ones in the first two decades of the twentieth century the sudden disposal of the corpse by authorities was a decided shock. While death practices changed over the course of the interwar period, domestic commemoration was slow to change in these decades. The First World War did not constitute a rupture in memorial terms, but the manner of death influenced how the families of the dead publicly articulated their loss. These articulations took similar forms to the disaster dead, who remembered their loved ones through memorial ephemera while telling people that they had died in particular circumstances. This positioning of the deaths as markedly different was in use before the First World War, and helped families to understand how they might frame their dead in socially accepted ways after loss in wartime. The state slowly overtook family responsibilities around death, and families reacted to this by deepening their outward connections to the deceased.

[25] See the Pathé Newsreels for the 1950 Knockshinnock mining disaster.

Constructing a History of Mass Death

Without being reductive, there are a number of similarities between the war and disaster dead of the early twentieth century which influenced how families mourned. The first are demographic: it was almost exclusively young men who died in these events. The majority of these deaths were working-class, and in both cases, the age of the men at death was largely under 30. The second similarity was based around practical workplace issues: these men were known to be in dangerous jobs, and their families were well attuned to the dangers they might face. But these groups were also linked in other ways—miners were rhetorically linked with soldiers before and after the First World War, with the language of service used to argue for increased workers' rights. Finally, and most importantly, the families had to contend with complicated local and national rules concerning if and when they could interact with the body of the deceased, dictated by local authorities and the War Office. Yet there were also differences. Across all deaths, religious differences dictated some familial aspects of memorialization. Regionally the war dead came from across Britain, whereas the disaster dead were concentrated within a specific locality. Temporally, the war caused individual deaths over a longer period of time, with some pinch points in major battles, while in disasters the deaths all occurred in a much shorter time. War deaths were also treated differently—from Imperial War Graves Commission headstones to Next of Kin Memorial Plaques sent by the British government, the way that these deaths were officially treated contrasted with the local authority burials, with no attendant personal domestic memorial, that the families of disaster victims could expect.

This is, on the whole, a book about the death of men. By the early twentieth century, mining was an exclusively male workplace, with the people who died assigned male at birth. In war, too, deaths were overwhelmingly gendered, although women died alongside men, albeit in non-fighting roles. Over one thousand women died doing war work between 1914 and 1918, but their deaths were subsumed into broader war narratives which emphasized the loss of men, not women. Overall, an estimated 722,785 British and Irish soldiers died during the First World War.[26] Of these, approximately 500,000 were under the age of 30. The majority of men who died on active service were unmarried, although the war created 203,283 widows and 355,211 orphans.[27]

[26] Jay Winter, *The Great War and the British People* (Basingstoke, 2003), 71.
[27] Winter, *The Great War and the British People*, 274.

Despite the high number of elite deaths, infantrymen, who enlisted, or were conscripted, from predominantly working-class backgrounds, comprised 450,000 of the total deaths.[28] There are no such complete figures for the disaster dead, although thousands died in mining disasters between 1900 and 1939. There are, however, figures which note similarities between the ages of the dead. Eighty per cent of the British Army were under the age of 30 for the duration of the First World War, with men under 25 most likely to be killed.[29] In a mining disaster, such as West Stanley, nearly 60 per cent of the men killed were under the age of 30.[30] The Gresford disaster had a similar proportion of dead in their twenties and thirties.[31]

The second point of similarity is, quite simply, that the work that these men were doing was very dangerous. This comparison hinges on working-class men's conception of the war as a type of labour. Janet Watson's work highlights the different ways that people saw their service in war, arguing that for many, especially working-class volunteers and conscripts, and professional soldiers and nurses, war work was seen as an extension of regular work.[32] There was a class divide with this conceptualization of labour, with middle- and upper-class volunteers more likely to view war work as a service for more abstract reasons, such as King and country.[33] Miners, seafarers, and those who worked in heavy industry were all acknowledged to be in high-risk jobs and the danger of death through sudden accident was widespread and constant.[34] For the purposes of this book, mining disasters are used as a comparator, but it must be noted that in terms of the total number of dead, accidents in which just one man died and industrial diseases were the main causes of death for colliery workers.[35] Mining disasters, rather than accidents, are

28 Winter, *The Great War and the British People*, 71, 83, 84.

29 Jay Winter, 'Demography', in John Horne (ed.), *A Companion to World War I* (Oxford, 2012), 251; Winter, *The Great War and the British People*, 76–83.

30 Demographics calculated from Eric Forster, *Death Pit* (Newcastle upon Tyne, [1969]), 22.

31 Michael Pollard, *The Hardest Work Under Heaven* (London, 1984), 181.

32 Janet S. K. Watson, *Fighting Different Wars: Experience, Memory, and the First World War in Britain* (Cambridge, 2004), 5. This attitude was echoed in other areas of the British forces. See Nathan Wise, 'The Lost-Labour Force: Working-Class Approaches to Military Service during the Great War', *Labour History* 93 (2007), 161–76. Thomas Stephens's doctoral work promises to be very illuminating on this point.

33 Watson, *Fighting Different Wars*, 7.

34 Roy Church, *The History of the British Coal Industry, Vol. 3* (Oxford, 1986), 584; David Stewart, *The Sea their Graves: An Archaeology of Death and Remembrance in Maritime Culture* (Gainesville, 2011), 7–10.

35 Church, *The History of the British Coal Industry, Vol.* 3, 586. For work on death from occupational disease see Arthur McIvor and Ronald Johnston, *Miners' Lung: A History of Dust Disease in British Coal Mining* (Aldershot, 2007); Arthur McIvor and Ronald Johnston, *Lethal Work: A History of the Asbestos Tragedy in Scotland* (East Linton, 2000); Roger Cooter and Bill Luckins (eds.), *Accidents in History: Injuries, Fatalities and Social Relations* (Amsterdam, 1997).

drawn upon because they marked moments where occupational mortality entered into the national consciousness, dominating ideas about work and death. Mining and soldiering were not exclusive to one another, and many miners saw active service. One miner found the numbing quality of the danger inherent within his profession useful when he joined the army, explaining that he 'became indifferent to the many dangers in the mine'. Talking about the psychological effect of the sudden death of a fellow miner, he said he 'might become apprehensive for a day or two, then the incident was completely forgotten. This training was valuable to me during the First World War when men were yielding their lives on a far larger scale.'[36]

Death at work was classed, racialized, and gendered. In professions with high occupational mortality rates, where working-class men dominated, their families had to live with death in a way that the families of middle- and upper-class professionals did not experience until the First World War. Junior officers, who were generally in their early twenties and from middle- and upper-class backgrounds, were particularly affected by heavy death rates during the First World War.[37] This led to the creation of the war myth of the lost generation, of a whole generation of young men wiped out by war. Middle- and upper-class families were hit harder by the loss of their sons than the rest of the population, and their dominance in literature cast this presumption into the cultural memory of war.[38]

Class and race combined in the war to create specific occupational hazards for different groups of workers. Stokers, for example, who worked in the dangerous part of the bottom of the ship, were more likely to be working-class Black men, leading to a high death toll among certain groups of racialized and classed naval workers.[39] Death in mining disasters was not racialized along the same lines as death in war. Well-paying hewer jobs, often worked by young men, were those closest to the coalface, the most dangerous position in the mine. Race and mining is still a woefully under researched area, although work by Norma Gregory is changing this.[40] Little is known about how many Black miners there were in the early twentieth century, let alone died in

[36] Thomas Jordan, quoted in John Burnett (ed.), *Useful Toil: Autobiographies of Working People from the 1820s to the 1920s* (London, 1974), 104.

[37] Winter, *The Great War and the British People*, 94, 98; Tomás Irish, 'Fractured Families: Educated Elites in Britain and France and the Challenge of the Great War', *The Historical Journal* 57:2 (2014), 524–8.

[38] Santanu Das, 'Reframing First World War Poetry', in Santanu Das (ed.), *The Cambridge Companion to the Poetry of the First World War* (Cambridge, 2013), 3–34.

[39] Jesse Ransley, 'Black and Asian Seamen of the Forgotten Wrecks of the First World War' (Maritime Archaeology Trust, [2014–18]), 11, 21.

[40] Norma Gregory, Black Miners Museum, https://blackcoalminers.com/ [Accessed 13.01.2023].

disasters.[41] Sometimes, wartime obituaries can shed light on this, such as the death notice of US-born Private William Gibbs, which described his work in a colliery before his death in 1917.[42]

These professional workplace dangers were recognized by trade unionists and newspaper reporters, many of whom rhetorically linked war service and mining. After mining disasters in particular, the press often employed the language of war. In 1901 the *Pontypridd Chronicle* declared: 'no soldier will face the bullets of an enemy more fiercely than a collier will face death in the deadly afterdamp when the sacrifice of his own life may be the means of saving others.'[43] These sentiments were echoed by Richard Haldane, Secretary of State for War, in a speech made shortly after the West Stanley pit disaster. Honouring the miners' deaths, Haldane declared: 'may we be found at our posts, as these brave men in the pit were found.'[44] These comparisons did not wane after the First World War and from the 1920s onwards the rhetoric of mining as bodily sacrifice was used to argue for increased workers' rights.[45] After the 1927 Marine colliery mining disaster, the *Western Mail* stated that the dead men 'were stricken with a soldier's wounds in a soldiers' battle.'[46] While there was a certain amount of political posturing in these comparisons, they linked mining and soldiering as careers that should be thought of in term of danger in the public eye, with the conditions of mining disasters equivalent to those of war.

For all of this public rhetoric about deaths, this book turns towards the domestic, to ask how families made sense of their loss. In particular, this book contends that families who lost a loved one in war or disaster had to find a way of domesticating 'abnormal' deaths which occurred in the workplace. Throughout the early twentieth century, dying in the home was the norm. Caring for the sick was a physical manifestation of love. Working-class families tended to the sick themselves, while and middle- and upper-class families were more likely to pay for a domestic servant or nurse to tend to the

[41] Rosemary Power, '"After the black gold": A View of Mining Heritage from Coalfield Areas in Britain', *Folklore* 119:2 (2008), 162.

[42] *Staffordshire Weekly Sentinel* clipping available at: William Gibbs, 'Lives of the First World War', https://livesofthefirstworldwar.iwm.org.uk/lifestory/1338255 [Accessed 23.06.2022].

[43] *Pontypridd Chronicle*, 1 July 1901, cited in Michael Lieven, *Senghenydd: The Universal Pit Village 1890–1930* (Llandysul, 1994), 71.

[44] *Durham Chronicle*, Friday, 26 February 1909, p. 3; *The Auckland Times*, 26 February 1909, p. 2.

[45] Susan Pedersen, 'Gender, Welfare, and Citizenship in Britain during the Great War', *American Historical Review* 95:4 (October 1990), 1006; Mike Mantin, 'Coalmining and the National Scheme for Disabled Ex-Servicemen after the First World War', *Social History* 41:2 (2016), 163; John Newsom, *Out of the Pit: A Challenge to the Comfortable* (Oxford, 1936), 64–7.

[46] *Western Mail*, 2 March 1927, p. 8.

dying.[47] Family members sat with the dying person and tried to be present at the moment of death. Witnessing death could be a highly emotional experience, and could be a deeply upsetting moment, with the capacity to be traumatic if the dying person was especially young, in extreme pain, or scared.[48] Families kept the corpse within the home until the funeral, and so it was some days after dying that the family finally said goodbye to the body of their loved one. In short, domestic spaces were linked with death and dying.

If death in the home was the norm, and understanding death as part of a domestic process was common, to experience mass death outside of the home was unusual. After war and disaster officials often took over the care of the corpse, and others regulated funeral services. Families were denied their domesticated understanding of death, and by re-domesticating it they created a way of regulating the emotions attached to these 'abnormal' and highly traumatic deaths. Understanding that this was a shared experience between war and disaster dead is key to unlocking commemorative similarities and experiences between the two groups.

Despite these shared features of death, there were differences, both in the types of death discussed but also among families themselves. Across all deaths, religious differences dictated some familial aspects of memorialization. This was partially recognized by the War Office, and small prayer books specific to Christian denominations and Jewish soldiers and sailors were given to men who had to read burial services and give prayers for the dead. Throughout the early twentieth century Britain was overwhelmingly Christian.[49] Some turned to spiritualism to try to reconnect with the dead, although they were a minority.[50] E. W. McFarland found that in Scotland the war prompted a mass crisis among Protestants who did not have a clear theology which dealt with mass death, as opposed to Scottish Catholics who could rely on sets of rituals that covered 'sudden death'.[51] For the faithful, their religious beliefs were undoubtedly of comfort. For Catholic families, Saint Barbara, the patron saint of miners, artillery, engineers, and people

[47] Strange, *Death, Grief and Poverty*, 45; Jalland, *Death in the Victorian Family*, 98.

[48] Strange, *Death, Grief and Poverty*, 35.

[49] Michael Snape, *God and the British Soldier: Religion and the British Army in the First and Second World Wars* (Abingdon, 2005), 20; also see Callum Brown, *Religion and Society in Twentieth-Century Britain* (Abingdon, 2006); Callum G. Brown, *The Death of Christian Britain* (Abingdon, 2001).

[50] Owen Davies, *A Supernatural War: Magic, Divination, and Faith during the First World War* (Oxford, 2018), 76.

[51] E. W. McFarlane, 'Passing Time: Cultures of Death and Mourning', in Lynn Abrams and Callum G. Brown (eds.), *A History of Everyday Life in Twentieth-Century Scotland* (Edinburgh, 2010), 260.

who faced sudden death, especially by explosions, helped those with no body to mourn.[52]

Different religious denominations had contrasting experiences of bereavement during war. Patrick Houlihan's work on Germany and Austro-Hungary has interrogated Catholic contemplation of the war, suggesting that transnational understandings of war saw loss and suffering on a universal scale, making individual loss easier to comprehend, and perhaps to bear.[53] Culturally and emotionally, families also put memorial plaques in local churches, special memorial services were held, and shrines were created.[54] However, these actions largely stayed in religious buildings. Spiritual beliefs and outward expressions of them do not always marry together, and personal belief is very difficult to access. In the first few decades of the twentieth century the majority of Britons were culturally Christian, and, while a minority found routine in weekly churchgoing, most were affected by popular practices which helped forge British identity.[55] Christian symbols permeated memorial material, through the inclusion of the cross, but any other overt reference to religious belief is generally lacking within domestic memorialization practices.

Regionally, there were differences in where the families of the war and disaster dead lived. The war dead could be very concentrated, especially if men had joined up for a local Pal's Battalion, but were also spread throughout the country.[56] Disaster dead were concentrated in individual towns and villages, although the families of the dead men could live considerable distances away. Adrian Gregory posits that the 1913 Senghenydd disaster, in which 440 men and boys died, roughly equated to the 10 per cent of national war dead in the First World War, arguing that due to the highly localized nature of the disaster, 'no British community suffered loss on this scale during the Great War'.[57] As Hester Barron's work on mining communities explains, miners lived and worked in very different settings: some lived in isolated villages, some in towns, some lived near other miners, others in communities filled with people of different occupations, but all were members of communities that represented

[52] Patrick Houlihan, *Catholicism in the Great War: Religion and Everyday Life in Germany and Austro-Hungary, 1914–1922* (Cambridge, 2015), 228.

[53] Houlihan, *Catholicism in the Great War*, 216.

[54] Connelly, *The Great War*, 25–48. Bryan Mclure's PhD also promises to be fruitful on this point.

[55] See Douglas Davies, *Mors Britannica: Lifestyle and Death-Style in Britain Today* (Oxford, 2015) for a nuanced discussion of how religion is spiritually and culturally mediated.

[56] See Geoffrey Moorhouse, *Hell's Foundations: A Town, its Myths and Gallipoli* (London, 1992), esp. pp. 60–79.

[57] Adrian Gregory, *The Last Great War* (Cambridge, 2014), 279.

more than just their job role.[58] Some collieries had more localized workforces than others, so although the families of disaster dead were usually reasonably locally concentrated, there were instances where young men had moved into the area for work.

The regions focused on in this book are skewed towards South Wales, North Wales, and the North of England. South Wales and the North-East of England led coal production across the early twentieth century. War deaths are taken from these regions, as well as cities including Glasgow and London. There were some regional variations in family mourning practices, such as engraved memorial glasses being more prevalent in the North-East of England, or a family in North Wales choosing to use Welsh in an In Memoriam card to a loved one. However, broadly speaking, the cultures of mourning which sprung up around war and disaster dead followed national patterns. This is not to say that local areas did not have specific customs, but that if they did exist they may have been oral, or their material traces lost to time. Much of the memorial material that has survived, in archives and families, is object- and paper-based, which points to elements of a homogenized culture of mourning ephemera across the early twentieth century.

In the First World War individual deaths happened over a period of years, with flash points during certain battles, whereas disaster deaths all occurred with alarming rapidity. For the families of disaster dead, although sudden, the deaths of their loved ones were known about within hours, if not days. It was only in disasters where men were trapped underground that the outcome could be measured in weeks. The families of the war dead, however, barring those of professional soldiers who were immediately at risk, were aware of the possibilities of their loved one's death while they underwent training, were deployed, and then in the days, weeks, months, or years that followed this to their demise. Due to the prolonged nature of the First World War, as well as the number of men involved, when family, distant relations, and friends are counted among the bereaved, most households were likely to have been affected by the death of a serviceperson.[59]

Owing to the number of dead and the manner in which they died, official recognition and involvement in death practices was heightened in the case of war. As Gregory argues, the hierarchy of sacrifice in the First World War centred on soldiers' suffering, leading to a devaluation of non-military

[58] Hester Barron, *The 1926 Miners' Lockout: Meanings of Community in the Durham Coalfield* (Oxford, 2010), 22–3.

[59] Gregory, *The Silence of Memory*, 19.

experiences, as lived by civilians.[60] Military deaths, and specifically lives sacrificed by soldiers in the war effort, were deemed the highest sacrifice. Suffering was central to this concept and civilians were highly aware that soldiers, and by extension their families, had paid a 'blood sacrifice'. This national construction of loss as part of a war waged by the state meant that the government response to death in military service attempted to honour the war dead. Chapters 1 and 2 of this book argue that the state assumed the role that families of the war and disaster dead usually undertook after the death of a loved one. Bodies were held by officials, funerals were arranged on behalf of the families, and, in the case of the First World War dead, bureaucratic paperwork came to regulate mourning. Chapter 4 extends this, exploring how the war and disaster dead were commemorated in the home. While there was a rich culture of creating mourning material, after the First World War the government attempted to shape national remembrance through sending Next of Kin Memorial Plaques into the homes of the bereaved. While families had their responsibilities taken away from them after the death of a loved one, the bereaved of war were subjected to much stricter memorial policies, which only emphasized the importance of personal memorialization.

Gendering Death

Although this book focuses on men in active service, there were other casualties of war, and the deaths of women and civilians, long neglected in the histories of war, are re-entered into the narrative in these pages. During the First World War aerial bombardments resulted in the deaths of 1,239 civilians, while coastal bombardments in December 1914 killed a further 127 civilians.[61] There were also over 15,000 non-military casualties in the war at sea.[62] Angela Woollacott suggests that between several hundred to over one thousand women likely died in munitions work alone, which, when the dead of other professions are added, is a considerable number.[63] There were several notable large explosions at munitions factories in the late 1910s, such as

[60] Gregory, *The Last Great War*, 135, 294.

[61] Susan Grayzel, *At Home and Under Fire: Air Raids and Culture in Britain from the Great War to the Blitz* (Cambridge, 2011), 21; Michael Reeve, '"Are we downhearted? NO!": Representing War Damage and Destruction following Bombardment on the First World War "Home Front"', *Critical Military Studies* (2019), 3.

[62] Winter, *The Great War and the British People*, 71.

[63] Angela Woollacott, *On Her Their Lives Depend: Munitions Workers in the Great War* (Berkeley, 1994), 9.

Silvertown (1917) and Chilwell (1918). These explosions killed both women and men, in numbers akin to medium-sized mining disasters. Few of the women who died were married—however, there were at least a handful of war widowers created upon their deaths, and sweethearts and fiancés who were not counted in any formal way. What this meant in practice was that whole families could be torn apart by war. In 1918 Catherine Carroll, a munitions worker, contracted gangrene and died after falling from a tram in the factory where she worked, shortly followed by her husband William, who died in hospital while on active service a month after his wife.[64] They left behind four children who were sent to be looked after by their grandparents.

The deaths of these other casualties of war were not commemorated in the same way as their military counterparts. Anne-Marie Hughes's work has shown that while the deaths of munitions workers were locally mourned, they were not given attention on a national stage.[65] Due to the 1914 Defence of the Realm Act, explosions at munitions factories were regularly concealed, although local and official knowledge often deviated. While the families of the dead were afforded respectable funerals, they never received official recognition for their loss in the same way that the families of servicemen and servicewomen did. There was some commemoration of women and munitions workers in the interwar period, but this was patchy and often locally mediated. Alison Fell argues that public memorials to women who had died, particularly nurses, created and unveiled in the 1920s, elevated their status to that of 'supreme sacrifice' which ideologically aligned their deaths with those of servicemen.[66] Munitions workers were not given the same level of prestige, but women who died in factory explosions were sometimes added to rolls of honour and were locally treated as having died on war service, even if they were not officially recognized as such.[67] Although both groups were, at various times, discussed in terms of sacrifice, the reality was an uneven approach to placing women and non-combatant workers within wider memorial culture in the interwar years. Civilian war dead were locally commemorated, and there were no national schemes of recognition for these others who lost their lives doing war work akin to the Cenotaph or the Tomb of the Unknown

[64] Women's Archive Wales, WaW0355.

[65] Anne-Marie Hughes, 'Death, Service and Citizenship in Britain in the First World War' (Unpublished PhD, University of Manchester, 2009), 74, 81.

[66] Alison S. Fell, *Women as Veterans in Britain and France after the First World War* (Cambridge, 2018), 22, 46–50.

[67] Fell, *Women as Veterans*, 194–5.

Warrior.[68] Much like miners and people who died on active service in the First World War, these war workers were commemorated in the home, and the means of their death discussed by the bereaved.

Women were doubly affected by death in the First World War. Not only were the lives of women who worked in nursing and munitions under threat, but women were nationally positioned as the natural mourners in wartime. National war commemoration focused on mothers, and lauded women who had 'given' their sons above all other bereaved.[69] Women, not men, were positioned as the primary mourners of the dead in the national eye. The 'labour of loss' fell on the bereaved, who tried to gain legitimacy for their private loss through external work, such as political activism and community organizing.[70]

Practically, women and children's living situations could rapidly alter after the death of a male breadwinner. To some extent the hardship a family faced after the death of a man depended on their geographical location and the level of support offered by family and friends. Women in County Durham, for instance, were particularly hard hit after the loss of their husband because of a lack of suitable work for women.[71] These economic pressures were recognized by the public, and after major disasters, both surviving miners at the pit and the general public donated money to the families of victims.[72] Catherine Welsby has highlighted the gendered dimensions of these relief funds, detailing the difficulties that the women of Senghenydd faced in obtaining financial assistance. For example, administrators attached moralistic conditions to the reception of assistance. In order to access the Senghenydd relief fund, women had to provide a marriage certificate, which was not always possible, and illegitimate children from cohabiting couples were given a paltry allowance compared to those born to married parents. Regular stipends could be stopped if the relief fund's executive committee judged that women were performing 'immoral acts', loosely defined.[73] Similar morally coded restraints were put on the benefactors of the Gresford fund. If a widow remarried, access to the fund was void, as it was assumed that her new husband would financially care for his new wife.[74] Families in subsidized or free

[68] Michael Reeve, *Bombardment, Public Safety, and Resilience in English Coastal Communities during the First World War* (London, 2021), 304–6.

[69] Gregory, *The Silence of Memory*, 33; Suzanne Evans, *Mothers of Heroes, Mothers of Martyrs: World War I and the Politics of Grief* (Montreal, 2007), 8.

[70] Damousi, *The Labour of Loss*, 161.

[71] Barron, *The 1926 Miners' Lockout*, 13.

[72] Ann-Marie Foster, 'The Barry Urban District Council, Disaster Relief Funds and Civic Society, 1913–1934', *Urban History* 48:4 (2021), 688–90.

[73] Catherine Welsby, '"Warning as to her future behaviour": The Lives of the Widows of the Senghenydd Mining Disaster of 1913', *Llafur* 6:4 (1995), 97–8, 104–5.

[74] Stanley Williamson, *Gresford: The Anatomy of a Disaster* (Liverpool, 1999), 57–8.

accommodation owned by the mining company could be swiftly given notice to leave, and the death of a breadwinner often precipitated a move of accommodation.

In histories of mining disasters, these were often the passive roles that women were given. Books which focus on mining disasters tend to examine individual explosions, most of which were Welsh disasters.[75] In these books women are resigned to the role of mourners, often in somewhat flowery prose. Women were, of course, impacted by death, but were also involved in explosions through care for the corpse, nursing, or as volunteers who either worked with bereaved families or raised money for disaster funds. Much like narratives of war, women involved in disaster were reimagined into the primary role of mourner to fit male expectations of their emotional role.

Studies which have linked widowhood to straitened circumstances after war have focused on the ways that women tried to demand state assistance due to loss of income. Erika Kuhlman has drawn attention to the war as a mass widow-making event, which had no comparator before 1914, the scale of which ensured that widows would become a politicized group as they sought recompense for their loss.[76] Damousi's work has shown that in Australia mothers' anger at the level of renumeration offered led to political activism, casting a wider net over the activism of bereaved women.[77] British women's relationship to the state through widowhood has been intimately charted by Angela Smith, who has shown that women used deliberate strategies to try to elicit aid from what they saw as an indifferent state.[78] Once pensions were granted, women were forced to abide by strict moral codes, regulated by patriarchal systems. Mothers could also try to claim monetary recompense for the loss of a working daughter. After the First World War, Mary Anne Jones tried to sue the Explosives Co. Ltd. after the death of her daughter from TNT poisoning. The company paid her a £20 lump sum to absolve themselves from responsibility for her daughter's death.[79] Despite these appeals, the loss of income from a husband, brother, son, or daughter

[75] Lieven, *Senghenydd: The Universal Pit Village*; Stanley Williamson, *Gresford: The Anatomy of a Disaster* (Liverpool, 1999); John H. Brown, *The Valley of the Shadow* (Port Talbort, 2009); Gordon L. Routledge, *Black Wednesday* (Carlisle, 2011).

[76] Erika Kuhlman, *Of Little Comfort: War Widows, Fallen Soldiers, and the Remaking of the Nation after the Great War* (New York, 2012), 3.

[77] Damousi, *The Labour of Loss*, 41–5.

[78] Angela Smith, *Discourses Surrounding British Widows of the First World War* (London, 2013), 11–12.

[79] Newspaper clippings on the Women and War Wales website; see entry for Elizabeth Anne (Lizzie) Jones, http://www.womenandwar.wales/search.php?func=search&searchfor=Jones&in_all=on#prettyPhoto [Accessed 28.01.2023].

was a deep blow to many working-class families, and working-class women felt the brunt of their unequal circumstances more sharply than most. Flashes of this are primarily seen in correspondence with institutions, and glimpses of the impoverishment of death can be seen between families and official bodies.

While there were very practical reasons why women could especially suffer after the death of a loved one, the historical focus on women as mourners gives a false idea of who grieved. Children, parents, spouses, and siblings, as well as the slightly more removed sweethearts, nieces, nephews, and other more distant relations, as well as friends, were all involved in family commemorations, in both passive and active roles. There was a highly gendered element to this. Grief was socially mediated, but national memorial events which placed widows and mothers in the role of mourner obscured the way that men could articulate their grief in public. Historically, this has meant that more attention has been given to women's role in mourning cultures, although there are notable exceptions to this.

Work on the history of men's emotional reaction to death points towards people who felt loss deeply but were excluded from memorial narratives. Laura King has shown that fathers are often artificially separated from family life, and constitute historical actors in their own right. As she argues, if we focus too much on separating gender, as has been done in work on mourning in wartime, we can 'obscure change elsewhere'.[80] Damousi is one of the few to have written about men's grief, specifically that of fathers, tracing the efforts that one Australian middle-class father made to remember his son through scrapbooking, befriending his son's comrades, and creating a network of the bereaved.[81] Focusing on soldiers' grief, Acton casts their writing as 'extended elegies for dead friends'.[82] In a British context, Linda Maynard's work is particularly attuned to the different expectations placed on middle and upper-class men, who were supposed to show a 'stiff upper lip' and support female relatives in their grief, which resulted in men often hiding from people to properly mourn their loss.[83] These traces are more visible because middle and upper-class men were more likely to write about it, and have these writings preserved. Gendered ideas of mourning were also perpetuated in public mourning practices. Corinna Peniston Bird's work on the representation of

[80] King, *Family Men*, 5–6.

[81] Damousi, *The Labour of Loss*, 57–63.

[82] Acton, *Grief in Wartime*, 107.

[83] Linda Maynard, *Brothers in the Great War: Siblings, Masculinity and Emotions* (Manchester, 2021), 199.

grieving men in public memorials notes that they have been silenced through their cultural depictions on, or erasure from, war memorials.[84]

The history of family memorialization in this period broadly runs alongside the re-articulation of family structure. Between the late 1910s and the late 1950s the family was increasingly articulated as an independent social unit, which emphasized complementary roles between men and women as parents and spouses.[85] Within First World War studies, there has been work on special family relationships and their importance to people on active service. Roper has suggested that the young men who fought had special relationships with their mothers and their comrades, both of whom provided emotional support.[86] Maynard has expanded this to show the importance of sibling relationships in war, citing brothers and sisters who could perhaps communicate more openly to each other than they could their parents.[87] Family mourning was caught up in this wider trend, which increasingly placed memorial weight onto the nuclear family.

Increased awareness that mass death through warfare was likely to happen again slowly permeated public consciousness during the interwar period. Throughout the 1930s the government led a concerted effort to shape the way that the public articulated and understood their emotions. This development of an emotional economy placed a high value on stoicism in the face of death and encouraged citizens to restrain articulations of grief.[88] This restriction was said not to come from the repression of emotions, but from an understanding of the feeling, and through it a means of self-regulation.[89] Susan Grayzel's work on air raids suggests that by the middle of the Second World War the responses of stoical citizens under fire 'represent the culmination of the acceptance that modern war destroyed civilian lives that began with World War I'.[90] Acton also draws attention to the stark divide between expectations for women after the First and Second World Wars. She argues that the 'glamourised' image of bereaved women, which lay alongside their stoical character in the face of adversity, was erased by the Second World War. Instead, suffering was to be silenced and hidden from view.[91]

[84] Corinna Peniston-Bird, 'The Grieving Male in Memorialization: Monuments of Discretion', *Journal of War and Culture Studies* 8:1 (2015), 45, 55.

[85] Laura King, *Family Men: Fatherhood and Masculinity in Britain, c.1914–1960* (Oxford, 2015), 6; also see Leonore Davidoff, Matt May, Janet Fink, and Katherine Holden, *The Family Story: Blood, Contract, and Intimacy, 1830–1960* (London, 1999).

[86] Roper, *The Secret Battle*, 5–6.

[87] Maynard, *Brothers in the Great War*, 3.

[88] Noakes, *Dying for the Nation*, 14.

[89] Noakes, *Dying for the Nation*, 59.

[90] Grayzel, *At Home and Under Fire*, 314.

[91] Acton, *Grief in Wartime*, 49.

For some family members, particularly children, their grief after family death before the Second World War could be silenced through social pressure. Following the conventions of emotions history, when feelings are expressed in these pages they are for the most part taken at face value: people use the language they are comfortable with to explain their emotional state to others.[92] Children and grief have largely been marginal to First World War studies, although Rosie Kennedy's work has been crucial to ensuring that children's experiences of war and loss are recorded.[93] Grief could profoundly affect family dynamics and alter both personalities and interpersonal relationships.

The death of a close relative could be especially difficult for children, not just because they were grieving, but because of the way that adults treated them. After his brother's death at Gallipoli, the working-class Yorkshire-born J. H. Armitage 'was not allowed out of her [his mother's] sight, for the next two years I was almost a prisoner at home, it was a relief to go to school and mix with other boys... [I] felt her possessiveness both stifling and traumatic.'[94] His mother underwent a dramatic personality change in her grief, and was filled with anger. Before her son's war pension was awarded she had some lean weeks, borrowing from family and neighbours to make ends meet, later avoiding those who had helped her. Armitage remembered that 'she seemed to hold a grudge, having a "Chip on Her Shoulder", and even shunned our neighbours treating everyone with suspicion and distrust'. She also developed the habit of talking to herself when she thought that nobody could hear her. As a child, this deeply upset her youngest son, for whom 'if there had been another child, or someone else that I could have talked to, it would have been a great comfort to me, but all that I would do was to listen and say nothing'.[95] The mother's grief, told through the recollections of her youngest son, suggests a distraught woman who was deeply affected by her son's death to the extent that her grief significantly affected her personal relationships.

Armitage was already dealing with a mother who was deeply grieving for her eldest child, but his loss was compounded by neighbours marginalizing his grief. He recalled that 'I did hear people say to mother "He's only a kid, he'll soon get over it and forget abbout [*sic*] his brother as he gets older".'

[92] Joanna Bourke, 'Foreword', in Lucy Noakes, Claire Langhammer, and Claudia Siebrecht, *Total War: An Emotional History* (Oxford, 2020), p. ix.

[93] Rosie Kennedy, *The Children's War: Britain, 1914–1918* (Basingstoke, 2014), esp. ch. 1.

[94] Burnett Archive, J. H. Armitage, 'Twenty Three Years or The Late Way of Life and Living by "The Exile"', 60.

[95] Burnett Archive, J. H. Armitage, 'Twenty Three Years', 62.

People would tell his mother that it was good she only had one child, not many, to look after, as some kind of consolation. For Armitage, 'it was not that easy for me to get over'.[96] For children who lost a close relative their grief was difficult. Their emotions were not necessarily centred or even acknowledged within familial or neighbourly circles, and people, when trying to comfort adult family members, inadvertently alienated children through dismissing their very real grief.

Throughout the book the term 'loved one' is sometimes used as a shorthand to denote the relationship of the family to the deceased. The term is not without its issues. In her study of working-class fathers Strange uses the term 'affection' instead of love, to negate the complicated overtones which come with using this term.[97] There are also practical reasons why this might be taking liberties with the families of the dead. In C. S. Peel's memoir of the war years she recalled:

> One woman with a very bad husband owned frankly that she would not be sorry if he were to be killed. 'But I 'spose he'll be spared, and the other as 'd be missed 'll be taken, for that's the way of things,' said she. 'It's the only time since I've been married as I and the children 'ad peace. The war's been a 'appy time for us.'[98]

The above is a stark reminder that for some there might be celebration or ambivalence, rather than mourning, upon the death, all of which serves to illustrate a central point: that family is messy, mourning is complicated, and the two combined do not necessarily lend themselves to neat understandings of how people historically grieved.

The Material of Emotion

The emotions explored in these pages can be found in a range of materials, in print, manuscript, and object form. The memorial material includes the textual—letters, diaries, and official forms—through to the visual—memorial plates, displays, photographs—and the in-between—In Memoriam cards, family rolls of honour, and memorial pamphlets. These have been found in a

[96] Burnett Archive, J. H. Armitage, 'Twenty Three Years', 61.

[97] Strange, *Death, Grief and Poverty*, 16.

[98] C. S. Peel, *How we Lived then 1914–1918: A Sketch of Social and Domestic Life in England during the War* (London, 1929), 172.

variety of spaces, such as administrative archives, museums, and private collections. Given the focus on family memory, oral histories and autobiographies have also been drawn upon to supplement the material. In these pages material culture is melded with oral and textual remnants to provide rounded expressions of grief. This approach aligns with the work of Elizabeth Hallam and Jenny Hockey, who have argued that grief, memory, and material culture must be studied in tandem in order to understand death and mourning.[99] They highlight the importance of objects, visual images, and texts in filling the space left by the dead in order to recall them.[100] This approach goes some way to providing an insight into people whose grief is not usually well-documented, such as working-class men, although much information, such as everyday conversations which recalled the dead, is hidden from historical view.

Both formal and informal archives of ephemera and objects have been drawn upon to demonstrate the range of memorial making across the twentieth century. Santanu Das has shown the importance of this approach in researching other arenas of war, emphasizing that non-textual sources are essential when studying the Indian Army.[101] Michael Twyman notes that, in part because of the institutional reluctance to engage with ephemera, private collections which are then made available for historians to study are important repositories of ephemeral material and the ability to work with these private collections is common within ephemera studies.[102] Private collections hold working and middle-class family archives, especially when bundles of belongings have been sold together, and can contain rich family sources. Their owners are also often rich founts of knowledge themselves, and some private collections (and collectors) have been used here to supplement archival sources.

There are weightings towards certain types of document for different social classes. The war myth of the 'fallen generation' has skewed cultural memory towards upper- and upper-middle-class soldiers, who were particularly affected by heavy death rates in the First World War. This meant that the elite families whose sons had eagerly signed up were far more likely to lose them than other social groups, and has been the basis of the national preoccupation

[99] Elizabeth Hallam and Jenny Hockey, *Death, Memory and Material Culture* (London, 2001), 3. Also see Ruth E. Toulson and Zahra Newby (eds.), *The Materiality of Mourning: Cross-Disciplinary Perspectives* (Milton, 2018).

[100] Hallam and Hockey, *Death, Memory and Material Culture*, 7.

[101] Santanu Das, *India, Empire, and First World War Culture* (Cambridge, 2018), 3–21.

[102] Michael Twyman, 'Editor's Introduction', in Maurice Rickards, *The Encyclopaedia of Ephemera* (London, 2000), p. vi.

with the 'fallen generation'. This is not to detract from any suffering that elite families faced—they lost sons, brothers, and uncles, and friends and family grieved deeply. It is, however, important to note that these families left more detailed and complete records of their grief than their working-class counterparts. These archives of elite grief have been the focus for much of the work on the family aspects of mourning after the First World War, including the writings of middle- and upper-class women, whose words are present within this book. The gendered ways that women were allowed to write about death, in particular death in the First World War, mean that emotive descriptions are more often, although not exclusively, penned by women.[103] The wealthy had recourse to memorial types that poorer families did not, such as commissioning an individual bronze memorial plaque for a church, creating a printed long-form memorial book, or the creation of a scholarship in their loved one's name. Middle and upper-class mourning cultures are included in the narrative here to provide a contrast to working-class experiences, which have been brought forward to articulate class differences in mourning practices across the twentieth century.

When focus is shifted to the memorial material and its place in family rituals, the printers and makers give additional clues to commemorative culture. A key point that has been ignored in death studies is that men, and often working-class men, were the makers and producers of memorial ephemera. It is they who overwhelmingly dominated the printing world as designers, printers, and distributors of these items. While some of their actions were of course designed to serve the market, as people affected by loss they helped shape the cultures of commemoration in a way that is often overlooked. They also showed their loss in quasi-public arenas, through commissioning In Memoriam columns, preparing Memorial Books, and, in the case of the First World War dead, through sending items and letters filled with emotion to the Imperial War Museum. The former two points are discussed in Chapter 3, and the latter in Chapter 5. Through their acts working-class men shaped mourning spaces and left traces of their feelings through letters and ephemera.

Despite memorial ephemera's popularity across the early twentieth century, it has, as a whole, escaped sustained historical scrutiny. Two exceptions are Carol Acton and Catherine Moriarty, who have both drawn attention to the affective importance of memorial ephemera within First World War mourning cultures. Acton argues that families who lost a loved one in war demanded

[103] Strange also found that this was the case when writing about Victorian and Edwardian grief: Strange, *Death, Grief and Poverty*, 212.

additional remembrance through memorial albums, which collected military remembrances of the dead.[104] Moriarty shows that memorial photographs could be used in multiple spaces, from street shrines to domestic display.[105]

'Ephemera', by their very definition, refers to items that are transient and short-lived: memorial ephemera, conversely, are designed to be kept, awkwardly breaking with the origin of its definition.[106] There is a sense of purpose to ephemera that makes them particularly pertinent as memorial items. Lisa Gitelman suggests that paper items such as tickets and receipts 'are patterns of expression and reception discernible amid a jumble of discourse, but they are also familiar material objects to be handled—to be shown and saved, saved and shown—in different ways'.[107] As Gillian Russell argues, these items can be performative, allowing particular social events to take place, which elevates the item into an active object.[108] If ephemera can take on practical meanings, then the ephemera of mourning takes on a particularly important role within wider social ritual. It transcended its role as a piece of ephemera that relayed a message and transformed it into a powerful tool for remembrance. Ephemeral items were also cheap to personalize, especially for families who could afford to include photographs, which became more and more common from the late 1910s, lending them an increasingly intimate air. It is in these small pieces of paper that we can see the memorial traces which allow people to create domestic legacies of memorialization which could, if preserved correctly, survive decades.

Families and Memory Work

The survival of these memorial forms are significant for historians researching this material, and this book is, in part, a study about where the domestic legacies of the dead have been stored, and how people's relationships to them have changed over time. The final third of this book asks how the family memory of war and disaster has interacted with larger cultural trends. A vital part of this interaction lies in the relationship between families and institutions. This section broadly argues that, when given the option, families of all

[104] Acton, *Grief in Wartime*, 23.

[105] Catherine Moriarty, '"Though in a picture only": Photographs and Commemoration', in Gail Braybon (ed.), *Evidence, History and the Great War* (New York, 2008), 34–8.

[106] Maurice Rickards, *Collecting Printed Ephemera* (Oxford, 1988), 174.

[107] Lisa Gitelman, *Paper Knowledge: Towards a Media History of Documents* (Durham, 2014), 3.

[108] Gillian Russell, *The Ephemeral Eighteenth Century: Print, Sociability, and the Cultures of Collecting* (Cambridge, 2020), 21.

classes placed their memory items into museum collections as a way of legacy building, although it finds that over the course of the past century the memory of individual family members have largely been subsumed by cultural memories of war and disaster. Many family historians are now working with people to reveal family archives, and ancestors are allowing researchers to work with this material. The results of this collaboration are changing the ways that we understand family dynamics, family archives, and historical practice.[109]

Scholars of memory studies have led the way in understanding how family and cultural memories are linked. As Astrid Erll writes, 'families serve as a kind of switchboard between the individual memory and larger frames of collective remembrance'.[110] Jan and Aleida Assmann have developed the framework which takes memories from the communicative to the cultural. Jan Assmann argues that cultural memory develops through stages of memory types: from communicative, to generational, before these memories are codified within cultural memory.[111] Anecdotes from a person's past can be transmitted in the form of communicative memory rehearsed within group exchange which lasts between eighty to one hundred years, extending beyond the life of a single family member and becoming part of the generational memory of their immediate ancestors.[112] Intergenerational memory transforms into a cultural memory when it is organized through visual cues, institutions of learning, and commemorative rites.[113] Larger interactions between individual and collective memories are only beginning to be theorized by memory scholars. Psychologists have suggested that the development of autobiographical memory is formed through dialogue between family narratives and cultural memory and that children learn to locate their identity in this ever evolving memory space.[114] Family memory as a site of meaning-making

[109] For example, see Laura King and Jessica Hammett, 'Family Historians and Historians of the Family: The Value of Collaboration', in Paul Ashton, Tanya Evans, and Paula Hamilton (eds.), *Making Histories* (Berlin, 2022), 237–50; Ashley Barnwell and Laura King, 'Family History Collaborators in Conversation', *International Public History* 2:2 (2022), 1–3; Tanya Evans, 'How Do Family Historians Work with Memory?', *Journal of Family History* 46:1 (2021), 92–106; Tanya Evans, 'Secrets and Lies: The Radical Potential of Family History', *History Workshop Journal* 71:1 (2011), 49–73.

[110] Astrid Erll, 'Locating Family in Cultural Memory Studies', *Journal of Comparative Cultural Memory Studies* 42:3 (2011), 315.

[111] Jan Assmann, *Religion and Cultural Memory: Ten Studies*, translated by Rodney Livingstone (Stanford, 2006), 24.

[112] Aleida Assmann, 'Memory, Individual and Collective', in Robert E. Gooding and Charles Tilly (eds.), *The Oxford Handbook of Contextual Political Analysis* (Oxford, 2006), 210–24; Aleida Assmann, 'Transformations between History and Memory', *Social Research* 75:1 (2008), 213–14.

[113] Assmann, 'Transformations between History and Memory', 55–6.

[114] Robyn Fivush and Natalie Merrill, 'An Ecological Systems Approach to Family Narratives', *Memory Studies* 9:3 (2016), 307. Also see Robyn Fivush, Tilman Habermas, Theodore E. A. Waters, and Widaad Zaman, 'The Making of Autobiographical Memory: Intersections of Culture, Narratives and Identity', *International Journal of Psychology* 46:5 (2011), 321–45.

has been a core part of sociological and historical approaches to identity formation.[115] Recent work suggests that an hourglass metaphor is useful for envisioning the communication between different forms of memory. In this, the two opposite ends of the hourglass represent individual and collective memory, with family memory as the point in the middle of the hourglass that larger and smaller memory types are processed through.[116]

The tension between micro and macro memory types is present in all modern memory of war and disaster. From the 1930s on, the death of soldiers was at the centre of the First World War myth. In mining communities, individual deaths in small accidents, not large-scale disasters, dominated cultural memory in the twentieth century. While the public memory of disaster was linked to the profession of the victims, disasters remained a relatively small part of the cultural memory of the communities they were experienced in. Within the South Wales coalfield the collective memory of disaster did not feature prominently in the decades following the Second World War. In a study of oral histories taken in the early 1970s in South Wales, David Selway notes that large pit disasters barely featured at all, unless experienced by a family member or when interviewees were part of the local community affected. Instead, miners talked about smaller accidents and disease caused by long years down the pit. Selway argues that it was only after the mines were closed, and the danger to workers gone, that big pit disasters began to attract wider remembrance in the coalfields.[117] Writing in the early 2000s, Douglas Davies notes how the weight of particularly bad disasters now fixes their names and sites within contemporary cultural memory.[118] Within popular cultures of mining, mass death has emerged as a popular trope, to the extent that Bert Hogenkamp drily suggests that 'a mining film without a disaster is like a Western without a shoot-out'.[119]

Family memory is linked to generational resilience. Often family memory is created through the rehearsal of stories about the family, told between children, parents, and grandparents, which forms a generational chain of living

[115] Anne-Marie Kramer, 'Kinship, Affinity and Connectedness: Exploring the Role of Genealogy in Personal Lives', *Sociology* 45:3 (2011), 381; Anna Green, 'Grandparents, Communicative Memory and Narrative Identity', *Oral History* 49:1 (2019), 90.

[116] Aline Cordonnier, Valérie Rousoux, Anne-Sophie Gijs, and Oliver Luminet, 'Collective Memory: An Hourglass between the Collective and the Individual', *Memory, Mind & Media* 1 (2022), 4.

[117] David Selway, 'Death Underground: Mining Accidents and Memory in South Wales, 1913–1974', *Labour History Review* 81:3 (2016), 196–209.

[118] Davies, *Mors Britannica*, 91.

[119] Bert Hogenkamp, 'A Mining Film Without a Disaster is like a Western Without a Shoot-out: Representations of Coal Mining Communities in Feature Films', in Stefan Berger, Andy Croll, and Norman LaPorte (eds.), *Towards a Comparative History of Coalfield Societies* (Aldershot, 2005), 90.

memory generally covering at least three generations. The ways family memory engages with and provides a counterpoint to cultural memory are only beginning to be explored by scholars. In Green's study of family memory in the south of England, she found that a family's remembered past was highly contingent on the longevity of previous family members and their ability to pass on family histories.[120]

Historians have pointed towards the ways that family memory can present complex narratives of war, which has been the focus of the majority of work on intergenerational family memory. In their research about the family legacy of the First World War, Roper and Rachel Duffett noted that participants in their study of the effects of the conflict all noted the war as a pivotal moment in their family, and the nation's, history, emphasizing tragedy and loss, but pointing to a wider range of understanding of war than is often assumed.[121] They argue that the soldier-centric narrative is somewhat countered through these understandings, although they acknowledge that family stories lean on popular public narratives of what war is.[122] James Wallis suggests that family history research, which reveals people's experiences in non-Western Front arenas of war, could similarly help dilute understandings of a homogenous war experience.[123]

These family narratives, whether simple or complex, are overwhelmingly gendered. Given the cultural masculinity associated with war and disaster, the histories that families recount are often ones which have unconsciously accepted that masculine memories are the ones that should be repeated. Keith Gildart has drawn attention to how autobiographies of miners emphasize the myths of 'solidarity, community, militancy, masculinity, and commitment to the politics of the left'.[124] Lucy Noakes has highlighted the gendered nature of family memory, arguing that older women are likely to describe male accounts of war when prompted about family experiences, obscuring the roles that women played in wartime.[125] Where women are mentioned, their suffering and resilience are highlighted, forming part of family narratives about strong

[120] Anna Green, 'Intergenerational Family Stories: Private, Parochial, Pathological?', *Journal of Family History* 38:4 (2013), 391. Also see Harald Welzer, 'Re-narrations: How Pasts Change in Conversational Remembering', *Memory Studies* 3:1 (2010), 16.

[121] Michael Roper and Rachel Duffett, 'Family Legacies in the Centenary: Motives for First World War Commemoration among British and German Descendants', *History & Memory* 30:1 (2018), 80, 106.

[122] Roper and Duffett, 'Family Legacies in the Centenary', 78–9.

[123] James Wallis, '"Great-grandfather, what did *you* do in the Great War?" The Phenomenon of Conducting First World War Family History Research', in Bart Ziino (ed.), *Remembering the First World War* (Abingdon, 2015), 25.

[124] Keith Gildart, 'Mining Memories: Reading Coalfield Biographies', *Labour History* 50:2 (2009), 154.

[125] Lucy Noakes, '"My husband is interested in war generally": Gender, Family History and the Emotional Legacies of Total War', *Women's History Review* 27:4 (2018), 617.

women who had to cope when men were taken away from them. Yet this reduces them to relatively flat historical roles. Their experiences of war and their complex reactions to loss are obscured by these family retellings, which has worrying implications for the long-term memory of war and disaster.

The final third of the book articulates how family memories of war are mediated through institutions which support cultural memory. Chapters 5 and 6 ask what happens when families are brought into contact with museums as institutions which often act as a pillar of cultural memory. It is in these spaces that the differences between war and disaster narratives are stark, with the First World War dominating memory cultures in a way that mining disasters do not. Chapter 5 shows that due to the quantity of personal material the Imperial War Museum collected in the 1910s and early 1920s, working-class families were able to place mementos of their loved ones in a national collection. The letters which accompanied the donations constitute an archive of family grief in their own right, and point towards families who felt that their loved one could gain national recognition through the inclusion of memorial material in this national museum. Chapter 6 follows longer-term memory trends of both the war and disaster dead. It argues that family memory hinged on memorial ephemera and objects created in the early twentieth century, but that some families lost the meaning attached to objects, and so had to re-imbue them with personal meaning.[126] In the 2000s, family histories were reinvigorated through the internet. Through online projects created for the centenary of the First World War, the families of the war dead were afforded an opportunity to publicly declare their relationship with their loved one in a way that was unparalleled by other mass death events in Britain.

The contours of family mourning after war and disaster in Britain changed and evolved over the course of the twentieth century. As families came to term with their sudden loss, they created and imbued memorial ephemera and objects with special meaning. These objects became powerful memory prompts, both within the family and outside of it. By placing these items into local and national collections the families of the war dead extended their family memory into the twenty-first century. But these memories were also subsumed by wider war narratives. The reasons that the historiography of war

[126] Personal relationships with objects are a keen part of social science practice. See Mihaly Csikszentmihalyi, *The Meaning of Things* (Cambridge, 1981); Margaret Gibson, 'Melancholy Objects', *Mortality* 9:4 (2004), 285–99; Liz Gloyn, Vicky Crewe, Laura King, and Anna Woodham, 'The Ties That Bind: Materiality, Identity, and the Life Course in the "Things" Families Keep', *Journal of Family History* 42:2 (2018), 157–76; also see Nicholas Saunders and Paul Cornish, *Contested Objects* (Abingdon, 2009) and *Matters of Conflict: Material Culture, Memory and the First World War* (Abingdon, 2004).

grief has focused on middle- and upper-class families are the same reasons that have meant that the cultural understandings of war have rested on the myth of the 'lost generation'. This has melded with family memory to create strong impressions of the First World War which often rely on commemorative tropes. Families of the disaster dead too are now bound by powerful class-based interpretations of the past, where large disasters, and not everyday work-based illness or accident, were the main scourge of pit workers. What has often remained in families is a strong desire to remember the dead. Through objects, ephemera, and tales about the deceased, families have sought to memorialize their dead over the past 120 years. Their fierce attempts to retain the memory of a loved one are, in many ways, proven by their inclusion in this book. Complex family relationships were distilled into small items of grief which were used as a commemorative buffer against mass memorial decisions that had been taken from them, and which have been both included in and excluded from memory-forming practices since the early twentieth century.

Family Mourning After War and Disaster in Twentieth-Century Britain. Ann-Marie Foster, Oxford University Press.
 DOI: 10.1093/9780191968129.003.0001

1

Receiving Death

The families of those who worked in dangerous spaces, be they military or industry based, knew that there was always a chance of death. Dying in war was a messy business. Bodies were pushed beyond their limit, mangled, and propelled into death. Soldiers died in battle, of wounds, and from sickness. These are the deaths that most people have a passing familiarity with, of people being torn apart by shells, violated by bullets, and asphyxiated by gas. Sailors drowned, were burned, or died from hypothermia in icy waters. This death-adjacent work was highly racialized. Men with Black, South Asian, and East Asian heritage were most likely to work in the dangerous engine rooms, where injury, heat exhaustion, and burns were likely, as well as a higher probability of death in the event of a shipwreck, since these roles were concentrated in the bowels of the ship. Women workers were also subject to harsh working conditions. Working-class women were poisoned in munitions factories, and nurses were exposed to disease and danger, sometimes fatally, during their working lives. Miners too faced dangerous work environments and could die of burns, asphyxiation, by being crushed, or, as with military and naval men, of slow-drawn-out diseases caused by impossible working conditions. Rescuers and workers recovering bodies would often discuss the horrific conditions they found the men in, and the suffering associated with such a death was the topic of many a local and national conversation after disaster. Social elements of dying were highly contingent on location—some people died surrounded by comrades, friends, and care givers, while others died alone.

Workers, their employers, and families all engaged in antemortem measures to ensure that in the event of a death bodies would be identified and next of kin notified. For all of this preparation, in the immediacy of death there was considerable confusion over the roles and responsibilities of various individuals. The state took the family's role by first registering a death and then taking over care of the body. This chapter deals with the messy part of death, between a loved one dying and their funeral. It concentrates on the various ways that families encountered death: from receiving news, to paperwork, receiving the summons to identify a body, and possibly taking it home. These practices differed: while paperwork and word-of-mouth communication were used for both war and disasters, war tended towards the former, and disasters the latter. Parallel timelines of immediate death practices emerged, from families who were close enough to be able to be near or with their loved one at their time of death, to families who were informed of a death well after the fact. There were multiple receptions involved in sudden death, and families found a way through these immediate emotional, bureaucratic, and communicative stages as best they could.

There were practicalities to be contended with in the immediate aftermath of death. Antemortem measures to identify the dead were married with postmortem ones to ensure that names would be associated with corpses. These measures ensured that the families of the dead would know if one of their members had died—however, in practice, this was a complicated and drawn-out process. Confusion was a key characteristic of war and disaster death, either through complicated bureaucratic processes or an anxious wait at the site of a disaster for news of a family member. Once families were informed of a death they, in turn, had to tell wider family members and friends. This was easier in the case of a disaster where the deceased lived locally, as news spread by word of mouth. In the case of war, with people scattered, letters were turned to in order to tell close ones of a death.

Running in tandem with this, deaths had to be registered, and the appropriate administrative bodies informed. The organized chaos of the early parts of death, in both war and disaster, reconfigured the ways the family and the state interacted with one another, with the state taking over the traditional family role of registering a body, foreshadowing the renegotiated roles both took on when handling the body of the deceased. During the First World War there was an increased bureaucracy of death—the official paperwork associated with death in the twentieth century. From forms to ensure that the correct next of kin details were present, through to War Office notifications of death, the families of the new citizen army were introduced to a death-based bureaucracy like never before. Military paperwork had long been necessary to control great numbers of troops. Charlotte Macdonald and Rebecca Lenihan's study of nineteenth-century British War Office records highlights the tension within soldiers' records, created to regulate identity, service, and financing for individual soldiers. They emphasise the records were created to 'detail individuals as constituent parts of the broader organisation whose entire formation stressed uniformity in the ranks', but which paid more attention to officers than rank and file, whose files were decidedly thinner.[1]

[1] Charlotte Macdonald and Rebecca Lenihan, 'Paper Soldiers: The Life, Death and Reincarnation of Nineteenth-Century Military Files across the British Empire', *Rethinking History* 22:3 (2018), 378–9.

By the early twentieth century Army paperwork took on a similar role to its nineteenth-century counterpart. Soldiers were to be registered, identified, accounted for, and distilled from a complex individual into a brief collection of words and numbers. The First World War saw this paperwork expand, not only in terms of the sheer number of people it had to process, but through the additional paperwork that people had to respond to. When a soldier enlisted he gave the details of his next of kin, to be informed if he was taken ill, wounded, or died, which replicated procedures for when a miner started work at a new colliery. In this seemingly innocent exchange of information lay a powerful transformation: the state assumed the role of the family and relegated them to the status of bystanders, unable to do anything but observe as the War Office assumed their bureaucratic role. While those whose loved ones died in disaster had a different relationship with bureaucracy, they were still touched by it through death registration and official inquests. Ultimately, in both war and disaster, families ceded control to officials, yet this took different forms in these varied workplace deaths.

In the case of disasters fortunate families could receive the body of their loved one. Not all bodies were allowed back into the family home, but for those that were, traditional death practices, which kept bodies in the home for several days before the funeral, could be enacted. This reception was not always met well, and families did not always accept that the body of their loved one had returned. The difficult emotions that emerged from sudden death, in the first wave of shock, were soothed as much as they could be by family, friends, and neighbours, who rallied around to offer succour. These various receptions, which took much of the usual family responsibilities away from those affected, prepared the families of the dead for the burials to come.

Controlling the Dead

The scale and confusion of the First World War brought with it a host of new bureaucratic problems: whole sections of civic society had to be mobilized, troops trained, and supplies moved. This movement of the living was contrasted with the stillness of the dead, who became an object for the Army to regulate. Soldiers and officials were well aware of the problems that could hinder families being informed of a death in a timely manner, and there was a significant amount of antemortem preparation to circumnavigate these risks. Death was prepared for both by officials who had to deal with paperwork following the event, and by individual soldiers and their families, who were well aware of the complications which could arise when trying to identify bodies in wartime.

The identification of the dead caused a constant problem for officials who, alongside individuals, sought to ensure that information pertaining to bodies could be collected. Identification methods slowly developed over the course of the early twentieth century in reaction to needs posed by war and disaster. The Army responded to increased pressure by the public for systems to identify the individual dead, and mining officials reacted to pressure from workers to be able to identify how many people were underground in case of disaster. The Army used identification tags, while mining officials implemented lamp check systems which gave some indication of the numbers involved in mining disasters. Neither system proved to be watertight, but were developed due to increased expectations around recognizing the individual dead.

The Army gradually increased its identification measures over the course of the late nineteenth and early twentieth centuries, largely responding to problems showcased through inadequate systems of registration. Army Form B.2067 was introduced in the late nineteenth century as an identification card which was sewn into uniforms (although most were simply placed in pockets).[2] However, these single cards were not of much use if the soldier had already been buried. Information about who was buried where, which could comprise a list of names, or simply the remembered knowledge of an officer, was of no use if the paper was lost or the officer himself did not survive. During the Second Anglo-Boer War, unless the dead were of a particularly high rank, or had been privately commemorated, soldiers who died were not buried with any form of identification, with simple iron crosses serving as a gravemarker, further complicating posthumous identification.[3]

The 1906 Geneva Convention made the identification and burial of the dead in war the responsibility of the victorious side, placing the onus on the holder of the field to carefully inspect all bodies in order to identify them.[4] Following the example of other European nations who had already introduced identification discs, and pressured by the Geneva Convention, single identity discs were introduced by the Army in 1906 as an attempt to record

[2] Sarah I. Ashbridge and Simon Verdegem, 'Identity Discs: The Recovery and Identification of First World War Soldiers Located during Archaeological Works on the Former Western Front', *Forensic Science International* (2020), 1.

[3] Thomas Laqueur, *The Work of the Dead: A Cultural History of Mortal Remains* (Princeton, 2018), 458.

[4] Ashbridge and Verdegem, 'Identity Discs', 2.

the men who died in combat. The disc was designed to be removed as proof of death. This was, in many ways, an improvement from the previous system, as the disc gave some proof that the bureaucratic measures put in place could begin, but was a far cry from a perfect system of identification. Single identity discs posed the opposite problem to the system of using identification cards: once removed, the body was left with no means of identification.

Despite immediate bureaucratic benefits, the single identity disc posed significant problems during the First World War. Upheaval on the battlefield, combined with reburials, meant that while the individual was marked as dead in official paperwork, their body was uncoupled from these documents which located the body after death. Soldiers, aware of these problems with the single identity discs, asked their families to send durable ones made out of metal, or made them themselves.

This was a potentially traumatizing experience for the family, who realized the significance of this request. Upper-class soldiers could request identity discs made from precious metal to be sent by their families. In a memoir written after the death of her son, Marie Connor Leighton vividly recalled sending him a silver identity disc:

> I knew what it stood for as I looked at it. It stood first and foremost for the fact that the boy who in himself was all earth and all heaven to me was in the army only one among many thousands—perhaps hundreds of thousands. It stood for a fearful confusion in which masses of men might get inextricably mixed up so that none could know who his fellow was; and it stood for a field on which there were many dead lying, and for grim figures walking about among those dead and depending for their identifications on some token worn by the still shapes whose lips would speak no more.[5]

Not only were families confronted with the hypothetical death of their loved one, they were aware that the items they were sending might be the only barrier between their family member and a nameless burial. These fears spoke of men who were so plentiful that they might not be recognized by those who had to bury them, and who might have to rely on these small items for their families to be informed that they had perished.

It became readily apparent to the War Office that families would not be satisfied if their loved one's body was lost within the milieu of the dead, unable to be located in a particular grave—if, indeed, they had been lucky enough to

[5] [Marie Connor Leighton], *Boy of My Heart* (London [1916]), 196.

be buried at all. Single identity discs were not fit for purpose, and so a new two-disc system was devised. Fabian Ware, by this time heavily involved in identifying the dead through his work with the Imperial War Graves Commission, was partially responsible for the design of duplicate identity discs, where one remained on the body while the other was removed as proof of death.[6] These were circulated from late 1916 and, although not foolproof, ensured that more bodies than under the previous system could be tracked, and paperwork as to their whereabouts updated.

Identification systems for mine workers developed in a similarly haphazard way. Largely, these systems revolved around the lamps taken down the pit. For the most part, surface workers knew who was likely to be down the mine at the time of a disaster. Combined with the conditions in mining disasters, which could destroy items on the body, there was less of a need to produce something to mark the individual dead, and items which informed management how many people were down the mine were prioritized. While the dead needed to be identified, this was generally done by colleagues and relatives, not by strangers (as could be the case in the Army).

By the early 1900s lamp checks were used to identify which miner had taken a specific lamp, which allowed people to work out how many men were underground in the case of pit accidents.[7] While this system was used in most collieries by the early twentieth century, the 1911 Coal Mines Act made a check system mandatory in all British mines.[8] There were some issues with these measures. It was only in the mid to late twentieth century that there was a three-check system which ensured that one disc was left in the lamp room, one was given to the banksmen when the miner was descending into the pit, and one was in the collier's possession, which proved that the lamp owner was in the mine. Before this, lamp swapping, loss of tokens, and lax application of these practices all led to confusion during various mining disasters. While these systems generally improved over the course of the early twentieth century, they only tended to show how many men were down the pit and who they were likely to be: they were not often used to identify the bodies of the dead.

Workplaces and the military both had systems in place to ensure that next of kin would be contacted in the event of a worker's death. In his

[6] Sarah Ashbridge, 'Military Identification: Identity Discs and the Identification of British War Dead, 1914–18', *British Journal for Military History* 6:1 (2020), 21–42.

[7] Lancashire Mining Museum, 'Miners Tally Checks', https://lancashireminingmuseum.org/2017/08/11/miners-tally-checks/ [Accessed 05.02.2021].

[8] Coal Mines Act 1911, Section 34.i.

autobiography, miner B. L. Coombes recalled that when he started work at a colliery in the early 1910s a clerk asked 'in a deep, sad voice for the address of my nearest relative so that they could be communicated with in case of accident or death'.[9] In the Army, the preparation for death through identity discs was married with systems to ensure that after death the individual's next of kin would be notified—however, much like the discs, the bureaucratization of death during the First World War was a slow process. It was not imagined that the war would last for as long as it did, or result in such a high number of casualties. When a soldier enlisted he gave the details of his next of kin, in case of injury or death. Through enlistment, the state assumed the traditionally familial mantle of completing death-related paperwork, and allowed the War Office to assume this bureaucratic role.

After war and disaster, representatives of the state, and not individual families, were expected to register deaths with the General Register Office (GRO). In peacetime families, sometimes aided by medical professionals, informed local registrars of deaths in the home. The 1836 Registration Act established the GRO, which centrally recorded all births and deaths in England.[10] Registrars oversaw the compulsory notification of deaths within the district they oversaw, and sent this information to the GRO, based at Somerset House. Following the 1874 Births and Deaths Registration Act, within five days of the death the closest family member to the deceased, or, failing that, a housemate, had to notify the registrar of a death in the home.[11] If the person died in a hospital, or in a charitable institution, the head of the organization reported the death.[12] After mining disasters, registration of death was submitted as part of the inquest. As a matter of course, coroners- inquests were held after most mining disasters to determine the cause of death of the men involved. Following the 1874 Act, families of those who were involved in an inquiry did not need to register the dead, and the paperwork from the jury involved was substituted in lieu of a formal death certificate for registration purposes.[13]

If a soldier died while on service abroad, the death was authenticated and the details transmitted to the GRO, which kept a permanent register of all military deaths overseas.[14] The Commander in Chief was responsible for the

[9] B. L. Coombes, *These Poor Hands: The Autobiography of a Miner Working in South Wales* (Cardiff, 2002), 17.

[10] Julie Rugg, 'From Reason to Regulation', in Peter C. Jupp and Clare Gittings (eds.), *Death in England* (Manchester, 1999), 216.

[11] Births and Deaths Registration Act 1874, ch. 88, 10–11.

[12] Births and Deaths Registration Act 1836, XIX.

[13] Births and Deaths Registration Act 1874, ch. 20, 3.

[14] Registration of Births, Deaths and Marriages (Army), 1879, 2.

lists and paperwork of Army deaths within their control, but once these records were sent to England, they became the legal property of the GRO.[15] If the soldier died on home soil, death registration followed the usual regulations. When under Army care overseas, the responsibility of informing the GRO fell to the state; when at home or on leave, responsibility once more fell to civilians.

In effect, after both war and disaster the legal mechanisms of registering the dead superseded familial control over this bureaucratic step. Although the death of an individual could, in peacetime, be registered by a hospital or an institution if they had died within its walls, the legal onus was generally placed on families to register the death of one of their own. How significant the registration of the death was to individual families is something that cannot be accessed—however, in terms of control, this distinction is significant. The state, embodied through the War Office or coroners, took this initial bureaucratic step away from families, hinting at the role they were to take in the long-term control of the dead. The registration was the first step towards full control of the dead, at the expense of the traditional family role. As a symbolic action it warned families that further control of the dead by official powers would be enacted.

Reporting the Dead

The mechanisms for relaying the news of a death to families were, at the beginning of the First World War, unfit for the large-scale conflict that unfolded. In 1914, no states had plans to document the dead in as much detail as was eventually required, preferring to rely on procedures developed after previous wars, which proved a thoroughly inadequate system as the war developed.[16] At the start of the war the Army still used burial regulations published in 1909. These regulations instructed that details about military deaths were passed on by the regiment, and were handled by the Adjutant General's Office, which provided administrative support for the Army. The guidance in the 1909 regulations simply stated that deaths should be reported to the Adjutant General's Office at the base they occurred. Those involved in burials removed the soldier's single identity disc and pay book, and sent them

[15] Registration of Births, Deaths and Marriages (Army), 1879, 3.

[16] Laqueur, *The Work of the Dead*, 460; Anne-Marie Hughes, 'Death, Service and Citizenship in Britain in the First World War' (Unpublished PhD, University of Manchester, 2009), 30.

to the office at the base. After receiving this information, the officer in charge was to 'telegraph the government concerned with the least possible delay the names of all officers and men who have been reported to him as dead, wounded, or missing'.[17]

Once war began this proved an inadequate system for recording the names of the dead, and both military and voluntary bodies were involved in recording and burying the dead. By 1916, the War Office Casualty Branch was responsible for bureaucratic procedures following death, issuing newspaper lists of the dead and individual death notices. They were informed by the men's units and the Red Cross, who created lists of the dead, and married these lists with the next of kin information at the Casualty Branch.[18] The office grew from several clerks to a staff of over 700, although the Red Cross continued to supply the department with names and information.[19] Red Cross involvement intervened in what was previously the dual responsibility of the family and the state. As Jay Winter argues, Red Cross members sometimes became stand-ins for families who were unable to search for the missing.[20] In this context, they acted as representatives for the family of the dead who would usually register a death, and gave support to help ensure that as many war dead as possible were recorded by the state.

Due to the confused nature of the war, families did not always find out about the death of their loved one through official channels.[21] In Britain, the families of ordinary soldiers received the news of their death via letter, with the families of officers being told by telegram. This was not necessarily immediate, and families could wait for some time to hear about the death of a loved one through official channels. A death notice from the War Office could be received after the family had been informed of the death by a letter from a comrade or religious leader who was present at the person's death. Due to bureaucratic errors, middle and upper-class families might only find out that their soldier had died from death lists published in *The Times*. The parents of Harry Taylor were two such unfortunates. Harry had been missing since 21 March 1918, but a telegram informing his parents of this had been overlooked. They had no time to grieve the fact that he had been confirmed dead before reading of it in the newspaper.[22]

[17] HMSO 'Field Service Regulations Pt. II Organisation and Administration 1909, Reprinted with Amendments 1913' (London, 1913), 165–6.

[18] Hughes, 'Death, Service and Citizenship', 30.

[19] Laqueur, *The Work of the Dead*, 461.

[20] Jay Winter, *Sites of Memory, Sites of Mourning* (Cambridge, 1995), 30.

[21] Andrea Hetherington, *British Widows of the First World War: The Forgotten Legion* (Barnsley, 2018), 15–21.

[22] Lilian Dalton, *Harry: Schoolboy and Soldier* (London, 1919), 51.

A notification of death from the War Office was not the same as a peacetime death certificate, and there was considerable confusion about the different types of paperwork received. There could be a substantial time delay between the family being notified that someone had died and receiving a death certificate. Many families did not understand that the death notice did not occupy the same legal status as a death certificate, and such was the delay between the two that in 1915 middle and upper-class families lobbied for a shorter gap between the death notice and the death certificate being issued.[23] Anne-Marie Hughes suggests that there may have been reasons for this, because the government was trying to rapidly process deaths in chaotic wartime circumstances, while hiding this from the families of the deceased, who needed to maintain some kind of morale as the war was still ongoing.[24] Even after the war had ended, the relatives of those for whom the Army was a career could find themselves surprised by the difficulty of access to the paperwork of death. Major A. G. Staveley's wife asked her solicitors to track down details of his death certificate seven years after his demise, as none had been issued in the interim.[25] Yet this discussion of the death certificate is, perhaps, getting ahead of ourselves, because in order to deal with bureaucracy families had first to receive the news of a death.

Receiving the News

The overwhelming majority of families who lost a member in war or disaster were not with their loved one as they died. During the First World War, if circumstances allowed, and messages were quick, private citizens could travel to France to be with their dying husband or son. While this opportunity was theoretically open to all, as the government was prepared to reimburse those who travelled for this purpose, in practice only those with a certain amount of private wealth could afford to take the trip.[26] For those fighting further afield, deathbed visits were not an option. When men were badly wounded and transported to field hospitals, their last hours were attended by nurses and orderlies who provided pain relief and comfort.[27] After disasters, the badly

[23] Hughes, 'Death, Service and Citizenship', 31.

[24] Hughes, 'Death, Service and Citizenship', 32.

[25] Commonwealth War Graves Commission Archive, efile, CWGC/8/1/4/1/1/87 (AA36539).

[26] Helen McCartney, *Citizen Soldiers: The Liverpool Territorials in the First World War* (Cambridge, 2005), 100.

[27] Christine E. Hallett, *Containing Trauma: Nursing Work in the First World War* (Manchester, 2009), 65–8; Jessica Meyer, *An Equal Burden: The Men of the Royal Army Medical Corps in the First World War* (Oxford, 2019), 110.

wounded were transported to hospitals, where, if close by, their family could attend their final hours, although these formed a distinct minority of the disaster dead. The majority of those who died in war or disaster did so without their family present.

The families of the dead received the news in a variety of settings: in a parlour, at the kitchen table, or at the site of an accident. Although in mining disasters the dead often passed away underground, sometimes with co-workers, sometimes alone, on the surface families who ran to the pithead were surrounded by people. Witnesses included concerned neighbours, workers from nearby mines, and young children. Ivor Jones, a colliery official at Seven Sisters, South Wales, recalled that his first impression of life 'in its tragedy and its blessings' came from seeing the aftermath of the 1913 Senghenydd mining disaster when he was 5 years old, later recalling: 'we were allowed, as children, very young then, to go as near as possible to the mine. And I could see those men brought up. And that gave me an awful feeling...the dead was being piled up. The women were crying, my own mother among them, but we had nobody underground as it happens, but every woman was crying...all the ministers were all helping out.'[28] These onlookers, young and old, formed the backdrop to the family experience at the pithead in the immediate aftermath of disaster.

Being informed that a family member had died was not a straightforward process: in wartime, the news of a death might not reach the family for some weeks, and a letter of condolence from an officer might reach the family before an official death notice. After a disaster the family might be able to wait near the disaster site, but others were informed of deaths via telegram. Thousands in wartime were denied even this comfort, as their loved one was listed as missing, offering a mixture of hope and despair for many. While confusion over wartime deaths was marked in weeks, months, and years, confusion after disaster could be measured in hours, days, and weeks. After mining disasters there was often confusion about who was down the pit at the time of the accident, and it could be days or weeks before any unrecognizable bodies brought up from the depths of the mine could be attributed to men missing from their homes.

In the case of mining disasters where families lived nearby, and could hear the blast, their experience of waiting for news of their loved one was measured in hours and days. They waited for survivors and rescuers to emerge to tell them of the fate of their loved one. Wives, parents, brothers and sisters of

[28] South Wales Coalfield Collection, VID/18, Ivor Jones.

the men in the pit who lived nearby would rush to the pithead seeking news of their loved one. After the West Stanley colliery explosion, women at the pithead were seen 'making frantic appeals for lost ones'.[29] After the 1916 Woodhorn mining disaster Tamar Armstrong was haunted by the fact that she ran to the pit hoping her sweetheart had survived, not initially thinking about her father, who, as she later discovered, was killed in the explosion.[30] In the immediate confusion of a disaster, knowing who was injured, or worse, was difficult to ascertain.

Not all miners worked near their families, which could delay news about a death reaching familial ears. Migration between counties was fairly common in mining communities in the early twentieth century, especially by young men with no dependants, but there were some married miners prepared to travel long distances for work.[31] The majority of miners tended to stay in one region, although they might change the colliery that they worked for several times throughout their working life. For families who lived far away from the mines their relatives worked in, telegrams and letters could be sent to inform them of news in the event of a disaster. During the 1910 Wellington Pit disaster in Cumbria, one woman, living in a different part of the county, was sent successive telegrams informing her that her brother was trapped in the pit, her cousin was missing in the disaster, and, eventually, that they had found her brother's body.[32]

Family members also rushed to the scenes of other types of disaster. In the immediate aftermath of railway disasters, families often attempted to visit the site of the tragedy and to search for news of their loved one. After the 1915 Quintinshill railway disaster, in Gretna, Scotland, wounded soldiers were taken across the border to the Cumberland Infirmary in Carlisle. The disaster happened when a troop train, carrying members of the 1/7th Battalion Royal Scots, crashed into a stationary passenger train, trapping a number of people. This was compounded by a third train ploughing into the wreckage of the first crash. The carriages were set alight, and the blaze became so strong that rescuers were unable to do anything to help those trapped in the wreckage. It is estimated that 226 people died in the disaster, 214 of whom were soldiers.[33]

[29] *Evening Chronicle*, 18 February 1909, p. 5.

[30] Mike Kelly, 'How the Woodhorn Colliery Disaster 100 Years ago Changed a Community', *Chronicle Live*, 13 August 2016.

[31] Roy Church, *The History of the British Coal Industry, Vol. 3* (Oxford, 1986), 215–24.

[32] Gordon L. Routledge, *Black Wednesday: An Account of the Wellington Pit Disaster, Whitehaven, in the Year 1910* (Carlisle, 2011), 7, 10.

[33] There is some confusion over whether 226 or 227 people died in the Quintinshill railway disaster. J. A. B. Hamilton, who produced the definitive account of the disaster, put the total at 226. His count is used in this book.

Many of the families of the dead lived in or near Edinburgh, in Leith and Musselburgh.

Community spirit often marked sudden disaster. An ambulance train from Carlisle conveyed many of the Quintinshill patients to the Infirmary, aided by a man who had been staying in Carlisle and heard about the accident and transported fifteen men over five journeys in his motorcar.[34] Scottish families who had been told that their loved one was injured were allowed to take a special train to visit them in Carlisle, but the families of those whose loved ones had died, or were missing in the confusion, were told to wait.[35] Some decided to make their way to the crash site independently to ascertain if their loved one had died.[36] The need for families to visit the wounded, and try to actively discover their family member's fate, was clearly recognized by military authorities who arranged the special train. This was an unusual occurrence after railway disasters and clearly marks the elevation of soldiers in wartime. The provision of transport to take family members to the crash site was significant in showing the military dimension of this tragedy, but families also travelled to the site before this special train was put on, emphasizing the length they went to in order to see if a loved one had survived.

Receiving the news of a death was, quite understandably, an incredibly difficult and upsetting moment. Hearing about the death of a loved one produced a range of responses, from tears to bodily stillness, and many family accounts of loss focused on the physical aspects of seeing or experiencing this sudden stab of grief. While receiving the news was a decided shock, families were not often isolated in their grief for long. In the case of a telegram, people ran to offer comfort. After disaster communities waited together for news of the dead. If one was informed of a war death through a letter, family, friends, and neighbours noticed soon enough. When there was a great distance between those affected by the death, letters assumed an enhanced role in providing a conduit for discussing the dead. Yet letters were not the only way of discussing the dead, and families and friends would visit each other to share in their bereavement.

While much has been written about the 'fictive kinship' of mourning in the twentieth century, the first group of people that the bereaved grieved alongside were friends and family.[37] There was a communal aspect to grief, and to

[34] Gordon L. Routledge, *The Sorrows of Quintinshill* (Wigton, 2002), 30–1.

[35] Routledge, *The Sorrows of Quintinshill*, 38.

[36] J. A. B. Hamilton, *Britain's Greatest Rail Disaster* (London, 1969), 69.

[37] On 'fictive kindship' see Jay Winter, 'Kinship and Remembrance in the Aftermath of the Great War', in Jay Winter and Emmanuel Sivan (eds.), *War and Remembrance in the Twentieth Century* (Cambridge, 1999), 40–60.

supporting the recently bereaved, which was a significant part of early twentieth-century death cultures. Nearly all of the accounts of families discovering a loved one's death show the various emotions which came to the fore when the news was received. These emotions were often expressed in a highly physical way, and people's appearances, their tears, and their bodily reactions all feature in accounts of receiving the news of the dead. Some family reports of receiving the news take on a heightened tragic nature. The most well-known of these is Wilfred Owen's family receiving a telegram informing them of his death on Armistice Day. But these tragic tales are echoed elsewhere. The author Marie Connor Leighton wrote about a family friend who had been expecting the return of her son on leave on Christmas Day and had delayed dinner until he arrived. Late in the evening, realizing that he was not coming back that night, she decided to continue the feast in his absence, not knowing he was dead.[38]

Leighton was also in the unfortunate position of writing about her own horror upon hearing the news about the death of her son Roland. On the day that Leighton and her husband had been expecting Roland home on leave they received the telegram telling them he had died. Leighton had been waiting for her son, and on hearing the opening and shutting of doors, initially assumed it was Roland. Thinking on it further, she fancied that 'something new and strange and heavy' had come into the air of the house.[39] Her husband entered the room where she was sitting to tell her of their son's demise:

> For minutes that were like years the world became to me a shapeless horror of greyness in which there was no beginning and no end, no light and no sound. I did not know anything except that I had to put out my hand and catch at something, with an animal instinct to steady myself so that I might not fall.[40]

This description, which focused on the loss of senses, is complemented by Leighton's description of her husband's grief, in which his physical appearance, including his motions and pallor, comes to the fore. Coming towards Leighton, the telegram clutched in his hand, there was 'something very odd about his step. And his face looks changed, somehow; sharpened in feature and greyish white.'[41] Leighton described grief as an emotional, visual, bodily, and spiritual presence, which affected nearly all of the senses. It was

[38] [Leighton], *Boy of My Heart*, 200.
[39] [Leighton], *Boy of My Heart*, 219.
[40] [Leighton], *Boy of My Heart*, 220.
[41] [Leighton], *Boy of My Heart*, 220.

overwhelming, and could manifest in particular ways, which encompassed the entire being.

The physicality of people's reaction to such news was also described by J. H. Armitage, a working-class man from Leeds, who was only a child when his older brother was killed at Gallipoli:

> I shall always remember the morning that the long buff coloured envelope came by the early post. Mother sat down and opened it then her face seemed to freeze like a mask. I remember asking her what the letter was about, after a while she said in a strange quiet voice – 'George is dead, he's been killed'. She said nothing else for what seemed like hours, she just sat there at the end of the long white table stareing [*sic*] straight in front of her.'[42]

The shock of the news affected his mother's voice, posture, and facial expression. Far from being able to immediately comfort her second son, who had just lost his brother, she was frozen and unable to do more than process the information contained within the delivered envelope. If Leighton's father's reaction was shown in his 'odd' gait, Armitage's mother's followed Leighton's through the absence of movement.

For middle-class children the news of a family death could precipitate a great deal of movement and travel to be reunited with the rest of the family. Mary Collisson, the daughter of a curate, was at boarding school when she was told of her brother's death. She was pulled out of class by her form mistress and taken to the Headmistress, who had the unfortunate task of breaking the news to her. Collisson later remembered that her immediate reaction was to seek comfort from her: 'I flung my arms round her neck and could hear myself saying "Oh! I did love him so." '[43] She was then sent to an aunt's in London, before they travelled home to be with the rest of her family. Not only was Collisson contending with a sudden bereavement, it was one that meant she had to travel to seek solace in her family, away from her school friends and boarding-school routine.

At the news of a death displays of emotion were common, and both men and women succumbed to tears at the news that a loved one had died. One woman recalled that, as a child, she witnessed 'a woman who had worked as a charlady for Grannie coming one day & throwing herself in Grannies [*sic*]

[42] Burnett Archive, J. H. Armitage, 'Twenty Three Years or The Late Way of Life and Living by "The Exile" ', 59.

[43] Burnett Archive, Miss M. Collisson, 'Memories of a Country Rectory', [6].

arms & weeping—Her son had been killed in France.'[44] When Collisson went home, immediately following her brother's death:

> the news from the War Office was known in the village as soon as it reached the Rectory and Mrs Ann Redman came running down, breathless, to bring her weeping sympathy. Soon after I got back Mrs Long came over—hastening to share our sorrow and try to bring comfort.[45]

The community aspect of grieving together, and of showing immediate support for the families of the deceased, was a significant part of many family experiences, whether a person died of sickness or through violence. Regardless of the mode of death, friends and neighbours came to mourn alongside the immediate family, sharing their emotions and showing their support for the bereaved.

Men too were prone to weeping at the news of a death. Herbert Asquith showed deep emotion after the death of his son in 1915, with his daughter-in-law Cynthia writing that he was 'heartbroken and just like a child—tears pouring down his cheeks'.[46] Shedding tears was not restricted to civilians, and servicepeople, witnessing death, often showed emotion in their grief. While weeping was more common in the early nineteenth century, from the 1870s onward emotional restraint was highly valued, and particularly taught to middle- and upper-class men and boys.[47] Natasha Silk has suggested that although men in the trenches were often expected to show a high level of emotional self-regulation tears were not uncommon.[48] André Loez argues that rituals of mourning which allowed soldiers to cry as part of the patriotic ceremony were a way of attempting to change the meaning of tears, from symptoms of emotional and physical distress to an homage to the heroism of the dead.[49]

While there were culturally coded ways and times in which emotions could be shown, as Thomas Dixon notes, 'the reality of the emotional life of military

[44] Burnett Archive, Jean Nettleton, 'Autobiographical Letter', 2:922, [2].

[45] Burnett Archive, Collisson, 'Memories of a Country Rectory', [6].

[46] Cynthia Asquith, quoted in Michael Roper, *The Secret Battle: Emotional Survival in the Great War* (Manchester, 2009), 220.

[47] Thomas Dixon, *Weeping Britannia: Portrait of a Nation in Tears* (Oxford, 2015), 202.

[48] Natasha Silk, 'Witnesses to Death: Soldiers on the Western Front', in Martin Kerby, Margaret Baguley, and Janet McDonald (eds.), *The Palgrave Handbook of Artistic and Cultural Responses to War Since 1914: The British Isles, the United States and Australasia* (London, 2019), 147–61.

[49] André Loez, 'Tears in the Trenches: A History of Emotions and the Experience of War', in Jenny Macleod and Pierre Purseigle (eds.), *Uncovered Fields: Perspectives in First World War Studies* (Leiden, 2004), 220–2.

men on active service was more turbulent than the image of the slow-pulsed, unimaginative, nonchalantly puffing Tommy would suggest'.[50] Linda Maynard records soldiers seeking private spaces to weep after the death of a loved one.[51] These emotions did not confine themselves to the immediacy of the war, and displays of emotion surrounding life and death extended into the interwar period. One officer, on finding one of his troops alive at a reunion after the war, burst into tears, 'crying because he thought he'd sent them all [his troops] to their death'.[52]

Emotions and grief are a tricky subject to interpret as the gap between the societal expectation of the ways that people should behave and the ways that they do behave is often vast. Middle and upper-class men were expected to provide support for their mothers and sisters, reserving strong emotions for their close male friends, although in private male loss was not as emotionally bounded as has been suggested. Julie-Marie Strange has drawn attention to the depth of grief felt by individuals who did not fit middle- and upper-class understandings of outward displays of mourning in the 1910s, with working-class men in particular stereotyped as unfeeling by members of other classes.[53] Bereaved men were, of course, deeply affected by loss but were expected to publicly articulate it in a specific way. Although this constrained emotional economy was to come into its own during the Second World War, the idea of the self-contained man had been in circulation since the late nineteenth century.[54] This had a gendered and a class-based appeal: women were not held to the same ideals of self-control, nor were working-class men and women, although both were discouraged from outward displays of emotion. As the First World War progressed, women were increasingly expected to show less emotion in public, although showing emotion was acceptable at commemorative events in the interwar years. Propaganda during the First World War began to emphasize that women needed to show emotional restraint when faced with the news of a loved one's death, although this most likely indicates that there was altogether too much weeping rather than too little during the period.[55]

[50] Dixon, *Weeping Britannia*, 208.

[51] Linda Maynard, *Brothers in the Great War: Siblings, Masculinity, and Emotions* (Manchester, 2021), 33.

[52] Mass Observation, Autumn 2014, K4506.

[53] Julie-Marie Strange, '"She cried a very little": Death, Grief and Mourning in Working-Class Culture, c. 1880–1914', *Social History* 27:2 (2002), 148.

[54] For more on emotions in the Second World War see Lucy Noakes, *Dying for the Nation: Death, Grief, and Bereavement in Second World War Britain* (Manchester, 2020), esp. ch. 2.

[55] Dixon, *Weeping Britannia*, 221–2; Hetherington, *British Widows*, 31.

A glimpse into the ways that upper-class family members were expected to publicly mourn is well illustrated by Vera Brittain's writing. Before the death of her fiancé, and indeed before she had begun training as a nurse, Brittain wrote a passage in her diary about Hilda Lorimer, who was one of her tutors at Somerville College. Lorimer gave a tutorial the day after she found out her brother had been killed. One of the other students had expected their tutor to 'be very much upset, but instead of this Miss Lorimer took the class with her usual thoroughness & care' and the only hint of her grief was that 'her usually bright hair was quite dull & her eyes dim & tired looking'. This prompted a discussion about the nature of grief among the students: Brittain's friend thought that this reaction meant Lorimer could not be very upset but Brittain disagreed, writing, 'for those who show least care deepest.'[56] The display of emotion, or lack thereof, was discussed at length by the young women. The calm stoical resolve shown by Lorimer was interpreted differently by members of Brittain's cohort, hinting at the difficulties posed when parsing the emotions of others after bereavement.

Once the immediate family heard about the death, they needed to tell others who had a close relationship with the deceased. During the First World War, the parents of the bereaved often had to tell their son's fiancée that their husband-to-be had perished. Constance Richardson became engaged to Michael Rudd during the early years of the war. When Rudd died in 1917, Richardson was working away from home in a munitions factory, and so she was told of his death via a letter, sent by his parents. She composed a letter to her mother, who lived in the same area as Rudd's family, writing, 'you will I expect by now, have heard the cruel sad news of dear Mike.'[57] News travelled so quickly by word of mouth that Richardson fully expected her family to have heard of her fiancé's death before she herself did. Others in Richardson's position had to tell their friends about the loss of their fiancé in person. Jenny Wrench, the sister of a deceased soldier, and his fiancée, Marie Lee, went to call on friends together to tell them the news of her brother John's death.[58]

Visits to break the news of a death were common in working-class communities, such as Richardson's. Miners who had escaped a mining disaster might have to tell the family of a victim that they had not survived. Although a little earlier than the majority of disasters discussed here, George Parkinson

[56] Vera Brittain, *Chronicle of Youth* (London, 1981), 149.

[57] Ann Kerry, *Connie's War: A young girl's life in the munitions factory at Gretna in the Great War of 1914–18 told in letters home to her family with additions by her daughter Ann Kerry* (Gwynedd, 2005), 32.

[58] Kerry, *Connie's War*, 18.

recalled being asked by a neighbour about the fate of her son after he narrowly escaped death in a pit explosion in the mid-1800s. In a memoir written decades later, he recalled how he reacted when confronted by the mother of one of the dead, who asked after her son:

> Alas! I had seen him, for it was her 'canny Bob' whose dead body I had passed at the bottom of the shaft. But what could I answer? How could I tell a poor distracted mother, hoping and fearing for her only son, that I had seen him dead? But she pressed the question… I tried to evade answering her directly, but she drew her own conclusions, which were all too soon confirmed.[59]

Parkinson could not face telling Bob's mother that he had died, although his awkward manoeuvring revealed what he could not say. Of course, following a narrow escape himself he was highly likely to have been in some kind of shock, but he was also placed in the impossibly difficult position of having to tell someone that their child was no longer living.

Telling families of a death was also difficult in wartime, and young officers in particular, who were tired and in mourning themselves, found it difficult to write to the families of men in their unit.[60] Chaplains also felt the strain of constant letter writing to the bereaved. In 1916 Reverend William Geare complained to his family that 'I do not think I have written so many letters in any four weeks in my life as I have here (some of them sad ones to wives or mothers of our heroes), and yet my bundle of unanswered letters never gets smaller.'[61] Soldier's comrades would also often write letters to the family, adding extra details about their deaths and comforting them in their loss. Often they described painless deaths, and there was an 'element of concealment' about the language used to describe death scenes in their letters.[62]

Letters which gave extra information about the death of a loved one were not always welcomed by family members. Knowing that death was painful, drawn out, and tragic could destroy the idea of a swift and painless death that many clung to.[63] This was, for some, a form of emotional protection. People were more than aware that war was bloody and painful. Letters home,

[59] George Parkinson, *True Stories of Durham Pit Life* (London, 1912), 52–3.

[60] Roper, *The Secret Battle*, 210–12; also Jessica Meyer, *Men of War: Masculinity and the First World War in Britain* (Basingstoke, 2011), 75–96.

[61] William Duncan Geare, *Letters of an Army Chaplain* (London, 1918), 45.

[62] Roper, *The Secret Battle*, 213.

[63] Carol Acton, *Grief in Wartime: Private Pain, Public Discourse* (Houndmills, 2007), 11–12.

although often censored, nonetheless told of danger at the frontline, the fear the soldiers faced, and contained general descriptions of the aftermath of battle.[64] Visits home allowed for frank conversations, which had the potential to reveal the true face of war. Civilians were also conscious of the war-wounded, especially if they lived in a town or city attached to a war hospital. Despite this, the toll of being told that a loved one had died in pain was still great.

Bill Williamson's grandmother received a telegram which informed the family of a death of one of its members on the same day that a letter saying he was in good health arrived. His aunt recalled that Williamson's grandmother

> 'Sat rocking her chair with grief and wringing her hands.' They heard later that he was not killed outright. Badly wounded, he was moved on to a stretcher to the sanctuary of the church near the front. Moments later the church was obliterated by heavy artillery fire. 'This news', said my uncle Jim, 'nearly killed Maggie.'[65]

The grief felt at the reception of the telegram and letter merged with the knowledge that the traditional transcript of a swift and painless death was not quite kept to; instead the brief hope that he might have lived was snatched away. The families of the deceased to some extent needed to experience a type of cognitive dissonance between the fighting they had heard described and the way in which their loved one died.[66] They could choose to acknowledge the circumstances their family member had died in, and the choice was important. It meant the difference between choosing, consciously or not, the belief that a loved one had died swiftly, or that they had died a horrific death.

Letters of comfort were sometimes offered in lieu of a visit because people found it hard to talk to the recently bereaved. Prior to the death of her son, Marie Connor Leighton avoided her friend, Mrs Orme, whose son had died in the war. Leighton contented herself with writing a letter of sympathy to the Ormes, 'not having the courage to go and offer that poor father and mother comfort that could be no comfort'.[67] She also noted the cathartic release that writing could have on the bereaved, writing, 'one young widow I knew attacked hers [grief] with a fountain pen and got the better of it valiantly by

[64] Meyer, *Men of War*, 16–20.
[65] Bill Williamson, *Class, Culture and Community: A Biographical Study of Social Change in Mining* (London, 1982), 152.
[66] Winter, *Sites of Memory*, 35–6.
[67] [Leighton], *Boy of My Heart*, 200.

writing screed after screed, not only to her relatives and friends, but even to her remotest acquaintances.'[68]

In colliery towns bereaved families would be visited by concerned relatives, friends, union officials, and religious leaders. After mining disasters in small communities families left their doors open so that friends and family could come and share in their tragedy, sometimes throughout the night following the disaster.[69] Often these visitors would try to comfort the bereaved in whatever manner they could. One widow from the 1931 Bentley colliery disaster recalled the local parson comforted her by discussing how her husband had died instantly, and so did not experience the horrific burns which many of the survivors of the immediate explosion later died of. He told her that 'he'd been through the war, but he'd never seen anything like that for the men to be alive', saying, 'if it's a consolation, thank God your husband was killed [instantly] like that.'[70] Words of comfort after mining disasters often revolved around the rapidity of death and the lack of prolonged suffering, mirroring discussions with the bereaved during the First World War.

Visits and physical comfort were also of great importance to the families of the war dead. Constance Richardson regularly wept over the loss of her fiancé, and wrote letters home describing the support she got from her co-workers at the munitions factory. Shortly after Rudd's death, she wrote to her mother explaining that she felt 'wretched'—'every now and then, quite unexpectedly, I'll start and sob, and I can't help myself... all the girls and the housekeeper were crying on Saturday because of me.'[71] The support that she received undoubtedly helped her, although she missed her mother and told her so in her letters home.

Physical support was so important that family members who were far away would sometimes try to visit their loved ones to comfort them. In 1915 Paymaster Paton was granted weekend leave to travel from London to Glasgow to comfort his mother after the death of his brother at the front.[72] In a cruel twist of fate, his train was one involved in the Quintinshill railway disaster, and so his mother lost two sons very close together.

[68] [Leighton], *Boy of My Heart*, 202.

[69] This was frequently reported on in press accounts of mining communities after disaster: see, for example, *Evening Chronicle*, 18 February 1909, p. 5.

[70] Lois Hill, quoted in John Woodhead, 'Essay in Oral History: The Bentley Colliery Disaster', *Labour History Review* (1975), 80.

[71] Kerry, *Connie's War*, 32–3.

[72] Routledge, *The Sorrows of Quintinshill*, 35.

Searching for the Missing

While some families of the dead were informed about their loved one's death relatively quickly, others were involved in a protracted effort to try to work out whether their loved one was alive or dead. Although some bodies were discovered after the war had ended, and some families were able to track down the site of their loved one's corpse based on the letters sent by comrades, hundreds of thousands of bodies were lost. For the families of these men, discovering that they had died did not come through a single letter, or being told by a neighbour, but was instead a protracted experience of hoping and searching, while fearing a death notification from the War Office. Families in this position were caught in a liminal space where they could not acknowledge a death or begin to grieve because they simply did not know whether their loved one was alive or dead. During the First World War men could be lost at sea, blown to pieces, buried, or their appearance altered beyond recognition, making identification impossible. Families might be told that their loved one was missing, and that they would eventually be listed as dead. However, by the time they received an official letter telling them to assume their relative had died, families, understandably, did not always believe this.

Finding out who was missing and who was wounded after major offensives was an enormously complex task. After battle, roll calls determined who in the regiment had survived. After a couple of days, lists of those who were missing (which could mean wounded, captured, or dead) were sent to the War Office, where they were compared with lists of men from hospital bases, and gradually whittled down. The list was sent to the Red Cross Inquiry Office for the Wounded and Missing, run by the Joint War Committee of the Red Cross and St John, where representatives began to enquire after the men on the lists, collecting information from the wounded that might help locate their missing comrades. From this, any new information would be passed back to the War Office, who would then send details to the families concerned.[73] When a soldier was initially reported missing, his family would be sent an Army B 104-83 form, informing them that 'the report that he is missing does not necessarily mean he has been killed'. Twenty-six weeks after a soldier had been declared missing, his wife received a letter transforming her separation allowance into a widow's pension, although, as Andrea Hetherington notes, great pains were taken to ensure that families knew that

[73] Richard van Emden, *The Quick and the Dead: Fallen Soldiers and their Families in the Great War* (London, 2011), 169.

this was a bureaucratic change and not one which should be taken as proof that their loved one had died.[74]

Families often supplemented this slow-working bureaucracy to trace the missing by investigating the whereabouts of their missing family members themselves. The families of missing servicemen attempted to find out where the body of their loved one might be through a myriad of ways, from asking friends and family, utilizing patronage networks, and attempting to persuade authorities to search for their loved one. This was a wholly class-based activity. The most immediate way of attempting to find out information to pass on to the relevant authorities was through personal connections, which was only possible in the case of upper- and uppermiddle-class families. If a family member was present in an area where it was thought more information could be gained, then they were asked to act on behalf of the parents or wife of the serviceman in question. The father of Private E. W. P. Kernot, who lived in Australia, asked his brother-in-law, based in London, to liaise with the Imperial War Graves Commission, the body in charge of finding and burying the dead, on his behalf, as he was closer and so could correspond at a faster and cheaper rate.[75] If a family member was an officer, in some position of authority, then the family used their networks to appeal for additional information about them in other battalions. In 1915 the brother of the missing Captain Robert Stuart, an officer himself, attempted to find out more information from the front, although he did not seem to further the family enquiry through his attempts.[76]

During the First World War middle and occasionally working-class families used local newspapers as a method of discovering information about their missing loved ones. One 'Personal Advertisement' simply read:

> If anyone can give Information of 36288 Pte. Alfred Scholefield, K.O.Y.L.I., missing since March 21st, will they kindly communicate with Lucas, Fenham Drive, Newcastle-on-Tyne.[77]

Some families used newspapers to announce that they had officially given up hope of finding them alive, and that they now assumed their missing loved one had perished. In a single 'Deaths' column in June 1919 two families

[74] Hetherington, *British Widows*, 20.

[75] Commonwealth War Graves Commission, efile, CWGC/8/1/1/4/1/24 (AA10356).

[76] Public Record Office Northern Ireland D1618/15/15/1, letter from A. Stuart, 15 October 1915.

[77] *Evening Chronicle*, 2 May 1918, p. 2. The Commonwealth War Graves website does not list Pte Alfred Scholefield among the war dead, suggesting that he survived.

decided that they would announce the news that they no longer assumed their soldiers were alive. One of the wives announced a funeral service for the 'deceased' in the same notice:

> LAMB:- Gateshead, 5, Marton Pl., missing on March 26, 1918, now reported killed on that date, Sergt. M.F. Lamb, 6th N.F., dearly beloved husband of Mary Jane Lamb (nee Foster) oldest son of Robert Lamb, 1, Hopper St., Gateshead: aged 29 years. Service will be held at St. Mary's Gateshead, on Sat., June 7. 3p.m. All friends and neighbours kindly invited. Deeply mourned by his loving wife and daughter Nellie.[78]

Some of these announcements, which declared that the missing were presumed dead, appeared quite some time after the assumed date of death. One notice that announced Second Lieutenant Frank Mansfield was presumed deceased appeared in the *Evening Chronicle* in June 1919. Frank was reported wounded and missing at Garelle on 3 May 1917. The date announcing his presumed death may have been insignificant, but it is possible that the announcement was posted on an emotionally significant date for the family.

Often a variety of search mechanisms were turned to, with the use of free Red Cross services mixed with private enterprise for those who could afford it. During the war, families of the missing could draw on a vast number of agencies set up to help accommodate the search for the missing. The voluntary Red Cross Inquiry Office for the Wounded and Missing was used in conjunction with private companies such as Cox & Co., and people were warned of the perils of using illegitimate companies who only promised results upon remittance.[79] Many of these private companies would demand a considerable fee, limiting them to wealthy families; however, all families were able to access the Red Cross voluntary services which offered to send out inquiries to find missing family members of all classes.[80] Where there was a choice, and where families had either social or financial capital, they were given recourse to a far wider range of mechanisms which they could use to try to establish what had happened to their loved one.

The upper-class Stuart family attempted to locate Captain Robert Stuart, son of the sixth Earl Castle Stewart, in a particularly wide variety of ways. He was reported missing in early November 1914, and his wife, Evelyn, began to search for him. Between November 1914 and December 1915 Evelyn Stuart

[78] *Evening Chronicle*, 5 June 1919, p. 2.
[79] Jalland, *Death in War and Peace*, 40.
[80] Winter, *Sites of Memory*, 35–44.

contacted the private company Cox & Co. Enquiry Service, as well as voluntary associations in different countries such as the Paris Branch of the British Red Cross Society, the International Red Cross Agency for Prisoners of War, the Salvation Army, the Prisoners of War Information Bureau, the Prisoners of War Help Committee, L'Agence internationale des prisonniers de guerre, Nos Prisonaires, and also pursued official channels of enquiry, such as contacting the British Legation in Berne, the American Consular Service, the Ministère de la Guerre, and the War Office. She attempted to track her husband through parcels sent via the Post Office, and put a trace on monetary transactions by contacting the American Express Company. Stuart also ensured that word about his loss was spread publicly, posting adverts in the British and French press, and had descriptions of him translated into all major European languages. She sent his photograph to prisoner-of-war camps in Germany, to be looked at by captured Gurkha troops who may have been present when he fell, as well as posting them in British prisoner-of-war camps so that captured German troops could report if they had seen him fall on the battlefield.[81]

The family drew on additional kin networks to collect information, and both Stuart's mother and mother-in-law proved particularly useful assets. Her mother-in-law asked family friends to search for her son, sending her information about secret prisoner-of war-camps where men were not allowed to write letters home.[82] Stuart's mother corresponded with those who saw first-hand accounts of his wounding, found the location of the Gurkha troops who fought alongside him in the battle where he fell, and contacted friends in Berlin asking them to help with their search.[83] It is clear that Stuart attempted to use all of the resources available to her in order to try to locate her husband. Ultimately, she lost hope, and her search for a living husband turned into a search for his body.

Many families found themselves in the same position as Stuart in searching for a corpse. Sometimes officers and comrades wrote letters to the family, warning them that they had seen their loved one die, but did not know what happened to his body in the melee of fighting.[84] Such letters were meant to comfort the families of the missing, for with the knowledge of certain death they could begin to grieve despite the lack of a body. For many, their 'missing'

[81] PRONI, D1618/15/15 Correspondence RE. R. S. Stuart 1914–15.

[82] PRONI, D1618/15/15 Correspondence to Lady Castle Stewart.

[83] PRONI, D1618/15/15 Private Correspondence to E. Stuart, wife of Robert Sheffield Stuart, *c.*1915.

[84] Acton, *Grief in Wartime*, 32–5.

family member ultimately did not return, and a protracted search for some physical remnant of the person would extend into the interwar years. The families of the missing often occupied a liminal space which delayed any immediate sense of grief. They did not have the short, sharp, shock of a death notification, but instead the drawnout pain of a long bureaucratic process. Given the emotional no man's land they occupied, for the hopeful, the confirmation of death, perhaps several months after their family member went missing, could be a cruel blow indeed.

Bringing Home the Dead

This timeline of loss was drastically contracted for the families of disaster dead. These families could have the body of their loved one back within the family home a day or two after receiving the news of death. This was a luxury not afforded to all whose loved ones died in a disaster—sometimes the person died too far away from home, or the body might have been sealed in the mine that was to become a final burial place. It was also a privilege that those who died overseas during wartime were not afforded, and their families had to wait years, sometimes decades, for their loved one to have a fixed grave. Recovering and identifying bodies was not an easy task. Rescues were dangerous and bodies fragile. Even if the bodies were recovered they were not always identifiable. After maritime disasters, photographs of the corpses were sometimes taken to aid identification at a later date and allow a burial service to take place, with the promise that the person in the grave might one day be identified.[85] For the families who were lucky enough to have a body, however, this made an enormous difference to the mourning processes. It allowed them to keep the body at home ahead of the funeral, which fell into usual working-class death patterns.

If at all possible, the bodies of the dead were recovered after disaster. The conditions in the mine after a disaster could pose considerable danger to the rescuers, because the carbon monoxide (commonly called afterdamp) left after an explosion lingered, and the possibilities of further explosions threatened to add to the death toll. It was not uncommon for people to die in rescue attempts, and workers were cautioned not to overextend themselves when bringing up the bodies of the deceased. An account of the 1901 Senghenydd

[85] National Maritime Museum, HIS/8, *Accounts of Wrecks & Disasters Which have Happened on the North Norfolk Coast Since 1860.*

colliery disaster described the lucky escape of George Benyon, who crawled through the afterdamp to bring back the body of William Thomas, which disoriented him so much that he could not speak for hours afterwards.[86] Risky attempts to retrieve the bodies of the dead also took place during the First World War, with soldiers being injured or killed trying to reach their comrades.[87]

Recovering these bodies was often a highly traumatic experience. Some miners had the unfortunate task of recovering the bodies of their family members. In a particularly tragic case, a member of the Ambulance Brigade at the Bentley colliery found the body of his son, Clifford Hayes, after the pit disaster there. Realizing that his son's section was in the affected area, he made straight for it, walking past men on stretchers in extreme pain. Passing the afflicted he recalled he 'seemed blind to all of this. I was near to being inhuman.'[88] For people who knew but were not related to the dead, witnessing their deaths was still highly upsetting. Survivors of the Quintinshill railway disaster were deemed to be particularly affected by their experiences. Soldiers who witnessed the carnage were quoted in local newspapers saying that it was worse than anything they had seen in the trenches.[89] A local man, Michael Moscrop, rushed to aid the victims of the crash, later commenting that for 'months and months' afterwards he could not eat roast beef because it reminded him of the smell of burning flesh, while many other witnesses suffered nightmares for some time after the accident.[90]

During disasters, the question of where to put the corpses of the victims when they were recovered was a problem. After mining disasters the bodies of the dead were, whenever possible, brought back to the surface and placed in offices or workshops at the pithead until they could be identified.[91] Due to the damage inflicted on the bodies of the workers it was often necessary to hide them until they were either made more presentable or could be neatly laid out to aid identification by other means. Spaces to host the dead were not as obvious for those making decisions after other disasters. After particularly bad railway disasters, because of the nature of the open space in which the

[86] Michael Lieven, *Senghenydd: The Universal Pit Village 1890–1930* (Llandysul, 1994), 65. There were two colliery disasters in Senghenydd in the early 1900s: the 1901 disaster, which killed eighty-one workers, and the 1913 disaster, which killed 440.

[87] Roper, *The Secret Battle*, 208.

[88] *Thomson's Weekly News*, 28 November 1931, quoted in John Church, *'It's like old wine to see you again, lass': An Account of the 1931 Bentley Colliery Disaster* (Doncaster, 1991), 17.

[89] *The Carlisle Journal*, 25 May 1915, p. 4.

[90] Hamilton, *Britain's Greatest Rail Disaster*, 92.

[91] National Coal Mining Museum, SR59, Oral Histories, 'Pretoria Remembered'.

accidents tended to occur, corpses were laid on the ground nearby. After the Quintinshill railway disaster, a small cottage, first used as a mortuary, became so full of bodies that the remains of the victims were simply laid on the grass and covered in makeshift shrouds.[92] Since railway accidents tended to be somewhat remote, and without the relatives of the deceased nearby, it was slightly less pressing, as well as less practical, to hide the bodies until they were transported to a mortuary for identification. Munitions explosions required whatever buildings were nearby to be used to house the dead. After a munitions factory exploded in Chilwell in 1918, a worker described seeing 'about 120 mutilated corpses laid out in the Church at Attenborough, most of them unrecognisable.'[93]

Once the bodies had been recovered the task of identifying the dead began. The state of the bodies could range from those which were intact, with people who looked as if they were sleeping, to pieces of flesh, barely recognizable as human. In the 1937 novel *Cwmardy*, written by the miner and activist Lewis Jones, bodies found by rescuers after a mining explosion were described as 'ghastly lumps of greasy putrefaction.'[94] When bodies were intact there could be an element of the uncanny. A man who helped carry bodies out from the mine after the 1910 Pretoria pit mining disaster recalled the effects of carbon monoxide poisoning on bodies, saying there were 'dead men shoved in tubs, like they were sleeping.'[95] The families of those whose faces were still recognizable were reunited with the body of their loved one relatively quickly. Bodies which were immediately unrecognizable had to be identified by colleagues or family members.

When a body was altered beyond recognition, usually because of fire, rock fall, or decomposition, items found on the corpse were used as an identification tool. They were placed on top or near the covered body and family members could then identify their loved one from these scant personal effects. As one reporter commented, 'proof of death is sometimes simply a tobacco pouch or pipe.'[96] After the 1913 Senghenydd mining disaster, rescuers would call the name of the person they thought the corpse was and this was verified by the items on top of their coffin.[97] This relied on family knowing their loved one's personal effects. In 1931, a father was asked about the experience of

[92] Dumfries and Galloway Archives, D37524.
[93] Burnett Archive, Lottie Barker, 'My Life as I Remember It', 2:37.
[94] Lewis Jones, *Cwmardy* (Cardigan, 2006 reprint), 117. [95] NCMM, SR59.
[96] *The Carlisle Journal*, 28 May 1915, p. 9.
[97] Glamorgan Archives, DWAW33, Transcript of recorded interview with Elizabeth Saunders, 1989.

identification by a reporter who caught him coming out of the makeshift mortuary. He replied, 'they showed me something that I could not recognise... my wife might know his belt, she once had to mend it. I am going to ask her now. They might be right about it being him.'[98]

Quite understandably, identifying the dead was often a deeply upsetting task. A newspaper report about the 1909 West Stanley mining disaster, where many of the bodies were badly burned, noted that when people were identifying the dead 'harrowing incidents were the rule, not the exception'.[99] After the Wellington pit disaster, where the bodies of the dead had to be left underground for three months before they could be recovered, a father broke down in tears at the Coroner's Inquest when speaking about having to identify his three sons.[100] As a general rule men were pressured into identifying the dead more than women, although who entered mortuaries varied greatly. At times this meant that men could be pressured into identifying the dead against their will. After the Bentley colliery disaster, one miner recalled his horror at being called by a nurse to identify a dead co-worker after the explosion, commenting, 'I daren't look at a man that's been in that bloody disaster', a protest ignored by the nurse, who scolded him and led him to the body of his colleague.[101] There were no strict rules about who should be allowed to identify the dead, but some care seems to have been taken to protect mothers of boys and young men who had died in pit disasters from seeing their remains, although this did not spare fathers the upsetting task.

The bodies of the dead were often cleaned and prepared for burial before being returned to the family home. This was standard practice, and the washing and preparation of the corpse marked an important part of the grieving process. In working-class homes the local layerouter, a woman who helped prepare the body, washed and clothed the corpse ready for burial. Laying out bodies was a task traditionally performed by women, who were either related to the deceased or who lived locally.[102] Occasionally family members undertook this task instead of the layerouter, as a final act of service.[103] In middle or upper-class homes, a nurse or trained servant would usually tend to the corpse.[104] Once the body had been washed and dressed, it would be kept in the house until it was time for the funeral. In the case of death from illness or

[98] *Doncaster Chronicle*, 27 November 1931, quoted in Church, *'It's like new wine to see you again lass'*, 19.

[99] *The Evening Chronicle*, 18 February 1909, p. 5.

[100] Routledge, *Black Wednesday*, 85.

[101] Herbert Barber, quoted in Woodhead, 'Essay in Oral History', 82.

[102] Mary Chamberlain and Ruth Richardson, 'Life and Death', *Oral History* 11:1 (1983), 35.

[103] Strange, *Death, Grief and Poverty*, 66.

[104] Pat Jalland, *Death in the Victorian Family* (Oxford, 1996), 210–12.

old age, the body was often kept at home for between five and ten days before it was buried.

It is incredibly difficult to say which of the traditional layingout rituals would have been followed in the case of different disasters. As Mary Chamberlain and Ruth Richardson have noted, war and mass death disrupt normal practices of preparing the corpse for burial.[105] In all likelihood, the mode of death and level of decomposition would have determined who prepared the body for burial. In the case of a badly damaged body, especially one that had been sealed into a coffin to be taken home, it is likely that a nurse would have prepared the body before it was sent home. Traditionally, laying out was a way of stopping bodily fluids from seeping through the coffin on the way to the burial site, so some packing of the corpse was probably performed, although this was probably done in the makeshift mortuary by a nurse or mortician who attended the corpse. In his memoir, R. A. S. Redmayne, HM Inspector of Mines 1908–19, recalled inspecting the makeshift mortuary after the Pretoria mining disaster, in which 344 men died. As he was inspecting the coffins, he was introduced to a young woman who told him that 'she, herself alone, had washed over one hundred of the bodies'. When asked why she had done so, she replied, 'Some one had to do it…I had lost one and t'other womenfolk mostly had.'[106] This act of service to her family and community honoured the dead in a practical and necessary way.

Once identified, the bodies of the dead were placed in coffins and families were sometimes allowed to take them home to await the burial. Families would have been intimately familiar with corpses in the late nineteenth and early twentieth centuries, as they usually stayed at home before their burial.[107] Working-class families with limited space would have lived alongside the corpse of their loved one for some time, with it occupying a central place in the home. When multiple family members died in the same blast, space had to be found to keep their bodies in the house. After mining disasters in the nineteenth century there were tragic reports of multiple family members placed on all the available spaces in the house, including the bed, the dresser, and the kitchen table.

Care was taken to place the body in a coffin to be taken home if at all possible. In the aftermath of a particularly bad disaster, a number of coffins were usually sent from the nearest town or city, and bodies were immediately

[105] Chamberlain and Richardson, 'Life and Death', 38.
[106] Redmayne, *Men, Mines, and Memories*, 155.
[107] Strange, *Death, Grief and Poverty*, 69.

placed into these caskets. By the time the first bodies were brought up after the 1913 Senghenydd disaster coffins had been sent from nearby Cardiff.[108] After disasters with a high number of deaths, supplies of pre-made coffins from nearby towns could be depleted, and bodies were packed into hastily produced caskets. The transport of these coffins to the site of the disaster was efficient and well organized. After the Quintinshill railway disaster, special trains from Carlisle and Glasgow were commissioned to bring the necessary number of coffins to the crash site.[109] Yet not every body was granted a single coffin. Because the bodies had been so badly mutilated in the fire which started after the trains crashed at Quintinshill, as many as three unidentifiable bodies shared a single coffin.[110] There is some anecdotal evidence of the same being true for mining disasters: after a particularly large and violent disaster placing assorted body parts in a single coffin to be buried was not unheard of.

The difficulty of identifying a body, combined with the shock of the event and the high numbers of dead, sometimes resulted in several families attempting to claim the same body, which prolonged their suffering and added an extra layer of pathos to the proceedings. After the West Stanley mining disaster three families tried to claim the body of one man.[111] Sometimes misidentification was only discovered after the body had been brought home. After the 1927 Marine colliery mining disaster, Robert Wilfred Button was mistakenly identified as Charles Monaghan and was laid out in the Monaghan family home awaiting burial for two days, until the family realized their mistake and returned him to the correct house.[112] In a large disaster these sorts of mistakes were not uncommon, and the added trauma caused by cases of mistaken identity can only be guessed at.

Just because the body of the family's loved one was returned to them did not mean that all members of the family recognized them as such. After the Pretoria mining disaster, Mrs Monks identified her brother Billy by the 'tommy tin' on his belt. As the body was in such a damaged state, the coffin holding Billy's remains was sealed, and the body returned to the family home. Monks's mother, when confronted with Billy's remains, 'wouldn't let him come in because it were a big coffin, wouldn't let him in, they said it's not my lad, it's too big…I don't convince [*sic*] it's me lad.'[113] It was only with some persuasion that Monks's mother accepted that it was Billy's body in the coffin and allowed her son inside her home. Tragic scenes such as this were

[108] Lieven, *Senghenydd*, 224. [109] Routledge, *The Sorrows of Quintinshill*, 33.
[110] Routledge, *The Sorrows of Quintinshill*, 34. [111] *Evening Chronicle*, 19 February 1909, p. 5.
[112] *Western Mail*, 4 March 1927, p. 5.
[113] National Coal Mining Museum, SR59, Oral Histories, 'Pretoria Remembered'.

reasonably rare, but do show the difficulty people could have in processing the sudden death of a family member. This was exacerbated by sealed coffins, which obscured the features of the dead and made the acceptance of their loss much harder.

If there was no body it became even harder to accept that a loved one had died. After a mining disaster at the Roachburn Pit, Cumbria, in 1908, one widow refused to believe that her husband had passed away. The Roachburn mining disaster had a small mortality count; one hewer died after becoming trapped, alongside two rescuers who tried to reach him. The mine flooded with peat water and they all drowned. Matthew Hillard, one of the rescuers, left a wife who could not accept he had died, confidently telling the *Farlam Hall Journal* that was reporting on the disaster that he would come back to her.[114] The majority of families whose loved ones died in rail and mining disasters were given their bodies, or knew where they were entombed. This was not necessarily the case for those whose loved ones died in the First World War and the high numbers of the missing created a group of people who existed in a liminal state.

Viewing the body of the deceased was only possible if the rescue party retrieved corpses swiftly. After some disasters bodies could not be immediately recovered because of the dangerous conditions in the mines. If the corpse had been left underground some time before being brought to the surface coroners refused to allow the dead to re-enter their homes, and they were held in a mortuary until burial. Heavily damaged bodies were also often kept away from the families, and wrapped in a shroud before being sealed into a coffin, to spare the family the distress of seeing their loved one in such a state. Despite this, after the 1913 Senghenydd mining disaster, one wife insisted her husband's sealed coffin be opened. The victim's daughter, who was 10 years old at the time, later remembered that the body 'was perfect except the skin had peeled off his face…The skin had peeled off his face but it was my father.'[115] Her mother's insistence was unusual—many families recognized that the coffins had been sealed to spare their feelings.

A particular problem for authorities was what to do with unidentified bodies. Not all men had families in the locality, and lone single workers were at particular risk of remaining unidentified. After the 1913 Senghenydd mining disaster three bodies were buried as 'Unknown'.[116] These unidentified dead

[114] Alistair F. Robertson, *January 28th 1908, The Story of the Roachburn Pit Disaster Reprinted to Commemorate the 100th Anniversary* (Alston, 2008), 35.

[115] Glamorgan Archives, DWAW33.

[116] J. Basil Phillips, *Senghenydd: A Brave Community* (Gwent, 2002), 164.

directly foreshadowed the approximately 200,000 bodies that were lost at sea or on the battlefield during the First World War.[117] For the families of these war dead, although they knew that their loved one had died, there was no known grave that could help direct their grief.

A disaster which linked both the war and disaster dead through a mass of unidentified bodies was the Quintinshill railway disaster. During this crash, identification discs, along with any other identifying features, were burned away.[118] The paper records of those in the battalion were destroyed in the fire and it was only through roll call, where only the living could speak, that the names of the dead were known. Once the wreckage had been cleared, only eighty-three bodies from the troop train could be identified. A further eighty-two bodies had been recovered but were not recognizable, and fifty men had to be declared missing by military authorities as their bodies had disintegrated in the heat of the fire.[119] These bodies could not be claimed by family members, and instead were kept in makeshift morgues until it was time for them to be buried.

Conclusion

Finding out about the death of a loved one was, and is, never an easy experience. The immediacy of death married physical grieving with paperwork. News of death was delivered in different forms, from hearing an explosion to receiving a letter. Individuals and families prepared for this potential loss by creating identification aids, so that not only would the state or mining company responsible for the men in question know who had died for their own records, but so that next of kin could be informed. People met the loss of a loved one with silence, weeping, and community support. Family and friends offered immediate support, and the physical shock of receiving the news became a part of many family's narratives about their war dead. Families of mining disaster dead were often close enough to the site of the accident to be able to travel to wait for news.

[117] Joanna Bourke, *Dismembering the Male: Men's Bodies, Britain and the Great War* (London, 2009), 229.

[118] Hamilton, *Britain's Greatest Rail Disaster*, 70.

[119] [Anonymous] 'Summary of Accidents and Casualties Reported to the Board of Trade by the Several Railway Companies in the United Kingdom, During the Three Months ending 30th June, 1915' (London, 1915), Appendix 1, Casualties as ascertained up to the 3rd July, 1915.

While the families of disaster dead often heard about the death of their family member relatively quickly, for the families of the war dead this could be a drawn-out process. The confusion of war and slow bureaucratic processes, coupled with the sheer numbers of men that these systems were working with, meant that families did not always receive timely information, and official letters could arrive after informal ones. Yet this paled in comparison to the protracted experience of loss that the families of the missing experienced. To them, receiving news about a death was not measured in minutes, hours, or days, but in weeks, months, and years. Families with social capital tried to circumnavigate the waiting process by using personal connections to uncover more information about the fate of their missing family member. Working-class families could seek information through public bodies or wait for updates from the War Office.

While there were significant differences in experiences between different groups involved in sudden death, there were also commonalities. Communities of friends and neighbours gathered around the bereaved. In working-class communities, people visited and wept with those who had lost a loved one; in upper-class families, where people might be separated by more distance, letters took on this role, although there was significant overlap across all classes. The most striking similarity is that deaths of war and disaster victims were registered by the state, taking this responsibility away from families. This action foreshadowed the control over the burial of the dead that officials enacted, further removing the family from their traditional roles.

Family Mourning After War and Disaster in Twentieth-Century Britain. Ann-Marie Foster, Oxford University Press.
 DOI: 10.1093/9780191968129.003.0002

2
Governing Death

On 11 November 1920 the body of an unidentified serviceman was laid to rest in the Tomb of the Unknown Warrior in Westminster Abbey. Within a week, somewhere in the region of 500,000 to 1 million people visited the tomb.[1] For those whose loved one had no grave, this was their representative body, located and reburied by the state. This control of bodies was common after mass death events, for the bodies of those who were identifiable as well as those whose names had become disconnected from the corpse. Families had already been in contact with the state through death notifications sent by the War Office; however, it is through the state control and burial of the corpse that we see how the government sought to regulate the deaths of servicepeople and disaster dead. Although this was a new experience, for middle-class families in particular, over the course of the nineteenth century the state gradually increased control over the bodies of its citizens, and after large disasters the families of the dead experienced local authorities stepping into their familial role.

The family of the dead conventionally controlled the body of their loved one, and the state only intervened if there was nobody to claim the corpse. Thomas Laqueur argues that by the late nineteenth century the British state had assumed a more visible role over the dead, hosting an increasing number of state funerals which asserted the dominance of civic society over individual families.[2] Yet these funerals were generally restricted to people on the extreme end of the class divide. Members of the aristocracy, or those who had been particularly prominent local or national public figures, could expect lavish treatment.[3] Similarly, if a family was in a state of abject poverty then the government assumed responsibility and buried the dead, although they did

[1] Adrian Gregory, *The Silence of Memory: Armistice Day 1919–1946* (Oxford, 1994), 24, 26.

[2] Thomas Laqueur, *The Work of the Dead: A Cultural History of Mortal Remains* (Princeton, 2018), 468.

[3] For example, Emma Darwin would have preferred her husband Charles to be buried in the family vault, instead of at Westminster Abbey. See Pat Jalland, *Death in the Victorian Family* (Oxford, 1996), 198.

so without any pomp or circumstance.[4] During the First World War the regulation of bodies expanded, and the state laid claim to the bodies of men who, although in the Army, were not of it. Joanna Bourke has shown how the state increasingly claimed men's bodies over the course of the First World War, through conscription, fitness, and, ultimately, death.[5] Timothy Ashplant, Graham Dawson, and Michael Roper argue that when the state assumed responsibility for the disposal of the corpse it regulated what were acceptable mourning cultures.[6] Laura Tradii suggests that this renegotiation of dead bodies after the First World War reimagined soldiers as members of Empire whose bodies were laid to rest among soldierly kin instead of along traditional familial lines.[7] While in previous wars the state had laid the bodies of those who perished to rest, with the exception of the small number of volunteers who died in the Second Anglo-Boer War, those who were registered by the Army had been career soldiers. The First World War was to change that and wrest control from families to create uniform cemeteries of the dead.

While for local disasters families were often in at least minimal contact with those in charge of burying the dead, in wartime contact with officials was solely through paperwork. This began with contact from the War Office when families were informed of the death, but intensified through grave-related documentation. As the modern state grew, so did the bureaucratic apparatus to support it, often through the production and dissemination of paperwork. As Patrick Joyce and Chandra Mukerji argue, the state is the centre of power, which is diffusely expressed through institutions of power, with different departments, people, and other forms of power that often conflict with each other.[8] In their reading of state power, it is regulated through materials, which allowed administrators, as those storing and moving the materials, such as documents, from site to site, a small amount of limited power, given the right circumstances.[9]

[4] Joanna Bourke, *Dismembering the Male: Men's Bodies, Britain and the Great War* (London, 1996), 211, 216–19.

[5] Bourke, *Dismembering the Male.*

[6] T. G. Ashplant, Graham Dawson, and Michael Roper, *The Politics of War Memory and Commemoration* (London, 2000), 10.

[7] Laura Tradii, '"Their dear remains belong to us alone": Soldiers' Bodies, Commemoration, and Cultural Responses to Exhumations after the Great War', *First World War Studies* 10:2–3 (2019), 256.

[8] Patrick Joyce and Chandra Mukerji, 'The State of Things: State History and Theory Reconfigured', *Theory and Society* 46:1 (2017), 2; Patrick Joyce, *The State of Freedom: A Social History of the British State since 1800* (Cambridge, 2013), 10–14.

[9] Joyce, *The State of Freedom*, 9, 16.

Bureaucrats inhabited a world where they both embodied power conferred through their status, but at the same time acted as part of a corporatized collective.[10] These bureaucrats were constrained by the system, and processes of bureaucracy were designed to work as a collective whole. If we follow Joyce's understanding of the state as diffuse, homogenous, and impersonal, Ben Kafka's reading of the 'psychic life of paperwork' shows the human influences which impact modern bureaucracy. The 'psychic life of paperwork' describes people's emotional reactions to paperwork as symptomatic of wider needs which may not be conscious or articulated, and which can clash with bureaucratic mechanisms, leading to feelings of frustration.[11]

While the state itself—and indeed, to a greater or lesser extent, the bureaucrats who handled paperwork—may have been impartial, families who relied on the state to inter their dead, and who were dependent on the bureaucracy of the Imperial War Graves Commission (IWGC), the body in charge of creating cemeteries for the dead, reacted emotionally to these bureaucratic processes. The paperwork of death was particularly important during the First World War, as the IWGC largely interacted with the bereaved through forms, letters, and other official documents. The management of death was relegated to a paper exercise, making it easier for families to feel personally attacked by the decisions made. The human component of the decision-making process was hidden, and families felt their only recourse lay through appealing to the person on the other side of the paper.

Times of crisis prompted mass control over the bodies of the dead. In the case of disaster deaths, local authorities organized funerals, overstepping the unspoken rule that families would control burial practices. Families were sometimes perfunctorily asked if they were happy with the arrangements, and might have the option to remove their dead for private burial, but the vast majority of funerals were organized by local representatives. In the case of war, not only did the state demand compliance from the bodies of those who enlisted or were conscripted, but regulated family experiences of bereavement through the paperwork required to create a personalized grave for individual soldiers. As this chapter demonstrates, the regulation of bodies by people external to them was an experience shared by the families of the war and disaster dead. Their loved ones had been engaged in high-risk occupations, died,

[10] Matthew S. Hull, 'The File: Agency, Authority, and Autography in an Islamabad Bureaucracy', *Language & Communication* 23 (2003), 288.

[11] Ben Kafka, *The Demon of Writing: Powers and Failures of Paperwork* (New York, 2012), 10–16.

and were now subject to control by powers outside of the family. As the rest of this book argues, because of this lack of involvement with death practices, and a loss of control over the burial of a loved one, families increasingly turned to domestic memorial forms. This chapter examines the relationship between families, bodies, and the state, by showing how the state's treatment of bodies alienated families from traditional forms of burial. While there was still reverence in the burials, and families were able to find comfort in the rituals provided for the dead, theirs was a jarring experience, and something was lost through their inability to decide how the dead were interred. Memorial words on headstones proved a particular point of contention between subject and state. Through complex bureaucratic systems, the families of the dead demanded that their voice be heard, although the response to this proved to be limited.

Burials and the Family

In February 1908 the Washington Glebe colliery explosion killed fourteen men. A few days after the disaster, the family of James Wake, one of the dead, waited in their home for the funeral procession to come and collect his coffin. The procession, accompanied by the banner of the Glebe Lodge of the Durham Miners' Association, the Washington Temperance and Hebburn Salvation Army bands, and thousands of onlookers, arrived at Wake's house having already collected the body of Robert Cowan, who was being buried in the same ceremony. Four men who died in the explosion were buried in the same grave that day.

In the local church, after hymns and a sermon, John Wilson, an agent of the Durham Miners' Association, gave a speech. According to the press:

> [Wilson] thought that the time had arrived when the workmen should have more assurance that they would go home hale and hearty than the results of our industrial life indicated was the case at present. He made no complaint. That was not the time. But he would say, as the mouthpiece of the mining industry, that the miner had the right to demand the highest safety that the highest science of the day could give him. They could not enter into the grief of the widow; they knew nothing of the miseries of the home which that day lacked its breadwinner. They did know, however, that owing to the Compensations Act, to the Miners' Permanent Relief Fund, and, he had no

doubt, to the generosity of their colleagues, the widows would not have to face the haunting spectre of poverty.[12]

The family of James Wake, his wife Sarah and their eleven children, did not actively participate in the ceremony, beyond sitting mutely. This was not the place for family mourning, but for formal and public tributes. Wilson explicitly stated that the onlookers could not understand the 'grief of the widow', nor did they attempt to, confining themselves to financial assistance. The funerals were large, public, and were not intended to offer the families involved in the disaster an intimate chance to say goodbye to their loved ones. The funeral of James Wake, and the lack of a public role of his family beyond being a spectacle of pity for onlookers, was a common sight after mining disasters in the early twentieth century.

Recovering and burying the bodies of those who died in mining disasters was of great importance to the families, and when men were entombed families went to great lengths to try to persuade mine owners to open the pit. The importance of funerals as a social rite was great enough to be passed down in family lore. Bill Williamson's uncle, also called Bill, once told him that his grandfather had gone to the funeral of a miner killed at work on a particularly rainy day: 'The lowering of the coffin into a sludgy grave upset [Uncle] Bill and afterwards, angry at the meanness of it all, he said to my grandfather that it would have been just as appropriate to leave the body in the pit. My grandfather reacted badly to this, saying, "If you did that we'd be no better than animals; you've got to have a proper burial." '[13] The emotional difficulty of processing pit deaths was met with anger at the everydayness of the burial. Strong emotions flooded communities when there was a fatal workplace accident, which could lead to tension around the appropriateness of the funerals which took place.

Burying a great number of unexpected dead caused problems for local authorities and funeral workers. Due to the high numbers of the dead, plots of land owned by local authorities were usually given to bury disaster victims in. This not only appeared to be a gesture of support for the families of the deceased, but mitigated the public health hazard posed by the sudden creation of what could be hundreds of corpses. After the Silvertown munitions

[12] *Durham Chronicle*, 28 February 1908, p. 5.

[13] Bill Williamson, *Class, Culture and Community: A Biographical Study of Social Change in Mining* (London, 1982), 88.

factory explosion in 1917, in which seventy-three people died, it was decided by the London Burial Board that a portion of the City of London cemetery would be set aside for the mass burial of victims, at no charge.[14] Similarly, after the 1913 Senghenydd mining disaster a new cemetery was opened as there were so many bodies to bury. The record book of, F. M. Coombes, conveys some of the strain individual funeral directors experienced after sudden disaster. Coombes was based in Gwent, South Wales, and was hired to help convey some of the fifty-two victims of the Marine colliery disaster to their final resting places in 1927. He organized thirty-two of the funerals, providing oak coffins, hearses, and horses, which totalled £649 9*s* 15*d*.[15] Coombes provided a mixture of individual and mass funerals, having to re-open the plot reserved for the mass grave of the disaster victims for burials that took place over multiple days.

After mining disasters, the bodies of the dead were not necessarily buried in individual graves, and mass graves, with multiple interments, were a common sight. The effect of these mass graves on the families of the dead has been strongly debated. Pat Jalland argues that families who lost a loved one in a mining disaster were afraid of the mass burial because of the association with a pauper death.[16] This follows from the work of Elizabeth Roberts, who notes that a pauper's funeral, paid for by the parish, was, to many working-class families, 'to bear a lifetime's stigma'.[17] Yet Julie-Marie Strange's description of a pauper burial, where 'the grave was little more than a hole into which the bodies of the abject poor were packed in flimsy coffins, with little or no ceremony', is a far cry from mass burial practices after disasters where large processions would accompany the dead, in new coffins, to their final resting place.[18] Indeed, there seems to be little evidence to suggest that families of disaster victims resented the communal graves shared by their loved ones. After the 1910 Wellington colliery disaster in Whitehaven, Cumbria, it was lamented that a mass grave had not been thought of sooner, as 'it would have been better and more fitting... if there had been two funerals only... to be all buried side by side', one for those whose families could identify their bodies, and one for those who could not.[19] There was comfort to be gained by burying the dead together after workplace disasters.

[14] Newham Archives, Silvertown Box 1. [15] Gwent Archives, D3335.5.

[16] Pat Jalland, *Death in War and Peace* (Oxford, 2010), 88.

[17] Elizabeth Roberts, 'The Lancashire Way of Death', in Ralph Houlbrooke (ed.), *Death, Ritual, and Bereavement* (London, 1989), 191.

[18] Julie-Marie Strange, *Death, Grief and Poverty, 1870–1914* (Cambridge, 2005), 7.

[19] *Whitehaven News*, 6 October 1910. Transcript provided by West Cumbria Mines Research, http://www.dmm.org.uk/news19/9101006b.htm [Accessed 18.02.2021]

Photographs of the dead being interred after mining disasters show carefully placed coffins in mass graves, foreshadowing images of state-led funerals for the civilian dead who died in bombardments during the Second World War. Lucy Noakes argues that after aerial bombardments in the Second World War, the state attempted to demonstrate that they were treating civilian corpses of the dead with the respect due to them.[20] She observes that the state attempted to imbue the burials of the dead with the same level of respect given to the First World War dead, who were buried in mass graves. Photographs show onlookers standing reverently beside graves strewn with flowers (see Figs. 1 and 2). While the ceremonies held in the 1940s were slightly different to those held after mining disasters in the preceding decades, with soldiers lining the streets and the dead being buried in multi-faith grave plots, the civilian outpouring of grief was highly comparable: people came to bear witness and bring floral tributes. Although the state-led tribute was not present in mass funerals after disasters, the respectability of the burials was. Those who died in mining disasters were given a culturally coded respectful burial, marked by common funeral practices, such as flowers, coffins, and a burial service read by a minister. Far from pauper graves, disaster victims were given an honourable burial. Although some families might have preferred individual graves, these conscientious funerals were at least within the realms of social acceptability.

Although these services were regulated by external powers in a civic space, how much these funerals should be read as civic rituals designed to draw the support of the local community is questionable. Ben Roberts has suggested that 'the civic funeral...was able to blend sombre decorum with recreational appeal and ceremonial symbolism'.[21] It is understandable that many came to pay their respects: mine workers in particular were a part of national networks of trade unions, and people who worked in nearby pits came to pay their respects to former co-workers and industry peers. Disasters were generally written about extensively by local newspapers. Even the censored Silvertown munitions disaster had illustrated editions of newspapers dedicated to the destruction wrought by the explosion.[22] The publicity afforded to

[20] Lucy Noakes, 'The "Worth" of Grief and the "Value" of Bodies: Managing the Civilian Corpse in Second World War Britain', in Zahra Newby and Ruth Toulson (eds.), *The Materiality of Mourning* (London, 2018), 176; Lucy Noakes, *Dying for the Nation: Death, Grief, and Bereavement in Second World War Britain* (Manchester, 2020), ch. 6.

[21] Ben Roberts, 'A Tale of Two Funerals: Civic Ritual, Public Mourning and Community Participation in Late Nineteenth-Century Middlesbrough', *Cultural and Social History* 13:4 (2016), 469.

[22] See *Daily Sketch*, 22 January 1917; 23 January 1917; 24 January 1917; 27 January 1917; 31 January 1917.

Fig. 1. Postcard, 'Burying in the Trenches, West Stanley'. Courtesy of Beamish, The Living Museum of the North, NEG 4273.

Fig. 2. Postcard, 'The Trench'. Courtesy of Beamish, The Living Museum of the North, NEG 6524.

them meant that they were destined to be large affairs. As was reflected on by the families of the dead, people were curious but compassionate. However, the large scale of these funerals disenfranchised the families of the dead. They were relegated to bystanders in their own family funeral.

As part of an attempt to make mass graves more appealing to families, care was taken to try to consult with them about the funeral plans. After the 1931 Bentley colliery disaster Lois Hill recalled the consultation with the families about the mass grave:

> I remember Mr Ballam of the Union asking us different things. Were we agreeable for this mass grave and the memorial? I know it was all taken out of our hands as regards the funeral. Mr Swan had that grave dug, and he lined it all with ivy and laurel. He said his biggest fear was the grave giving way, because they stampeded it. Massed bands; every denomination. It's a terrible ordeal. Len's mother, she said she couldn't go to the funeral if she couldn't see him. So me dad asked, and Dr Dunner, the Health doctor, said he couldn't be seen again. They said, 'You'll see him if you get your own undertaker.' Well, she never forgave my dad for a bit. It seemed to turn her brain. She couldn't believe that he was dead if she didn't see him, she said. We had to console her, anyway, and we got her round. We had mounted police to get us back. It were such a crowd. They were sitting on roofs and all sorts, going down there. We were four hours from Winninpeg Road to Arskey cemetery. There were such a lot. It's curiosity, a lot of it. Sympathy, too.[23]

Hill's memory of the experience, that the family were, in theory, consulted about the burial but that any decisions were entirely taken away from them, did not necessarily seem to cause her upset. Presumably cost prevented her mother-in-law from hiring an undertaker so that she could view her son's body again, although given the doctor's refusal to show her the body, which was very badly burned, this decision may have been made to protect her.

In Hill's experience, trade union workers acted as the mouthpiece for the bereaved families. While it is impossible to know how common this was after mining disasters in the early twentieth century, it indicates a strong union presence which gave voice to family decisions. As at James Wake's funeral, union men were also heavily involved in regulating family experiences after

[23] Lois Hill, quoted in John Woodhead, 'Essay in Oral History: The Bentley Colliery Disaster', *Labour History Review* (1975), 81.

sudden disaster. Union representatives worked with and on behalf of bereaved families, to act as an intermediary between local authority and the mass bereaved. While this gave individual families a voice, it is unclear how much agency families felt they had within this system.

The funerals which followed a major disaster were tremendously popular affairs and thousands of people flooded into villages and towns for the occasion. On the first Saturday following the 1909 West Stanley colliery disaster 131 men were buried. Local newspapers estimated anywhere between 70,000 and 200,000 attended the funerals.[24] The North-Eastern Railway Company ran special trains to accommodate some of the increased traffic into the village, and twenty-five ambulances were placed on hold in case of emergencies in the crowd.[25] Even after a disaster which incurred a smaller loss of life, such as the Washington Glebe colliery explosion in which fourteen men died, the number of observers at the funerals reached nearly 20,000.[26] These funerals were a chance for local groups to publicly show their respect for the deceased, and funeral processions were often made up of various local and industrial groups. After the 1918 Chilwell munitions disaster a worker recalled that, during the mass funeral for the victims, she, alongside colleagues, represented the 'A shift' of the filling store, but that 'every work place had their mourners Filled Shell, Empty Shell, Melt Houses, Press Houses, Mills, Experimental House not forgetting clerical and canteen workers'.[27] The community strength shown in these funeral processions was considerable, and recognized the local loss the disaster imparted to the area.

Large funerals for people involved in the war effort were arranged by local authorities and attended by thousands of people. The 1915 Quintinshill railway disaster fused the burial of soldiers with the mass burial of disaster victims. Due to the unidentifiable state of the bodies, it was decided that there should be a mass burial for members of the 1/7th Battalion, Royal Scots who died in the accident. The Quintinshill bodies were transported back to Leith in preparation for the funeral. On the day of the funeral, the procession to the gravesite was marked by a lack of family visibility in the parades. Perhaps due to the difficulty of knowing to whom each corpse belonged, the families of the deceased were nowhere near individual coffins as they processed solemnly through Leith. The men were buried with full military honours in Rosebank

[24] *Durham Chronicle*, 26 February 1909, p. 4; *The Auckland Times*, 26 February 1909, p. 7.
[25] *Durham Chronicle*, 26 February 1909, p. 4; *Durham County Advertiser*, 19 February 1909, p. 8.
[26] *Durham Chronicle*, 28 February 1908, p. 5.
[27] Burnett Archive, Lottie Barker, 'My Life as I Remember It', 2:37.

Cemetery.[28] This decision was also made after other disasters, such as the Chilwell munitions factory explosion, where the few identifiable bodies were taken by families to be privately buried, with the rest interred in a mass grave.[29]

Some wartime disasters prompted special services for people who were deemed particularly heroic in the face of extreme danger. After the Silvertown munitions factory explosion, a funeral procession was meticulously planned for four select victims: Sub-Officer Vickers, Fireman Sell, Winifred Sell, and 'the infant child of Fireman Betts'.[30] The event was ticketed and only select members of the local community were allowed into the church, mostly local dignitaries and those who had aided in the aftermath of the explosion.[31] Once again, the pomp and ceremony of the burials alleviated the fact that they were experiencing what could otherwise be perceived as a shameful pauper burial. Those in wartime were offered funerals to honour their sacrifice, mirroring large funerals for other disaster dead, although the funerals of those who died in war service were often more regulated than those of the disaster dead, through tickets and military processions.

Although families had little say in the ceremonies that accompanied the burial of their loved ones in a mass grave, friends could pay their respects to the dead through being actively involved in the funeral service. Harry Clarke, a survivor of the Bentley colliery disaster, remembered that he 'helped to carry Joe Pritchard to the communal grave'.[32] The survivors of the Quintinshill railway disaster were also present at the funeral of their comrades. The survivors of the crash were initially sent to Liverpool to join the rest of the battalion. They were sent by train, which compounded the trauma of their past experience. As one man recalled, 'it was a nightmare trip. Our nerves were shattered, and every time the train slowed or took a corner we gasped and braced ourselves for the worst.'[33] They had been placed aboard the ship bound for the Dardanelles when a message arrived excusing all but the surviving officers from sailing to attend the funeral of their former battalion members and they arrived back in Edinburgh the day before the funeral of 102 of their comrades. The funerals, as well as being a way of beginning to grieve, were

[28] The burial of miners with full military honours when they had been in the forces was also common.

[29] Burnett Archive, Lottie Barker, 'My Life as I Remember It', 2:37.

[30] Newham Archives, Silvertown Box 1, Order of Service for Sub-Officer Vickers et al.; letter from W. P. Bicknell, 25 January 1917.

[31] Newham Archives, Silvertown Box 1; ticket for the Public Funeral Service; plans for the funeral.

[32] Harry Clarke, quoted in Woodhead, 'Oral History', 73.

[33] Quotation in J. A. B. Hamilton, *Britain's Greatest Rail Disaster: The Quintinshill Blaze of 1915* (London, 1969), 73.

also a moment where the trauma of the event could be compounded. Survivor guilt, although rarely explicitly discussed, was also presumably present in some of the men. Often colleagues took part in these funerary rituals in a highly public sphere and paid their respects to their dead friends and colleagues, but the emotional effects of this were manifold.

The Nearly Absent Dead

While there were difficulties faced by families involved in a funeral, some families had no body to mourn at all. In mining disasters where the pit had to be sealed, often because of the ferocity of the fire still burning in the depths of the mine, the corpses of the dead were left in the pit works until the fire subsided. Sometimes bodies were retrieved from the pit after some months had passed and the mines were safe to enter again, but this was by no means a certain occurrence. When an inrush of water was involved it could take months for the pit to be drained and bodies to be retrieved, if they were recovered at all. This left the families in a state of limbo. They knew there was a body that they might be able to bury at a later date, but without one it was very difficult to begin to fully process the death.

The decision to close the mines, leaving the bodies of the dead in situ, was not made lightly. In his memoirs R. A. S. Redmayne, Chief Inspector of Mines 1908–19, commented on the difficulties managers faced when making this decision:

> I know that sentiment weighs heavily in the consideration of a problem of this nature and that there is an intense desire on the part of relatives of the dead to see and bury the bodies. But I do not believe that the management of a colliery is justified in allowing persons to risk their lives in order to recover dead bodies...I know that it sometimes requires a higher moral courage to resist a natural impulse and prohibit persons from undertaking (and undertaking oneself) a hazard of this nature than to allow the venture to be undertaken.[34]

Condemning 'reckless bravery', he argued that the colliery manager's role was to prevent lives lost in 'useless rescue work'.[35] The decision of whether or not

[34] R. A. S. Redmayne, *Men, Mines, and Memories* (London, 1942), 168.
[35] Redmayne, *Men, Mines, and Memories*, 167.

to close the pit rested with figures of authority, who were often of a different social class, and who bore the brunt of the wrath of families who were unhappy with this decision.

After the 1934 Gresford mining disaster, nearly all of the bodies were sealed in the pit, remaining underground to this day. Of the 266 dead, the bodies of only twelve men were brought to the surface, including one brought up five months after the disaster when the sealed pit was briefly opened for examination and one of the rescuers' corpses could be retrieved from the pit entrance.[36] Ithel Kelly, the last manager of the Gresford colliery, Trustee of the Gresford Relief Fund, and local expert on the disaster, thought that the original decision to not recover the bodies was made 'because to subject the next of kin to viewing someone that they couldn't recognise, [and] just the badness and the hazards of going through it, just wasn't on.'[37] A similar explanation was offered by Margaret Clapper, whose brother had died in the disaster. Clapper's family was visited by Henry Walker, Chief Inspector of Mines 1924–38, who explained that recovering the bodies would be too difficult, and that the body of John Clapper, who had worked close to the coal face where the explosion had happened, would have been blown to pieces. Reflecting on it decades later, Clapper recalled that Walker said 'I'm not going to get any [bodies]. I'd rather let it be their grave.'[38]

The decision not to rescue bodies from the Gresford pit was highly unpopular among the families of the men who were entombed, who lobbied officials to force them to retrieve them. Some of the Gresford widows protested at conferences set up to discuss the issue of the remains, in which the bereaved had no official say, demanding news and making their own views known.[39] One woman wrote to request the body of her brother be brought up, saying, 'the shock may be over with some people but it is not over in my home.'[40]

The families of the dead also attempted to plead with mine owners to help them recover the bodies of their dead after other disasters. Mary Mitchell lost her son in the Wellington pit explosion. It took seven months for the bodies of the 136 dead to be brought up from the pit.[41] Mary's son was one of those sealed in the pit for the duration. She corresponded with colliery officials and

[36] Beverley Tinson, *The Gresford Letters: Aftermath of a Disaster* (Gwespyr, 2009), 31–2.
[37] Ithel Kelly, quoted in Tinson, *The Gresford Letters*, 64.
[38] Margaret Clapper, quoted in Roger Laidlaw, 'The Gresford Disaster in Popular Memory', *Llafur* 6 (1995), 137.
[39] Laidlaw, 'The Gresford Disaster in Popular Memory', 135–6.
[40] Tinson, *The Gresford Letters*, 104.
[41] Gordon L. Routledge, *Black Wednesday: An Account of the Wellington Pit Disaster, Whitehaven, in the Year 1910* (Carlisle, 2011), 171–2.

the landowner of the site the colliery was located on, Lord Lonsdale, asking them to supply information about the pit reopening so that she could retrieve the body of her son. She explained that:

> Since the dreadful calamity, I have been nearly distraught with trouble I have never had a nights sleep since the dreadful affair happened. If I had any idea when the bodies of the poor victims would be recovered, it might make me a little easier in my mind, and if it be in your power to give me any information whatever, it would tend to relieve a broken-hearted mother's anxiety.[42]

Another woman, corresponding with her friend, and whose letter was published in a local newspaper, simply wrote: 'if they [the wives] could only get them, dead or alive, they are quite prepared to have them any way now.'[43] These appeals to people in positions of power mirrored pleas from families in the First World War to people who might be able to influence the treatment of their dead, which showed an astute awareness of who had the power to influence decisions about the bodies of the dead.

These types of absent bodies posed religious problems about how to impart burial rites, although local religious leaders found solutions to this. When a body was irretrievable, burial services were spoken over the pithead instead of a cemetery wherever possible. After the 1909 West Stanley mining disaster, the bodies of two men, John Rodgers and William Chaytor, could not be retrieved. Father Dix performed a private Catholic service for Rodgers and the vicar of nearby Beamish separately performed a public Anglican ceremony at the pithead for Chaytor. The latter service, 'despite the unceasing rain', attracted hundreds of witnesses.[44] Whenever possible the nature of the service at the pithead followed the religious practices of the deceased and their families. In some cases, such as the 1901 Senghenydd mining disaster, different Christian denominations held joint memorial services.[45] After the Gresford disaster, eight days after the explosion a memorial service was held at Wrexham Parish Church, where the first sentences of the burial service were uttered in lieu of a traditional funeral.[46]

[42] Whitehaven Archive, TCNB 6–71. [43] *West Cumberland Times*, 18 May 1910, p. 2.
[44] *Durham County Advertiser*, 2 April 1909, p. 7.
[45] Michael Lieven, *Senghenydd: The Universal Pit Village 1890–1930* (Llandysul, 1994), 68.
[46] Michael Pollard, *The Hardest Work Under Heaven: The Life and Death of the British Coal Miner* (London, 1984), 181.

Sometimes the name of a victim was engraved on a family headstone in a local churchyard, although this did not always offer particular comfort to the family. A widow whose husband died in the Gresford mining disaster recalled in an interview that 'it was awful... you can't describe it... it was so terrible... they didn't have a chance of getting him home. It was awful, awful... his name's on the stone in the cemetery... me Mother and my little girl are there, but my husband isn't, only his name.'[47] When the pit closed in 1973, the only part left standing was the pithead which was to act as a monument to the entombed men. Following a grassroots campaign, led by the sister of one of the entombed men, a public memorial was erected in 1982.[48]

For some families whose loved one was entombed in a mine, the lack of a burial space was deeply upsetting. For others, there was some comfort to be had knowing where the body of their loved one was, and that there had been some form of burial service read over the pit. Others were granted a grave, and families largely seemed to draw comfort from mass burials. These mixed experiences of death and burial were to foreshadow and echo experience in war, when the state tried to locate, bury, and rebury the dead.

Negotiating Death

During the First World War the place of the family and their involvement with burials of the dead led to heated public debates. Throughout the conflict, the state assumed control of servicepeople as part of their war service, extending their control into the realm of the body. The history of state growth during the First World War has been traced through its intrusion into the everyday lives of its citizens. Hallmarks of the modern surveillance state, such as passports, identity cards, and birth certificates, all had their origins in the conflict.[49] By 1924 the growth of new state bureaucracy was so great that the Interdepartmental Committee on Administration of Public Assistance

[47] Blodwen Bryan, quoted in Tinson, *The Gresford Letters*, 51.

[48] Laidlaw, 'The Gresford Disaster', 136–8.

[49] John Torpey, 'The Great War and the Birth of the Modern Passport System', in Jane Caplan and John Torpey (eds.), *Documenting Individual Identity: The Development of State Practices in the Modern World* (Princeton, 2001), 256–70; Nadja Durbach, 'Private Lives, Public Records: Illegitimacy and the Birth Certificate in Twentieth-Century Britain', *Twentieth Century British History* 25:2 (2014), 305–26; Rosemary Elliot, 'An Early Experiment in National Identity Cards: The Battle over Registration in the First World War', *Twentieth Century British History* 17:2 (2006), 145–76; André Keil, 'The National Council for Civil Liberties and the British State during the First World War, 1916–1919', *The English Historical Review* CXXXIV:568 (2019), 620–45.

recommended a citizen's advice service should be created to help people navigate these new structures.[50]

These new bureaucracies were not necessarily coherent, and the state relied on voluntary associations to augment its services, including ones to register and bury First World War dead. It has been well established that by the early twentieth century the boundary between the state and civic society was decidedly porous. This 'mixed economy' of state and voluntary service had its roots in the first decade of the twentieth century, where the implementation of Liberal social legislation, and the creation of the proto-welfare state, led to an increasing recognition of the value of charitable services as complementary to government provision.[51] Peter Grant argues that the war acted as a catalyst for this developing mutual interest, with the sheer amount of aid generated during the conflict leading to an increasingly professionalized charitable sector, which the state encouraged.[52] The War Office relied heavily on the Red Cross for assistance when registering graves, and the formation of the IWGC, responsible for reinterring the dead in their final resting place, began as an arm of this voluntary organization.

The IWGC began as a voluntary British Red Cross Unit, led by Fabian Ware, in 1914. The Unit began to collate the graves of the dead, slowly becoming incorporated into the Army. By early 1915, the Unit used Red Cross vehicles and personnel but were supported by Army supplies, before becoming formally incorporated into the Army later that year.[53] The Unit continued to gain power and authority. In February 1916 it became the Directorate of Graves Registration & Enquiries (DGRE) and in 1917 it was transformed by Royal Charter into the IWGC.[54] The IWGC organized the battlefronts into seven zones, and Grave Registration Units (GRUs) were formed to record the dead in individual areas. In its early days, two junior registration officers began a card-index register of the graves. This bureaucracy was slowed by

[50] Oliver Blaiklock, 'Advising the Citizen: Citizens Advice Bureaux, Voluntarism and the Welfare State in England, 1938–1964' (Unpublished PhD, King's College London, 2019), 29.

[51] Frank Prochaska, *The Voluntary Impulse* (London, 1988), 72, 82; M. J. Moore, 'Social Service and Social Legislation in Edwardian England: The Beginning of a New Role for Philanthropy', *Albion* 3 (1971), 37. The phrase 'mixed economy' often refers to the welfare state and was coined by Geoffrey Finlayson in 'A Moving Frontier: Voluntarism and the State in British Social Welfare 1911–1949', *Twentieth Century British History* (1990), 202; also see Pat Thane, *The Foundations of the Welfare State* (Cambridge, 2008), 143.

[52] Peter Grant, *Philanthropy and Voluntary Action in the First World War: Mobilizing Charity* (London, 2014), 168–72.

[53] Philip Longworth, *The Unending Vigil* (Southampton, 1967), 1–28.

[54] Peter Hodgkinson, 'Clearing the Dead', *Journal of the Centre for First World War Studies* (2017), 35.

Army units and clergymen who moved around, or lost the records which gave details of the graves of the soldiers they had buried.

While the war was still ongoing, burying the dead was a drawn-out process hampered by the atrocious conditions on the fighting fronts. Graves could be hastily dug, ill mapped, paperwork concerning their location could be lost, and areas where soldiers had been laid to rest earlier in the war were later destroyed. Wherever possible, soldiers were buried, although often this was a hasty affair undertaken by comrades, religious personnel, or pioneer troops who followed the main infantry to bury the dead.[55] From 1915 bodies were interred in cemeteries, giving some semblance of order to the chaos, although changing lines of war and the carnage wrought upon the battlefield could destroy these graves. In some ways, the families who dealt with the headstone paperwork were lucky. At the end of the war, 170,000 British soldiers were missing in France and Belgium alone and, unless their bodies were later discovered, families of these men had to be content with the name of their loved one engraved on a memorial to the missing.[56] After the war ended, the IWGC worked to concentrate the bodies in these scattered graves into larger cemeteries where they could be cared for properly. Bourke has drawn attention to battlefield burials and their likeness to pauper ones, arguing that mass interments on the battlefields were, in essence, 'common interments'.[57] Men were buried quickly, often in mass graves, and with little ceremony, bearing heavy resemblance to the state funerals conducted for paupers. Yet their reburial, and the care the state took in creating peaceful cemeteries for British soldiers, suggests that they were keen for families to understand that the bodies of the dead were being cared for.

The decision not to repatriate the war dead was announced in 1918 and led to a public debate over who should get to dictate where soldiers were buried. This pill was somewhat harder to swallow because the 130,000 men who were invalided back to Britain and who died on home soil were buried in a mixture of IWGC and civilian graves. The families of these servicepeople were sometimes able to attend a funeral and visit their grave.

For people who were lucky enough to have their loved one identified, the anger and upset at the lack of repatriation of bodies could be intense. Sarah Ann Smith, whose only son died in 1918, founded the British War Graves Association in 1919 to lobby for the repatriation of the war dead. By 1922 the

55 Bourke, *Dismembering the Male*, 214.

56 Ross Wilson, 'The Burial of the Dead: The British Army on the Western Front, 1914–1918', *War & Society* 31:1 (2012), 23.

57 Bourke, *Dismembering the Male*, 219.

association had over 3,000 members.[58] One of the key means of trying to get this decision overturned was through a petition sent to King George V. Those who signed the petition listed their name and their relationship to the dead, with wives, mothers, sisters, brothers, husbands, and nephews all appearing on the list.[59] What is particularly notable about this petition was that by listing their relationship to the deceased the families of the dead attempted to demonstrate their claim through blood. Ultimately the petition was ignored, although the IWGC was forced to produce literature to support the decision. They commissioned Rudyard Kipling to write a pamphlet sent to every next of kin which boldly claimed that moving the bodies would be 'a violation ... of the desire of the dead themselves'.[60]

In the aftermath of the war the British Army found it difficult to recruit men to staff the Graves Concentration Units, whose task was to exhume and rebury the dead in newly formed IWGC cemeteries. In the spring of 1919 the British Army used German prisoners of war, as well as dominion Grave Detachments to unearth the dead. These included the Chinese Labour Corps, of whom 1,500 died in this clean-up phase and were buried alongside the men they had previously exhumed.[61] The War Office hoped to recruit 15,000 men to help clear the battlefields and identify the dead, using extra pay as an incentive to help produce volunteers, but by June 1919 only 4,347 men had come forward to reinter the dead in France and Belgium.[62]

It was during a protracted process of initial burial, reinterment, and, eventually, through gravemarkers that the family were in direct contact with the state through the IWGC. The IWGC created ledgers and memos tracing deceased soldiers' whereabouts. When the family of the dead sent a letter asking if they had found the body of a loved one, for information pertaining to a person's grave, or requested updates about how quickly the IWGC was working, an 'enquiry file' (efile) was opened. Although many efiles have been discarded over the years, and the ones that were kept focus on cases where the IWGC felt they set some kind of precedent, they nonetheless offer an insight into the sorts of correspondence the IWGC had with bereaved families. While the information contained within the efiles is skewed because of this filing system, they are broadly representative of the type of information circulated, and patterns of help given, during the interwar years.

[58] Alison S. Fell and Susan Grayzel, 'Women's Movements, War and the Body', in Ingrid Sharp and Matthew Stibbe (eds.), *Women Activists between War and Peace* (London, 2017), 232.

[59] Commonwealth War Graves Commission, WG 783 Pt 1. Petition [1919].

[60] Rudyard Kipling, *The Graves of the Fallen* (London, [1919]), 15.

[61] Laqueur, *The Work of the Dead*, 468.

[62] Longworth, *The Unending Vigil*, 58.

Finding the graves of the dead was fraught with difficulty, and both during and after the war families wrote to the IWGC asking them for information about the location of their loved one's body. During the war, if the IWGC received a request for a grave location that it could not answer, a 'Form H' was sent to the Commanding Officer of the battalion the soldier was from to ask if they could give any information or a map reference of the place where the deceased was last seen. If this was not possible, the officer was to give details of the Unit that relieved them, so the IWGC could continue searching for the grave.[63] At the end of the war, before bodies could be reinterred, a vast search for the missing took place. Now aided by the Army, GRUs sectioned their territory, and searched for individuals whose graves might have been overlooked or unrecorded while the fighting happened. This continued until 1921, when Sir Laming Worthington-Evans, Secretary of State for War, said that owing to the difficulty of finding 'invisible graves', special searches would, from then on, only be carried out if relatives or friends could produce 'from their own knowledge evidence where the body of an officer or soldier may be found'.[64] Once the dead had been found and recorded, the IWGC faced the enormous task of reinterring them in formal cemeteries, so the land could be returned to French and Belgian farmers, a task that would take them years.[65]

While the GRUs swept the battlefields immediately after the war, they also acted on family information about the dead. In September 1918 the IWGC received a letter from Major General E. A. Wardrop who asked for information about Captain H. E. Chapman, who was 'seen to be knocked out by a machine gun bullet'. It was reported that two German soldiers had picked him up and placed him under cover, but that no more had been seen or heard of him, although as he had his identity discs it was possible that someone had buried him and marked the grave. No further correspondence regarding Chapman was received until 1919, when his mother began to make enquiries. Chapman's family were able to afford travel to France to attempt to find the grave of their son and in October 1919 Captain Chapman's mother sent a blistering attack on the bureaucracy she encountered there:

> No communication has been received at the office of the Graves Registration Camp Roizel [*sic*] respecting him... I had begged you to forward details of

[63] See, for example, the case of Lt J. D. C. Dennis. Commonwealth War Graves Commission, efile, CWGC/8/1/4/1/22 (AA10103).

[64] *The Times*, 10 November 1921, p. 14.

[65] Romain Fathi, '"We refused to work until we had better means for handling the bodies": Discipline and the Australian Graves Detachment', *First World War Studies* 9:1 (2018), 37.

> clothes etc, which I gave you, that would help them identify the body if found. You speak in your reply of 21st Aug 19 of the information I have [sent] having been noted, but it is quite useless to keep such information on the shelves of the [Law] Office when the only place if could be of any use wd be in the hands of the officer working on the spot. If other cases are treated as negligently as mine it is not to be wondered at that so many are still 'missing.'[66]

Her complaint highlighted the delay in information flow between the central offices in London and the regional ones where the searches were taking place. In many ways, this is not surprising—the sheer amount of logistical paperwork in circulation undoubtedly meant that some people's cases were missed—but here she suggests that this was a deliberate policy of bureaucratic neglect.

Families encountered the IWGC's complex set of rules through instances like these. The IWGC was formed of multiple departments in various stages of working through the implications of various rules and regulations. That the efiles were kept, as proof of precedent, is indicative of a vast organization with many moving parts, which had the power to disrupt and contradict each other. It is through these instances of family dealings with the IWGC that we glimpse the profound impact that the bureaucracy of the dead could have on the living. While families were able to control some aspects of their loved ones' graves, gaining closure in finally seeing them, others entered into protracted disputes with the IWGC, which influenced their understandings of whom this bureaucracy was supposed to benefit. This was only heightened when it came to providing headstones for the deceased.

Marking Graves

Once the dead had been found they were permanently laid to rest. The state control of the space that the dead were buried in disrupted peacetime norms of families owning, or renting, plots of land where their immediate kin could be buried.[67] Peacetime ownership of a grave allowed families to install a headstone: however, a minority of grave owners chose not to purchase one, because

[66] CWGC, efile, CWGC8/1/4/1/1/23 (AA10143).

[67] Patrick Joyce, *The Rule of Freedom: Liberalism and the Modern City* (London, 2003), 89–90.

of cost, or because they did not see it as important.[68] Having a permanent grave was of importance to many families, as it allowed them some sense of closure in the knowledge that their dead were being cared for. As Carol Acton notes, some families were overwhelmingly pleased with IWGC cemeteries, noting that one family, visiting the grave of their loved one ten years after his death, could only 'grieve spontaneously' once the grave was in front of them.[69] However, others were deeply upset that they had surrendered control to the state. Complicated emotions emerged from the push and pull of private and public grief as the wartime bereaved were asked to honour their dead's sacrifice, allow gravesite control by the state, and potentially cope with mixed feelings. The benefit of having a worthy grave for the dead combined with upset that this grave was not only potentially some distance away but that its design had been dictated by others.

While graves were undoubtedly important to many, the extent to which families cared about headstones is unclear. Strange has shown the fluidity of working-class attitudes towards graves in the late nineteenth and early twentieth centuries. By the late nineteenth century, plots of land where multiple people could be buried, one on top of the other, were available to purchase for between £1 and £5. Due to the cost of a family burial plot, multiple families could share the same dedicated space in cemeteries, all contributing to the cost. Alternatively, payment might be made to inter a loved one in a stranger's plot. The use of headstones was varied: some families could afford them, others attempted to use makeshift gravemarkers, which were often removed by cemetery boards. Some families did not bother with a headstone at all, either because they could not afford one or because it did not hold a particular importance for them.[70] Attitudes towards headstones were influenced by money and emotional ties to the grave, low-cost substitutes for stone monuments might be acceptable.

This complex relationship with headstones can be seen after mining disasters. Many of the men who died in mining disasters had some kind of temporary named marker above their grave. Some of these were hastily erected, such as the wooden crosses bearing namecards paid for by the Urban Council to mark the graves after the West Stanley disaster.[71] Others took the form of small stone memorial headstones. Some were to individuals, and others were

[68] Strange, *Death, Grief and Poverty*, 179.

[69] Carol Acton, *Grief in Wartime: Private Pain, Public Discourse* (Houndmills, 2007), 44–5; also see David W. Lloyd, *Battlefield Tourism: Pilgrimage and the Commemoration of the Great War in Britain, Australia and Canada, 1919–1939* (Oxford, 1998), 46.

[70] Strange, *Death, Grief and Poverty*, 131–93.

[71] *Consett Chronicle*, 5 March 1909, p. 6.

mass memorials in a churchyard with the names of all of the victims engraved. These gravemarkers were not necessarily permanent. This may not have been of particular concern to the immediate family, based on their understanding of how important the grave was.

In the case of the First World War dead, headstones constituted an area of high tension between families and the IWGC. Often, in letters to the families of the deceased, friends and comrades wrote that the dead, at least, had 'a good grave', which implies a burial service or a named marker.[72] Linking the body to a headstone was a highly important gesture. Knowing where a grave was, and investing it with the personal meaning bestowed by a marker, was helpful, although not always necessary, to the long-term emotional health of families who lost someone in a traumatic way.

During the First World War, wherever possible, soldiers were initially buried and a marker was placed on their grave. At this point soldiers who had not previously been given one had a temporary wooden cross with a metal nameplate placed on their grave. The dissemination of these wooden crosses was, by 1916, highly organized. Army Form W.3314, 'Instructions Relating to Burial Returns', was issued to chaplains on the Western Front and highlights the precision of the exercise by this point in the war:

> The G.R.U. responsible erects crosses on the site of the grave as soon as practicable. Crosses are at the same time kept ready at each G.R.U. office, and can be obtained with metal inscriptions, with only a few minutes delay. In cases where it is desirable for battalions, etc., to erect the crosses themselves, it is requested that the Chaplain or other Officer filling up this form shall name in space B. any convenient place where the crosses can be handed over by the G.R.U. to transport going up to the position.[73]

The markers were photographed by a travelling photographer, and sent to the families if they so desired. This practice seemingly stemmed from a Victorian custom of sending photographs or drawings of a gravesite to relatives unable to visit in person.[74] After the war was over the bodies in these scattered graves were interred in larger cemeteries where they could be cared for properly. As part of this process the wooden gravemarker was replaced with a stone marker. Families were able to request that they were sent the wooden cross

[72] Laqueur, *The Work of the Dead*, 487.

[73] Public Record Office Northern Ireland, D3019/1/5.

[74] Pat Jalland, 'Victorian Death and its Decline: 1850–1918', in Peter Jupp and Clare Gittings (eds.), *Death in England* (Manchester, 1999), 247.

which it replaced, although there were cases of them getting waylaid, or one family member declaring that they did not want it only for another to say that they did. These practices extended to the graves of those who died of wounds on British soil, and widows were asked if they wanted a wooden cross placed on their husband's grave before a permanent headstone could be created.[75]

It was recognized that there would be many visitors to the gravesites, and the IWGC hastily prepared the graveyards for guests throughout 1919, although it was many years before each soldier had an individual headstone. The uniformity of war graves was paramount to the IWGC's mission. The remains of those who died were supposed to rest, undifferentiated from one another, with class, race, and religious boundaries minimized through the distinctive IWGC headstone, although in reality only European troops received these promised graves.[76] This largely stemmed from the 1918 Kenyon Report, the response of Sir Frederic Kenyon, Director of the British Museum and adviser to the Commission, which emphasized that 'equality of treatment' should be key.[77] The Commission, following his recommendations, provided uniform headstones decorated with the relevant regimental crest and with the soldier's rank, name, and date of death. As Sarah Tarlow writes, this had the effect of reducing the 'complex modern individual to an almost pre-modern, substitutable person, remembered only as a soldier and in the same way as any and every other soldier'.[78] Gravestones were provided free of charge and were put in place unless a family had already managed to erect a private gravestone before the IWGC asked them to use one of theirs.

Personal inscriptions of up to sixty-six characters on the IWGC gravestones were allowed at the family's own expense, although not all families availed themselves of this offer. The cost barred some families from participating in this commemorative action, such as the wife of Private J. B. Slipp, who could not afford the extra expense this incurred, or the family of S. Davies, whose mother supplied the commemorative words 'ever in our thoughts', underneath writing 'I do not agree to pay the costs He gave his life freely & if this cannot be put on freely leave it off'.[79] These inscriptions were

[75] CWGC, efile, CCM52610, Pte J. Harding.

[76] Michèle Barrett, 'Subalterns at War: First World War Colonial Forces and the Politics of the Imperial War Graves Commission', *Interventions* 9:3 (2007), 451–74; Michèle Barrett, 'Dehumanization and the War in East Africa', *Journal of War & Culture Studies* 10:3 (2017), 238–52; Michèle Barrett, 'Sent Missing in Africa: Briefing Paper for *The Unremembered*' (2020), 1–29.

[77] Frederic Kenyon, *War Graves: How the Cemeteries Abroad will be Designed* (London, 1918), 7.

[78] Sarah Tarlow, *Bereavement and Commemoration: An Archaeology of Mortality* (Oxford, 1999), 157.

[79] CWGC, efile, CWGC/8/1/4/1/3/27; efile, CWGC/8/1/4/1/1/170 (AA51372).

heavily monitored by the IWGC, and requests for memorial words not in keeping with the Commission's outlook were regularly refused.[80] The Kenyon Report commented on this possibility, explaining that 'it is clearly undesirable to allow free scope for the effusions of the mortuary mason, the sentimental versifier, or the crank', but instead a small personal inscription, paid for by the family, 'of not more than three lines' would be allowed, although the Commission was to have 'absolute power of rejection or acceptance'.[81]

Some families chose to make the intangible tangible, and after the First World War some chose to memorialize their loved ones by engraving their last words to their families on their IWGC headstone. The wife of Private G. H. Pratt, of the East Lancashire Regiment, had his last words to her, 'God be with you till we meet again', engraved on his IWGC headstone as a permanent reminder of both his last moments with her and the Christian hope that they would indeed meet once more.[82] In so doing, his wife linked her husband's literal, corporeal, goodbye with a spiritual Christian farewell which spoke of reunion. These small connectors, of a highly personal meaning being broadcast by the family in an unseen way, offer a new understanding of the commemorative words chosen. Deliberately chosen to be displayed in a public place, they show the intimate connection between home and grave that could be created.

As much as the IWGC insisted that families could personalize the gravestone, in practice requests to do so were not always well received. In 1920, the IWGC contacted the parents of Jack Mainwaring to ask if a memorial headstone could be erected in the British cemetery in which he was buried. The Mainwarings agreed to this on the condition that his rank be excluded from the headstone. This caused some official trouble, and after several internal discussions it was decided that, as there was one existent precedent of a family omitting rank, it would be accepted in this case and a letter was sent to Jack's parents informing them of the decision. However, in June 1921, just before the gravestone was about to be engraved, a letter from the Principal Assistant Secretary was sent to Mainwaring's parents asking them to consider the matter further. It was argued that:

> The impression gathered by anyone visiting the cemetery, reading the inscription as you propose to have it, might be that he [Mainwaring] was

[80] Sonia Batten, 'Memorial Text Narratives in Britain, c.1890–1930' (Unpublished PhD, University of Birmingham, 2011), 196.

[81] Kenyon, 'War Graves', 10.

[82] CWGC, efile, YP/1411.

> reduced in rank and it was desired to conceal this fact. At best the omission of the number and rank, particulars which appear on all other headstones erected over War graves, might be regarded as due to carelessness in engraving the headstone. I feel myself it is hardly fair to the memory of your son himself, nor to his comrades, to suppress what might be called his military identity.[83]

This complete reverse in attitude towards the parents' autonomy and their control over the gravestone led the parents of Second Lieutenant Mainwaring to change the inscription. Mainwaring's father replied, explaining that 'although both my wife and myself would prefer our sons [*sic*] rank not to appear on the headstone on reading your letter we think it only right to leave the matter entirely in your hands'. The Principal Assistant Secretary replied, saying that 'this is a matter to which the Commission has given serious thought' and further attempted to legitimize their decision by invoking the ghost of their son, by stating that it was 'in the interest of the dead themselves'. This official reaction to the personal wishes of the parents helps to highlight the tension which ran through this memorial initiative. It signalled that, although the parents were the private holders of their son's memory, both publicly and bureaucratically, the state, through the Commission, decided that his military status trumped any parental wishes.

In extreme cases of problems with IWGC bureaucracy, families could be refused IWGC headstones. The IWGC made the decision not to erect a war grave over the burial place of any soldiers who died after 31 August 1921, or those whose death was not directly caused by serving during the conflict.[84] In practice, these rules were sometimes flexible. Sergeant C. C. Poole was one of a minority of servicemen who, as a result of wounds received in service, died on British soil. Poole died in September 1921 due to heart failure, having been discharged from the Army in 1919 with gunshot wounds and 'valvular disease of the heart'. He was buried in an IWGC plot, and his widow, Mabel Poole, was determined to erect a suitable memorial to her husband after his death. This was in accordance with wider family wishes and in 1922 Poole's father wrote to the IWGC to request a memorial to place on his son's grave. The IWGC responded that because he had died after their cut-off date, and because it was unclear whether his death was due to war wounds, they could not place a memorial stone on his grave.

[83] CWGC, efile, SL18509. [84] CWGC, efile, CWGC/8/1/4/1/1/161 (AA49102).

In 1922 Poole commissioned a headstone from a local sculptor, who wrote to the IWGC, as owners of the grave, asking them to approve the design. After receiving no reply, Poole, assuming that this meant that after their initial refusal her husband was after all to be given a Commission grave, wrote again to the IWGC. In February 1923 she wrote to the Commission explaining that she understood other relatives with soldiers buried in an IWGC plot in Gloucester Cemetery had been asked to fill in a form with details of the epitaph they wanted engraved on their IWGC headstone. She explained that, because she had been overlooked, she was enclosing the information she wished to be carved on the headstone. Poole knew that forms were being sent, and knew enough about them to replicate the information requested. The IWGC, as they had done with her father-in-law, again refused her request for an IWGC headstone for her husband. Poole wrote a controlled but critical reply:

> I was more than surprised to hear that my late husband is not entitled to a memorial stone. He died in 1921 & death was directly attributed to War Service & wounds or he wouldn't have been in receipt of full Pension. I was refused permission by the W.G.H. to have a stone erected at my own expense & was informed that memorial stones were being erected to every soldier buried on that plot. It is rather like the 'Dog in the Manger' kind of treatment.[85]

'Dog in the manger' treatment, a reference to Aesop's fables, implied that the IWGC was wilfully blocking access to something that she needed even though it gave them no benefit. In this letter Poole invoked the bureaucracy of the war pension scheme to further legitimize her claim with a sister-organization to the pensions office.

Caught between the cemetery's insistence that all the headstones were being replaced with IWGC ones, and the IWGC's insistence that this was not the case, she turned to the Mayor of Gloucester for assistance and the Town Clerk began to act as a mediator. The Clerk believed he had found a suitable answer to the problem, and proposed that a headstone be erected, in the same style as the other IWGC headstones, but at Poole's expense. Unbeknownst to the Mayor, the Land and Legal Advisor for the IWGC had been contemplating a similar proposal, and a 1923 report recommended that the IWGC 'let her erect one at her own expense as grave at edge of plot and probably

[85] CWGC, efile, CWGC/8/1/4/1/1/161 (AA49102).

wouldn't be noticed'. Both the Town Clerk and the IWGC were happy with this proposal, and the IWGC contacted Poole in mid-March to tell her that due to the 'special circumstances of this case' they would allow a headstone of the Commission's standard design to be constructed for £3 10*s* 0*d*.

The proposal that the IWGC would construct a gravestone at Poole's expense, mediated by the Town Clerk, should have ended the dispute. Poole refused their offer, arguing that because she would be 'paying for it I might be allowed to erect one according to my own choice as there are other stones on the plot not of the standard design'. Different IWGC departments approached this problem with different solutions: the Land and Legal Advisor suggested it would 'be the simplest course to allow her to do so' but the Controller and Financial Advisor instead argued that 'the best way of dealing with this matter would be for the Commission to put up the headstone at their own expense'. The IWGC as a whole were strongly resistant to individual memorials on their plots, which seems to have influenced their final decision. This was also a time-sensitive matter, as the IWGC gravestones in the plot for those who were entitled to them were set to be unveiled in June—it was desired that Sergeant Poole's headstone should be ready by this date so they could present a uniform landscape of graves.

In May 1923 the IWGC informed Mabel Poole of their decision to construct a Commission headstone, adding, 'the Commission hope the course will meet with your approval'. Ultimately, Poole was granted her wish, although at the expense of a protracted argument which exposed bureaucratic weaknesses in the IWGC. Her appeal to people in authority, to act as mediators in her case, was all that she could do to add weight to her claims and, ultimately, these tactics bore fruit. Yet it is clear that this was done somewhat reluctantly, and her perseverance paid off because the IWGC did not deem her husband's grave to be in a particularly focal part of the gravesite. Her case begs the question of what happened to those who were not as persistent, and who did not reach bureaucrats with sufficient powers to make decisions about matters such as this.

The families of the war dead had very little control over the graves of their loved ones. In keeping with state control of the bodies of the living in the final weeks, months, and years leading up to their death, the state also controlled the graves of the dead. The only way of individualizing the dead was through a small inscription which was vetoed if it was deemed to be unacceptable by the IWGC. Individual families tried to circumnavigate these official regulations, although the power was usually with the IWGC, and resolutions which suited all parties often only happened if the family had a powerful advocate to act on their behalf. These negotiations through local officials who might be able to leverage the situation are reminiscent of appeals made by families of the disaster dead whose loved ones' bodies were entombed. These appeals were all through letters, and formed part of the paperwork of death that families increasingly encountered.

Family and bureaucratic time did not always work in tandem, and different priorities characterized interactions between the bereaved and those who controlled the body. Waiting for news of a grave created or confirmed could seem like a lifetime to some. Once the IWGC forms were sent the Commission were working to a deadline to create headstones for the dead, and internal memos reminded staff to prompt families for their choice of memorial words.[86] While to the IWGC this was a bureaucratic necessity, for families it was a considered and debated choice of words to include on the final resting place of their loved one. Perhaps this is where the core problem with IWGC bureaucracy lay. What was a simple piece of paperwork for the War Office was a death notification for a family. What was a simple form requesting an epitaph for the IWGC could be days and weeks of emotional decision making for the next of kin. The bureaucracy of death had the power to shape family mourning, protracting grief through the slow progression of irregular paperwork, and casting a long shadow over those who had to deal with these paper-based reminders of death.

Conclusion

In times of crisis, the families of war and disaster dead suddenly found that the bodies of their loved ones were not solely their property any more. In peacetime, families generally organized the funerals of their loved ones, and it was rare for this to be taken out of their hands by local or national authorities. For the disaster dead, families might have been lucky enough to keep the body of their loved one in the home before the funeral, but once the funeral procession began the family were no longer in control. In the case of disaster local authorities assumed familial power. In wartime the state, through a governmental body, assumed the mantle.

Over the course of the early interwar period, the bureaucracy of death encountered by the families of the war dead could profoundly shape their experience of loss and their relationship to the state. The gap between the

[86] CWGC, efile, CWGC/8/1/4/1/87 (AA36539).

perceived power of the state by the families and the reality of this was stark. Families imagined a state which could mobilize whole sections of society, supply vast armies, and keep track of its soldiers. Once these soldiers were no longer living, families were confronted with a vast bureaucracy developed throughout the war to try to trace their army of the dead, but which could not possibly satisfy all individuals. From the outset it was an impossible task. Families lucky enough to know where their loved one was buried were confronted with a slow-moving system of burials and reburials, which resulted in letters asking the IWGC where their loved one was and when he might get a permanent headstone.

Although the families of the deceased did not control the burial of their dead, the types of funeral on offer wildly differed. The bodies of the dead were (re)interred in their final resting place with funerary rituals after war and disaster. Sometimes these were arranged by individual families, but more often they were organized by the state or local authorities. Large funerals of the disaster dead stood in almost direct opposition to the quiet reinterments of the majority of the war dead.

During the First World War there were, of course, many who could never hope to have a gravestone. Thousands of bodies went missing during the conflict, and their names were engraved on large reverent memorials, one monument assuming the role of hundreds of individual graves. Similarly, families who lost loved ones at sea, particularly naval families, did not expect a body to mourn. Instead war memorials and gravestones on family plots, where a name could be added, were common ways of memorializing the dead.

There was a cultural expectation that bodies would be recovered and buried, although whether families expected a gravestone is debatable. During the war great emphasis was placed on giving the war dead a respectable burial, so families would feel that their loved one had been honoured for their sacrifice. The uniform cemeteries created were an attempt to assure the families of the dead that there was a safe and quiet place for the dead to be buried. But, as the option to provide a personalized inscription hinted, families wanted more control over their memorial narrative than this system allowed. This control could not always be enacted in the public space of burials, but instead developed through acts of domestic memorization.

Family Mourning After War and Disaster in Twentieth-Century Britain. Ann-Marie Foster, Oxford University Press.
 DOI: 10.1093/9780191968129.003.0003

3

Printing Death

On Saturday 20 February 1909, in the columns of the Newcastle upon Tyne newspaper the *Evening Chronicle*, Alice and Michael posted a death notice for their sons:

> Martin—Stanley, 2 Manx Street, in the explosion, aged 21 years, John Willie, beloved son of Alice and Michael Martin, known as Johnson; also Joseph, beloved son of same, aged 14 years. Interment on Sunday. All friends kindly invited.[1]

Theirs was one of twenty-eight death notices posted in the column that day, announcing the dead of the West Stanley colliery explosion, with more printed in other local newspapers across the region. This marked one of the first memorial acts that the Martins would undertake for their sons, expressing their love and sorrow through print media.

Across the first four decades of the twentieth century there was a rich print culture of death which spanned the whole of the British class system. Print developments during the nineteenth century meant that previously expensive memorial customs, such as sending ornate memorial cards, morphed into plainer, more affordable, practices. For the primarily working-class families of the war and disaster dead, this meant that by the turn of the century printed memorial material was both culturally expected and relatively affordable for all but the poorest families. People could select memorial material which reflected their feelings towards the dead, and the tragic circumstances of those who died in mass death events formed a subset of memorial material. Highlighting the mode of death, or choosing a memorial form that reflected that, such as a memorial card emblazoned with a military motif, allowed families to mark their dead as special.

Families adapted pre-existent social mourning cues to articulate their loss in quasi-public spaces. Working and middle-class families posted death and In Memoriam notices to the local newspaper, while upper-class families sent

[1] *Evening Chronicle*, 20 February 1909, p. 2.

obituaries to local and national newspapers. There was a tension in this, as the newspapers that they sent these notifications to were also often the same places where gruesome details of the deaths the families were notifying their communities of were sensationalized. After mining disasters the results of coroner's inquests, and upsetting descriptions of the state of the bodies, were printed in local newspapers. Similarly, during the First World War newspapers gave some sense of the horrific conditions those in the armed services could find themselves in. Upper-class families were haunted by casualty lists, printed publicly in *The Times*.

The newspaper was the most public way that families announced the death of a family member, but commissioned memorial ephemera were also an important tool for remembering the dead in the early twentieth century. People of all classes sent In Memoriam cards to close friends and families, so that they could privately remember the dead. Wealthy families might, in special circumstances, such as the death of a son on military service, commission a memorial book, for private family use. These external grieving prompts were printed or created within the first few days, weeks, and months of the family hearing the news of a death, but also provided points of annual remembrance. Ephemera were crucial to the mourning process, with grief elevating their role from necessary social items to ones which were highly valued by family and friends, the production of which could lend some small catharsis to the maker.

These printed worlds of the dead allowed the families of people whose bodies had been controlled by others a way of reclaiming their death narrative. Although this was culturally constrained and socially mediated, memorial ephemera often marked the first real decision that the family could make about the treatment of their dead in public. This was, perhaps, only a small gesture of control—however, the importance of this to individual families should not be overlooked. It was through the words, images, and forms of memorial material that families began to construct the legacy of their loved one.

Printing News of the Dead

Family remembrances to the dead were printed in newspapers which actively shaped the way that local and national publics understood and engaged with war and disaster. Most people encountered accidents and disasters through the pages of the newspaper.[2] Miners and newspapers had an uneasy

[2] Paul Fyfe, *By Accident or Design: Writing the Victorian Metropolis* (Oxford, 2015), 31.

relationship, with the press casting miners either as heroes, working underground in terrible conditions, or as being squalid, political, and stubborn.[3] After mining disasters, workers were lauded for their heroism, and articles which praised rescuers and provided horrifying detail about deaths underground were common.

Although newspapers glorified the rescuers and the dead of disasters, they also revelled in the tragedy created by large-scale death and singled out particular families for mention in their columns. Local newspapers regularly mentioned people who were notable for the exceptionally tragic nature of their loss, such as Mrs Dixon, who lost her husband in the 1908 Washington Glebe disaster. The *Durham Chronicle* noted that 'Dixon, we were informed, had been married about twelve months ago [to] the widow of a man formerly killed at the Glebe Pit, and therefore great sympathy is felt for Mrs Dixon in her bereavement.'[4] After the 1931 Bentley mining disaster, the press interviewed rescuers who talked about the terrible burns the miners faced, as well as the particularly haunting scenes of mutilated corpses they came across.[5] The same types of news report followed the 1915 Quintinshill railway disaster. *The Carlisle Journal* described how 'one young woman, who had been married only three weeks, identified her dead husband in the public mortuary'.[6] These pathos-laden tales which received special merit were, in part, a calculated way of arousing public sympathy for the families of those affected. This reporting style emphasized human loss in disaster narratives as paramount. In attempting to sell newspapers by relating these tragic stories editors and reporters placed the emphasis of the story on the bereaved, highlighting the grief felt by families in the wake of the sudden disaster. Newspaper reporting of disasters was sensational and described death details in a way that accounts of military wartime deaths simply did not.

In wartime, descriptions of ruined landscapes and wounded soldiers found their place in the pages of the newspaper. Although news reports were not as detailed as after disasters, families were still aware of the horrific circumstances in which their loved ones died. Wartime photographs, films, and word of mouth descriptions supplemented official news channels. Helen McCartney's work has stressed the close ties between the home and fighting

[3] Roger Laidlaw, 'The Gresford Disaster in Popular Memory', *Llafur* 6 (1995), 28; David Selway, 'Death Underground: Mining Accidents and Memory in South Wales, 1913–74', *Labour History Review* 81:3 (2016), 201.

[4] *Durham Chronicle*, 28 February 1908, p. 5.

[5] John Church, '*It's like old wine to see you again, lass': An Account of the 1931 Bentley Colliery Disaster*' (Doncaster, 1991), 18.

[6] *The Carlisle Journal*, 25 May 1915, p. 6.

fronts, showing that details about fighting conditions, including information about the type of death encountered, came to families from letters and discussions with comrades on leave.[7]

For upper-class families in the First World War *The Times* became a site of tragedy, as casualty lists were published, in some cases informing the family of a wound or death before an official letter had reached them. This created a mass anxiety among newspaper readers. In her wartime diary, Vera Brittain expressed this with the comment 'I may well dread to open *The Times*.'[8] She was not the only one. In later life Harold Macmillan recalled that 'one scarcely dared to read the newspapers, especially if a new battle had begun to rage'.[9]

After mining disasters it was not uncommon for newspapers to reprint the findings of the inquiries in some detail. After the 1909 West Stanley disaster comments about the state of the bodies, with 'parts of their heads blown away', and other graphic details, were published in local newspapers.[10] The *Consett Chronicle* went as far as to publish a list of the dead with the cause of death next to the name underneath, giving such intimate details as 'in some cases the mouth and nose appeared filled with coal dust, suggesting that some of the men might have died from suffocation'.[11] This intimate information, known to the families and those who lived in the area, was reported widely in the local and national press.[12] Even if the manner of death was not published, a list of names and addresses often was. On rare occasions, this also happened after munitions explosions, such as the 1917 Barking explosion in which thirteen women workers were killed.[13] Sometimes, the addresses of the deceased were reprinted on memorial ephemera, adding an extra layer of intrusiveness to family grief.[14]

The families of war and disaster dead knew that their loved one's death was likely to be spread through newspaper lists in some form, with varying amounts of information about the violent nature of the death circulated. There was a cultural expectation that details of the manner of death would be told when a loved one had died in a mass death event. Families posted newspaper notifications and memorial reminders in newspapers which,

[7] Helen McCartney, *Citizen Soldiers: The Liverpool Territorials in the First World War* (Cambridge, 2005), 89–95, 107.

[8] Vera Brittain, *Chronicle of Youth* (London, 1981), 213.

[9] Harold Macmillan, quoted in David Cannadine, 'War and Death, Grief and Mourning in Modern Britain', in Joachim Whaley (ed.), *Mirrors of Mortality: Social Studies in the History of Death* (London, 1981), 198.

[10] *The Auckland Times*, 19 February 1909, p. 5; *The Evening Standard*, 18 February 1909, p. 5.

[11] *Consett Chronicle*, 5 March 1909, p. 6.

[12] *The Times*, 18 February 1909, p. 12.

[13] *The Times*, 11 August 1917, p. 3.

[14] Beamish Museum, GS 04.08.2010.

as well as providing a way for individual families to grieve, did so in the same pages which spread information about these often gruesome and deeply upsetting deaths. This tension between the needs of the family and the conventions of the wider community and the press formed an uncomfortable background to the printing of memorial ephemera.

Newspapers, Death Notices, and In Memoriam Columns

Immediately after the death of a loved one, families posted death notices in local newspapers. These were rapidly printed, and could be in press before wider death lists were circulated. In the case of mining disasters, these notifications happened before the results of inquests were announced. After this initial announcement, families returned yearly to the newspaper to post an In Memoriam message. Not every family felt the need or could afford to do this, but they were a popular form of annual commemoration throughout the twentieth century. These notices represent a clear area of continuity in death practices after war and disaster, with families using pre-existent methods of announcing the death of a loved one. Announcing the death of a family member was a significant step within 'normal' death practices, and families thought of these announcements as socially expected. Where the announcements differ is in extra sentences highlighting the violent mode of death suffered, through mention of disaster or explosion, and in the phrases, 'killed in action' and 'died of wounds'. This constituted a subtle but significant shift in death notice language. Families wanted readers, be they friends, acquaintances, or unknown members of the public, to know that the death they were reading about was a particularly tragic one. The reasons for this could be complex, and vary from practical reasons, such as not wanting to relive a disaster, to social ones, such as marking a family's loss as a 'blood sacrifice'.

The Births, Marriages, and Deaths sections of local newspapers were an important feature of everyday life in the early twentieth century, providing a means of communicating family events to friends and acquaintances, but also to the wider world. Families used newspapers to announce the death of their loved one and give details of the burial service, as well as to thank people who had assisted them during their bereavement. These columns were made possible by the development of the provincial press in the mid-1860s.[15] Due to the telegraph's rise as a means of quickly transmitting information, local

[15] Maurice Milne, *The Newspapers of Northumberland and Durham* (Gateshead [1971]), 21.

newspapers quickly grew in popularity throughout the end of the nineteenth century, as they were able to combine international news with local reporting. As their popularity grew, so did people's involvement with them as a way of communicating family news through the Births, Marriages, and Deaths section.

Death notices, as small inexpensive announcements, not usually more than a couple of lines in length, were where the family could announce the death of a loved one, and details of the funeral, to the wider world. They performed the task of telling the community about the dead in a way accessible to all but the poorest members of society. They followed conventional patterns, although people were able to choose certain phrases, or include a quotation, which could personalize the text. In his study of death notices in *The Times* between 1785 and 1985, Udo Fries argued that death notices slowly moved towards increasingly rigid phrasing, with not much scope for individualization by the 1980s.[16] In a study of Irish death notices, Ciara Breathnach and David Butler point towards what they tell us about social mobility, positing that for the Catholic middle class in particular, death notices came to represent upward mobility during the mid-nineteenth century, picking up in popularity for working-class families the century after.[17] While the death notice was culturally constrained, by the twentieth century it was a cultural norm across most of Great Britain and Ireland, albeit one which contained local and regional subtleties.

The notices usually included the name of the deceased, their street address, details of the immediate family left behind (parents, spouse, and children), and, often, details of the funeral. It was not uncommon to see multiple family members' deaths announced in the same notice if they had died in rapid succession. Death notices were cheap for the family to print and prices remained broadly stable across the first few decades of the twentieth century. In 1909, the *Consett Chronicle* charged 2*s* to announce a birth, marriage, or death.[18] In 1927 the *Western Mail* charged 1*s* 6*d* for the first twelve words of the announcement, with an extra 9*d* for sets of six additional words.[19] Some newspapers waived printing fees for death announcements during the First World War.[20]

[16] Udo Fries, 'Two Hundred Years of English Death Notices,' in Margaret Bridges (ed.), *On Strangeness* (Tübingen, 1990), 62.

[17] Ciara Breathnach and David Butler, 'Death Notices and Obituaries in Provincial Irish Newspapers, 1820–1900', in James Kelly and Mary Ann Lyons (eds.), *Death and Dying in Ireland, Britain and Europe: Historical Perspectives* (Sallins, 2013), 252, 256, 266, 272.

[18] *Consett Chronicle*, 5 March 1909, p. 5.

[19] *Western Mail*, 4 March 1927, p. 1.

[20] My thanks to Helen McCartney on this point.

These announcements were by no means used only by those who had been bereaved in violent circumstances, but they were flagged as special through their wording. The death notices section was filled with people who had died from sickness. Yet the manner of their death was rarely mentioned, unlike the announcements of people who died because of their involvement in war or disaster. These sudden deaths were marked as special deaths, outside the norm and of social note. In the case of large disasters, the columns of local newspapers were often filled with numerous death notices from bereaved families. The reasons for this are multifold and overlapping. Families wanted to gain recognition for the sudden death of a family member, have their work recognized (be it mining or military based), alert people to the cause of death so that uncomfortable questions were not asked of the newly bereaved, or simply because it was an established convention.

Funeral details were a key feature of death notices. These could range from small announcements intended for friends of the deceased, to notices which drew hundreds of mourners from the local community. After the Quintinshill railway disaster a death notice in *The Carlisle Journal*, which announced the funerals of the two railway workers who died in the crash, ensured that their funeral was attended by thousands of mourners.[21] After the West Stanley mining disaster, the high coverage given to it in both local and national newspapers, combined with an announcement of the time and dates for the funeral procession, led to an attendance that the *Durham Chronicle* estimated was between 70,000 and 80,000, and *The Auckland Times* claimed equated to nearly 200,000 mourners.[22]

During the First World War, death notices could mark significant bureaucratic and emotional points in a family's journey towards (often uneasy) acceptance that a missing family member was likely dead. In June 1919, the family of 2nd Lieutenant H. L. Frank Mansfield announced that although he had been 'reported wounded and missing at Garelle, May 3, 1917, [he] is now officially presumed to have died on or after that date'.[23] On the same day, the Lamb family announced that they were holding a memorial service for Sergeant M. F. Lamb, who went 'missing on March 26, 1918, now reported killed on that date'.[24] Some families decided to announce this not in the death notices column but in the In Memoriam column instead—such as the family of Joseph Wheatley, who posted that he had been reported missing in 1918,

[21] *The Carlisle Journal*, 28 May 1915, p. 10.
[22] *Durham Chronicle*, 26 February 1909, p. 4; *The Auckland Times*, 26 February 1909, p. 7.
[23] *Evening Chronicle*, 5 June 1919, p. 2.
[24] *Evening Chronicle*, 5 June 1919, p. 2.

but was since presumed dead.[25] This was publicly significant, and it is telling that these families used the death notices column, instead of the slightly further removed In Memoriam one, to inform the local community that they now officially recognized their loved one as dead. The social code of using death notices as a method of mass communication proved strong, even in the case of abnormal timelines of death.

The Births, Marriages, and Death section also allowed families to thank the wider community that supported them in their bereavement with a Notice of Thanks. Following the West Stanley disaster, Mrs Hodgson offered 'her heartfelt and sincerest thanks to her relatives and the general public for the many condolences, floral tributes, tributes of respect and other kindnesses shown her in her recent bereavement'.[26] In 1917, Mrs Jennison and her family thanked 'kind friends and neighbours for letters and sympathy in the great loss of her dear husband, Lance-Corporal Fred Jennison, who died of wounds in France'.[27] These posts, although less common than death notices, provided an opportunity for families to acknowledge communities of support that helped them in their grief. The posts usually emphasized the helper's role as a good neighbour, as well as acknowledging debts of aid outside of the traditional people whom one would be able to thank, such as the general public. Although Notices of Thanks were not overly popular columns in the early twentieth century, when used they formed a significant space where the family could show appreciation to the wider community while subtly reminding them of their ongoing feelings of loss.

When paper shortages affected newspapers during the First World War, editors ensured that they continued to print death notices, because of their importance to the structure and saleability of the newspaper. Signs of this strain were increasingly apparent in the Advertisements section of the *Evening Chronicle*. By mid-1916 the editors included notices informing readers that due 'to the pressure on our advertising space we have been obliged to hold over a number of Advertisements'.[28] By 1918 the editors told the readers that 'owing to the great pressure on our space, we are unable to accept any further Advertisements for the "Evening Chronicle" until further notice'. Despite pressure on this source of revenue, the editors were keen that families should not be affected by these material constraints, and continued to reassure their readers that 'an exception will be made in regard to Births, Marriages,

[25] *Durham Chronicle*, 25 March 1921, p. 1.
[26] *Consett Chronicle*, 5 March 1909, p. 2.
[27] *Evening Chronicle*, 2 May 1918, p. 2.
[28] *Evening Chronicle*, 6 June 1916, p. 2.

Deaths'.[29] Not only was the column seen as an important feature by those who used it, but its social value was clearly understood by those in charge of producing it. Given the limited newspaper space the paper shortage produced, by valuing the 'Births, Marriages, and Deaths' columns above advertising, the editors sent a clear message about the social role of the newspaper.

Families could personalize their message to the community further through including an image of the dead in local newspapers. These were fairly uncommon in the early years of the twentieth century, although they became popular during the First World War. After a disaster, the images of individual dead were not included in death notices, although they were often available in memorial pamphlets printed by a local newspaper firm. During the First World War, however, advances in printing techniques meant that newspapers started to print the images of individual soldiers. While this was, as a rule, not continued in local newspapers after the war, there was usually a regional illustrated newspaper people could submit their loved one's photograph to.

While it is impossible to fully estimate how many families sent photographs of their loved ones to local newspapers during the First World War, we can get a vague sense of the scale of the phenomenon. It was certainly not every family who submitted an image to a newspaper, and it seems to be a distinct minority who did submit their loved one's photograph to illustrated newspapers. However, it is clear that a significant number of people felt compelled to commemorate their dead in this way. A crude examination of the digitized collection of First World War soldier images taken from the *Illustrated Chronicle*, a newspaper which covered the North-East of England, finds that out of the 23,683 images sent by family members, 3,821 of them were of servicemen who were killed outright, 899 who died of wounds, 227 who were lost at sea, and a further 920 of soldiers labelled 'missing'.[30] Approximately 25 per cent of those whose images were featured in the *Illustrated Chronicle* died or were missing as a result of the war, double the national percentage of wartime combatant deaths.[31] Families who lost a loved one posted images of the dead at a higher rate than one would expect if each soldier were represented. This could have been because of the geography of the deaths commemorated, as northern Pals battalions often suffered heavy losses, but presumably also indicates a desire on behalf of the bereaved to publicly mark their dead,

[29] *Evening Chronicle*, 2 May 1918, p. 2.

[30] The *Illustrated Chronicle* digitized collection is available on flicr, https://www.flickr.com/photos/illustratedchroniclewwl/ [Accessed 21.07.2020].

[31] Jay Winter, *The Great War and the British People* (Houndmills, 2003), 72.

leading to a high rate of engagement with this ephemeral form which became a site of memorialization.

Death notices were not limited to publication in local newspapers, and can be found in the pages of professional magazines. Among certain professions, the death of a member of staff might be announced in trade magazines and newsletters in addition to a death notice in the newspaper. Company magazines were popular from the 1880s, but became increasingly professionalized after the First World War, transitioning from a collection of pieces aimed at reasonably small groups of clerical workers, edited by company staff, to magazines with professional editors which appealed to the whole of the company.[32] These magazines were particularly popular among railway workers, as a professional group who were particularly close knit.[33] The times and dates of funerals were sometimes posted in workplace magazines, such as the funeral of Captain K. J. Maples, who worked in the Solicitor's Office of the Great Western Railway, whose memorial service was announced in *The Railway Gazette*, the day before it was due to be held.[34] During the First World War *The Railway Gazette* had a regular 'Roll of Honour' section where the deaths of railwaymen who had been given leave to go and fight were memorialized. Sometimes these announcements included men who had worked for the magazine themselves. In 1915 the column announced: 'We regret to record that Lance Corporal W. J. Clarke, one of the five members of the staff of this journal who enlisted last September, has died from wounds received during a recent engagement.'[35] Company magazines constituted another extended community with which the family could feel they needed to share the news of their loved one's death.

There was a class element to whether a family posted a death notice, an obituary, or both. An obituary was a longer form of a death notice, reserved for those who were socially elite, or particularly notable in some way.[36] The family of Captain W. Langdon, of the Cheshire Regiment, commissioned both

[32] Michael Heller, 'Company Magazines 1880–1940: An Overview', *Management & Organizational History* 3:3–4 (2008), 186.

[33] Hannah Reeves, 'An Exploration of the "Railway Family", 1900–1948' (Unpublished PhD, Keele University, 2018), 21–4.

[34] *The Railway Gazette*, 28 May 1915, p. 557.

[35] *The Railway Gazette*, 28 May 1915, p. 541.

[36] For work on obituaries see: Zsófia Nagy, 'The Changing Nature of Death and Mourning: An Analysis of Hungarian Obituaries (1961–2000)', *Mortality* 23:2 (2018), 151–72; Bridget Fowler and Esperança Bielsa, 'The Lives we Choose to Remember: A Quantitative Analysis of Newspaper Obituaries', *The Sociological Review* 55:2 (2007), 203–26; Bridget Fowler, 'Mapping the Obituary: Notes towards a Bourdieusian Interpretation', *The Sociological Review* (2004), 148–71; Gary L. Long, 'Organizations and Identity: Obituaries 1856–1972', *Social Forces* 65:4 (1987), 964–1001.

obituaries and death notices.[37] Langdon came from a well-off Anglo-Jewish trade family in Manchester. He was educated at Rugby and Oxford, and was building his career in law when he was killed. His education, as it did with so many public-school-educated men, clearly played a role in his decision to fight, as he enlisted for the Public Schools Battalion of the Middlesex Regiment in September 1914.The collection of printed memorials to Langdon not only allows us to see the types of information in circulation, but also shows how rapidly these items were published, as well as their geographic spread. An obituary or a death notice for Langdon was included in twenty-nine separate publications. These ranged from local newspapers, to newspapers focusing on trade, school magazines, and national coverage in *The Times* and through the *Jewish Chronicle*, with pictorial coverage in the *Manchester Evening Chronicle,* the *Manchester Evening News*, the *Altrincham Guardian*, *War Illustrated*, and the *Illustrated London News*. Some newspapers contained multiple postings, such as the *Chester Courant*, which in a single issue posted three types of death notice for Langdon, including one in a special 'Killed in Action' column. The first announcements were made six days after his death, and, although most were published within a couple of weeks, some were published later, with the most extreme example printed a full six months after Langdon's death. While some of the accounts of his death may have been copied from one another, it nonetheless shows the considerable range of people to whom Langdon's family passed the news of his death. This reach was a privilege not afforded to everyone, but shows the different types of newspapers which upper and upper-middle-class families used to announce the news of a death. Families from a lower socioeconomic background would post a death notice in a local newspaper, perhaps extending this to a trade magazine if the man who died was well-established in their career.

After the family posted a death notice, one of the clearest ways that families continued to mark their loss was through annual In Memoriam posts in the local newspaper. These were yearly remembrances, usually posted on the anniversary of death, which were slightly longer and allowed more personalization than death notices commonly held. Work on In Memoriam columns stresses their social importance, emphasizing the rituals they uphold. Sheila Adams suggests that these notices were used by the bereaved as a

[37] Captain Langdon 'Obituary Book' digitized by the Jewish Museum, London, https://www.jews-fww.uk/jewish-museum-london-jewish-military-museum-collections-personal-possessions-1391.php [Accessed 5.06.2020].

way of maintaining a 'sense of social and biological continuities in their life-histories'.[38] Tony Walter emphasizes their dual nature, suggesting that some people saw them as a way of expressing their grief without upsetting others, but that others understood the notifications as a social expectation that would be posted long after the dead had ceased to be remembered in private.[39] For some, both of these assertions might have been true. Writing about First World War In Memoriams, Sonia Batten highlights that these posts contained a particularly freighted significance for families whose loved ones were missing, because the families of these dead lacked the choice of engraving a small remembrance on an Imperial War Graves Commission headstone.[40] For many, from families whose loved one had a grave to those who did not know the whereabouts of their family member's body, these acted as printed social reminders of community-based mourning rituals, and, for some at least, were of genuine lasting importance as a public reminder of loss.

The business of printing death was a revenue source for local newspapers, which could be cynically exploited. Local newspapers were so involved with the production of In Memoriam columns that they would remind readers to post commemorative words to the newspaper to print. In 1910 the *Consett Chronicle* published an almanac with the names of all the dead they had provided a Death Notice for in the past year, to 'be hung up in every house for ready reference' so that they could send an In Memoriam to the newspaper in time for the anniversary of their relative's death.[41]

Following the death of a loved one, family memory of the dead was extended both inside the family and externally throughout the years and sometimes decades that followed. For families who had lost someone in the First World War in particular, the In Memoriam column provided a point of community memorialization separate to local and national public remembrance on 11 November. This public recognition was equally important for those whose loved ones had died in a disaster, although this memory was different to that of the war in that communities grouped together on the anniversary of mining deaths to console one another. Those who lost people in the First World War were less likely than the families of disaster dead to have a day when community members perished en masse. By publishing the date of

[38] Sheila Adams, 'Women, Death and *In Memoriam* Notices in Local British Newspapers', in Kathy Charmas, Glennys Howarth, and Allan Kellehear (eds.), *The Unknown Country: Death in Australia, Britain and the USA* (London, 1997), 98.

[39] Tony Walter, *On Bereavement: The Culture of Grief* (Buckingham, 1999), 51, 144.

[40] Sonia Batten, 'Memorial Text Narratives in Britain, c.1890–1930' (Unpublished PhD, University of Birmingham, 2011), 108.

[41] *Consett Chronicle*, 5 February 1910.

death in a public space, private grief was briefly projected onto the outside world, forming a point of memory which stood apart from local and national memorial initiatives.

In Memoriam notices were generally posted by the parents of the deceased or a spouse, although siblings, sweethearts, and extended family and friends also posted remembrances. The year following a death was the most popular time for a memorial to be posted, but some families and friends posted yearly messages for decades after a loved one's death. Stylistic commonalities can be seen among all of the postings in the predominantly working-class notices examined here; stock phrases such as 'ever remembered' were prevalent, and the date of death was always mentioned. Those doing the remembering were guided by a standard form of memorialization, and could choose a mixture of verses and sayings, but did not offer an intimate message which strayed out of socially acceptable bounds. As with death notices, the manner of death was mentioned in these posts. This was also extended to civilian deaths in wartime, such as the post for George Bentley, 'who was killed in the air raid on Jan 29, 1918'.[42] There were also practical differences in how local newspapers framed the obituaries of those who died in war. The *Durham Chronicle* began a 'Roll of Honour' column during the First World War as a military equivalent to the In Memoriam column in the newspaper. This was repeated in the years after the war, appearing less often as the frequency of memorials to the First World War dead also dwindled, before being resurrected in the Second World War, although it was never as popular in the 1940s as during the First World War and its immediate aftermath.

In Memoriam posts nearly always contained a snippet of a poem or a small rhyming verse, which reflected the circumstances of death. For example, In Memoriam notices following mining disasters tended to focus on the immediacy of loss, containing phrases such as 'his death was sudden, the shock severe, we little thought the end was near'.[43] Variations of this phrase were repeatedly mentioned in poems and funeral cards to victims of mining disasters, giving the choice of words for public consumption a broader memorial meaning, as loss was understood in this rhetorical form over several ephemeral forms. The verses selected for publication after the First World War tended to emphasize duty and the nobility of loss.[44] This was also true of other conflicts. An In Memoriam for Private Henry Cave, who died in the Second

[42] *Acton Gazette*, 31 January 1919, p. 2.
[43] *Durham Chronicle*, 29 March 1935, p. 2.
[44] Batten, 'Memorial Text Narratives', 197.

Anglo-Boer War, was posted by his family for several years after his death in 1902.[45] The types of poem selected for Private Cave's memorial verses were similar to those chosen by parents in later conflicts.

To contextualize family loss, remind the community of the extent of suffering, or perhaps to save money, the merger of memorials for different family members was reasonably common throughout the interwar period. In 1920 one family posted in the *Durham Chronicle*:

> KNOX.—In loving memory of my dear husband, Robert, who was killed at Framwellgate Colliery, 5th March, 1920; also in proud and loving memory of my dear son, John Robert, missing 26th October, 1918. 'Thy will be done' is hard to say, But what God gives He takes away. Always remembered by his loving wife and family.[46]

The Knox family clearly saw the death of Robert, in a mining accident, and John, who went missing in wartime, as interlinked, despite the significant difference in their dates of death. This merger of war and peacetime deaths as linked through their sudden and traumatic nature, and, in the case of John, without the sense of closure that a death notification from the War Office brought, signified the family's loss on a broader scale. The Knox family saw the two types of sudden death as worth memorializing in tandem, a not uncommon occurrence for families who lost multiple members in tragic ways, because of their extreme nature.[47]

The majority of people who posted In Memoriam notices were parents or spouses; however, other family members, friends, and sweethearts also contributed to this memory-keeping practice. Unique to First World War death practices were sweethearts who posted In Memoriam notices. Laura Alder, Walter Tilling's sweetheart, posted annual In Memoriam notices for four years after his death, until 1921.[48] The partner of a different soldier posted the poem ''Tis sweet to know we'll meet again, Where parting is no more, And that the one I loved so well, Has only gone before.'[49] These types of message contribute to what Carol Acton describes as the glamorized role of the

[45] *Durham Chronicle*, 19 February 1909, p. 12; *Durham Chronicle*, 15 February 1907, p. 12.
[46] *Durham Chronicle*, 3 March 1920, p. 1.
[47] Also see the Ashman family, *Durham Chronicle*, 19 February 1909, p. 12; 23 March 1917, p. 2; 30 March 1917, p. 2.
[48] *Evening Chronicle*, 2 May 1918, p. 2; 2 May 1919, p. 2; No newspaper, January–June 1920; 2 May 1921, p. 2.
[49] *Evening Chronicle*, 16 June 1916, p. 2.

bereaved sweetheart.[50] This constructed view of the sweetheart who publicly and privately mourned was given an elevated social status because she had sacrificed herself through her lover.[51] These bereaved women marked their relationship in a public space, and claimed the same right as wives to be publicly remembered as the dead person's romantic companion. These sweethearts used mourning traditions, generally reserved for the family, to announce their continued grief, marking them as intimate with the deceased.

Multiple family members, and occasionally friends, typically posted In Memoriam notices for a couple of years after their loved one's death. After this, family members might continue the tradition alone, or these public remembrances might tail off. Private John Storey died in 1916, and the year following his death saw In Memoriam notifications from 'his loving friend, Annie McLean, in Canada', his 'loving sister in law Mary, and brother-in-law Tom', and 'his sorrowing mother, father, sisters, only brother Tom; Pal, L/C Walker, brother-in-law Kit'.[52] Although less common, possibly because of the costs involved, and the fact that there were more opportunities for in-person mourning, these sorts of multiple posts also happened after mining disasters. The year after Charles Chivers's death in the Washington Glebe disaster his wife and son, mother and father, and brother, sister-in-law, and their family all posted separate notices in the *Durham Chronicle* in his memory.[53] Friends of the deceased also posted In Memoriam notices, or were mentioned in other family's notifications if they had been unfortunate victims of the war. In 1920, a family posted an 'In Memoriam' for their son, Lance Corporal Gilbert Messenger, and his 'dear chum and dear friend Jack (Nicholson)', killed in 1917 and 1918 respectively.[54] As a general trend, the men who were commemorated by multiple people at once were not often memorialized for as long a time as those who only had one group to remember them, whose postings lasted for multiple years, sometimes decades.

These annual remembrances indicate the significance of this public memorial moment which ran outside of national commemorative timelines. Lance Corporal Dodgson's family posted an annual In Memoriam notice until 1950, continuing after the death of his mother in the early 1940s, and his father in the mid-1940s.[55] Similarly, Mr and Mrs Laing posted a small notice

[50] Carol Acton, *Grief in Wartime: Private Pain, Public Discourse* (Houndmills, 2007), 18; also see Jane Potter, *Boys in Khaki, Girls in Print* (Oxford, 2005), esp. chs. 2 and 3.

[51] Acton, *Grief in Wartime* (Basingstoke, 2007), 18.

[52] *Evening Chronicle*, 25 May 1917, p. 2.

[53] *Durham Chronicle*, 19 February 1909, p. 12.

[54] *Cumberland News*, 10 January 1920, p. 1.

[55] The last post appears in the *Durham Chronicle & Chester-le-Street Chronicle*, 31 March 1950, p. 2. The last mention of Dodgson's mother was 24 March 1939, and his father 23 March 1945.

to their son who died 'in action on the Somme' nearly every year until 1941.[56] The wife and children of Private Joseph Pratt posted 'In Memoriam' notices until 1943, when there was a year's silence, after which there was one more notice, this time from his sons and daughters only.[57] One woman posted an In Memoriam to her husband, Wilson Forrest, who died in 1918, and their son, who died in 1932, as late as 1960.[58] Strong memories of the deceased were not necessarily transmitted to sons and daughters, who, when the primary carriers of personal memory of the deceased had died, did not continue with the tradition of posting a yearly 'In Memoriam' notice for a significant length of time. While these columns were of great importance to the primary mourners, they were not generally continued by descendants, suggesting that the long-term memory of the deceased is not to be found in these columns.

These columns also have the potential to shed light on queer relationships in the early twentieth century. John Wilson Hall, who after the first posting referred to himself as Lance Corporal John T. Dodgson's 'pal Jack', posted an 'In Memoriam' notice remembering his friend from the year after Dodgson's death, until the early 1930s.[59] Dodgson's In Memoriam postings pose interesting questions about the visibility of mourning in queer relationships in the interwar period.[60] Helen Smith's work has shown that the period following the First World War was one which was relatively welcoming of men whose sexuality and emotional states were fluid.[61] Matt Cook has drawn attention to the multi-textured experience of queer relationships in the early twentieth century, arguing that 'the strength of their [people's] connection' is paramount to understanding queer relationships at the turn of the century.[62] The relationship between Jack and Lance Corporal Dodgson was clearly a powerful one. Jack's postings took place over a far longer time period than any other man's to a non-family member examined during the research for this book.

[56] *Durham Chronicle & Seaham Weekly*, 29 August 1941, p. 2.

[57] *Durham Chronicle & Chester-le-Street Chronicle*, 9 February 1945, p. 2.

[58] *Durham Chronicle & Chester-le-Street Chronicle*, 25 March 1960, p. 8.

[59] He regularly posted in the *Durham Chronicle* at the end of March every year until at least 1930. The copies of the *Durham Chronicle* between 1930 and 1935 have been destroyed and he did not post again after 1935.

[60] For methodology of reading queer history see Laura Doan, *Disturbing Practices: History, Sexuality, and Women's Experience of Modern War* (Chicago, 2013). Also see Kit Heyam, 'Gender Nonconformity and Military Internment: Curating the Knockaloe Slides', *Critical Military Studies* 6:3–4 (2020), 324–7.

[61] By queer I mean any relationship outside of heteronormativity. For more on this see Matt Houlbrooke, *Queer London: Perils and Pleasures of the Sexual Metropolis, 1918–1957* (Chicago, 2005); Helen Smith, *Masculinity, Class and Same-Sex Desire in Industrial England, 1895–1957* (Houndmills, 2015).

[62] Matt Cook, 'Domestic Passions: Unpacking the Homes of Charles Shannon and Charles Ricketts', *Journal of British Studies* 51:3 (2012), 622.

While the language stayed within the heteronormative roles of British society, the time frame did not, and suggests a deep and meaningful relationship which had been lost, and an individual who was deeply loved and profoundly grieved. This was the purpose of the In Memoriam columns, to publicly declare remembrance and affection to the bereaved in a socially constrained way. Through doing so individuals could show their communities the depth of their affection for the deceased, providing a public trail of relationships and loss.

The Ephemera of Remembrance

Families did not just announce to friends and acquaintances that someone had perished, but sent memorial material to remember them by. This material was selected from a vast print culture of mourning, and allowed families to memorialize the dead in personalized, domestic ways. Through the creation and dissemination of memorial ephemera families could create memorial narratives which honoured the dead. How they did so largely depended on their financial circumstances: working-class families printed In Memoriam cards, middle-class families would augment these with memorial pamphlets, and upper-class families would commission memorial books. Sending memorial items, including photographs of the deceased, to the friends and extended family of the deceased was common practice for families who could afford it. Writing in 1920, A. Temple noted that she had 'given hundreds' of photographs away after the death of a family member, who died while working as a nurse in 1915.[63] While not every family had hundreds of people to send items to, or indeed the finances to support this, people did print limited numbers of memorial items to send to their loved ones. Each printed memorial type followed the same memorial purpose; they were designed as keepsakes for families and close friends, but the form of these memorial items was dictated by the relative wealth and cultural status of the individuals involved.

In Memoriam cards, colloquially known as memory cards, were a highly popular way of commemorating the dead, and were common throughout Western Europe between the mid-nineteenth to the mid-twentieth centuries. They evolved from lacy ornate items, common in the early decades of their use, into plain, dull-coloured, chromolithographed cards, which became

[63] Imperial War Museum, EN1/3/DEA/003/3(146).

popular around the turn of the century.[64] Memorial cards usually comprised a cover with some kind of memorial image, a commemorative verse printed on the verso, a personalized memorial on the recto, which included the deceased's name, age, date of death, and a plain back cover with a printer's mark on it.[65] The cards for war and disaster dead were usually printed on the same card stock as those which commemorated people who died from illness. The verse selected for print would often focus on tragedy, duty, or heroism. In war and disaster In Memoriam cards there would also usually be an extra line somewhere in the message, stating that the person died in a disaster, accident, or explosion, or naming the battle the deceased was killed in, or providing a more generic 'Killed in Action'. There was a cultural understanding that this was the correct mode of address, learned from previous In Memoriam cards produced which referred to the tragedy in question. It seems likely that printers and families drew on earlier examples of death in tragic and unexpected circumstances, such as mining disasters, to dictate how In Memoriams to the dead of the First World War would be presented.

During the interwar period In Memoriam cards were part of the accepted demarcation of war and disaster deaths in the quasi-public sphere, showing a remarkable stability throughout the period. In much the same way that a death notice became widely used as a way of announcing the death, the production and dissemination of memorial cards was a step that the bereaved were expected to take, reasonably quickly after the death. These cards were sold by local printers, who were often linked to the newspapers in which the death notice would appear. Part of the reason that these memorial items were so common was that they were readily available and remarkably easy to produce. Printers bought blank stock of the patterned cards, and overprinted the details of the deceased, advertising their services next to the Births, Marriages, and Deaths columns. An advert in the *Consett Chronicle*, placed by Eleanor Neasham, a local printer connected with the newspaper, advertised their 'very Large and Artistic Assortment of memorial cards'. These cards were generally affordable: in 1909 memorial cards cost 2*s* 6*d* for the first twelve, with the price decreasing to an additional 1*s* 6*d* for each successive dozen ordered.[66] Assuming that at least one card was for the person who commissioned them, the remainder would be reserved for close family and friends, although in the case of larger family networks this would be extended.

[64] Maurice Rickards, *The Encyclopedia of Ephemera: A Guide to the Fragmentary Documents of Everyday Life for the Collector, Curator, and Historian* (London, 2000), 155–8.
[65] 'Verso' refers to the left-hand page of the open pamphlet, 'recto' to the right-hand page.
[66] *Consett Chronicle*, 5 March 1909, p. 5.

The designs on the cards, chosen by families, were a way of visually communicating feelings about the dead. The card stock that families could choose from included both religious and secular iconography (see Figs. 3 and 4). White lilies (purity), bluebells (faithfulness), ivy (fidelity), snowdrops (death, rebirth), sundials (passing of time), urns (a classical allusion to death), and crosses (Christian faith) were all featured on In Memoriam cards.[67] These images of plants and flowers, of classical allusions, and of metaphors for time were an extension of the Victorian visual language of death. The blank cards could be used to memorialize individuals or groups, and after large disasters printers would produce mass memorial cards on the same card stock as individual family tributes to sell at the funerals of the deceased, which named all

Fig. 3. Memorial Card for John West Arnold (recto). Courtesy of The Bodleian Libraries, University of Oxford, John Johnson Collection of Printed Ephemera, Funerary Box 3.

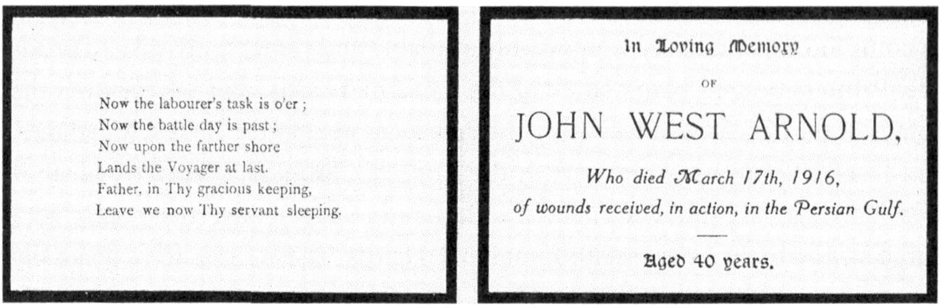

Fig. 4. Memorial Card for John West Arnold (interior). Courtesy of The Bodleian Libraries, University of Oxford, John Johnson Collection of Printed Ephemera, Funerary Box 3.

[67] Beamish Museum, Mining Disaster Ephemera, F.245; National Mining Museum, YKSMM:1999.88; YKSMM:1999.90; YKSMM:1992.1404; John Johnson Collection of Ephemera, Funerary Box 3. For a nuanced discussion of floriography see Beverley Seaton, *The Language of Flowers: A History* (Charlottesville, 1995).

Fig. 5. Mass Memorial Card for Angel, Vickers, and Sell (interior). Courtesy of The Bodleian Libraries, University of Oxford, John Johnson Collection of Printed Ephemera, Funerary Box 3.

of those who died, or were made in memory of all the dead of a certain disaster. Mrs Burgess, based in London, was a particularly prolific printer in this genre, especially after civilian disasters during wartime. Regional printers were also involved in this trade and printed items following local disasters (see Fig. 5). This blurred the line between personal and private memorial, and posited disaster deaths (including those in war) as those which affected whole communities, which helped boost sales of mass In Memoriam cards in the wake of disaster.

Over the course of the war In Memoriam card design developed to include militarized designs. Many families chose traditional card designs, but some chose to refer to a military death through their card selection. Some cards were overt in their reference to the First World War. One card included explicit imagery, with prints of troops, cannons, and cavalry, as well as a cross, laurel wreath, and the words 'Pro Patria Mori'.[68] Special cards could be commissioned for naval deaths, such as the memorial card for John William Booth, who died in the Battle of Jutland, which featured an anchor crowned by a laurel wreath.[69] The family of Private W. M. John Evans, of Caerau, in Cardiff, who died at the Somme, chose a card with a laurel wreath representing a hero's death in the centre, with a cross behind, two Union Jacks either side of the composition, and the words 'For his country's sake' in ornate font below.[70] Inside the card, a halftone printed image of his head and shoulders, in full military dress, was included. The memorial verse in this card is one which focuses on the heroism of his life, but also the bittersweet loss of the

[68] IWM, K.98/1562.

[69] First World War Poetry Digital Archive, 'In Memoriam card for John William Booth', http://ww1lit.nsms.ox.ac.uk/ww1lit/items/show/5999 [Accessed 21.06.2020].

[70] St Fagans National Museum of History, 58.418.15.

lack of a grave on Welsh soil. The opening lines, 'Nameless, his grave on a battlefield gory, Only a cross o'er a mound of brown earth', present a particularly bleak image, one not quietened by the second stanza, which begins 'None near to mourn him, save willows that, weeping, Bend o'er his grave'.

Families selected both the cover image and appropriate verses for the In Memoriam card. The bereaved could either view the available verses at the printer's office, or could be sent a printed copy of the selection the printers offered. Their choice of verse was a constrained but significant one as it allowed families to communicate how they felt to friends and family, albeit within a series of predetermined choices. The printer A. McCallum, who boasted the 'largest stock' and 'most varied assortment' of memorial cards in Newcastle-upon-Tyne, told prospective customers 'we can alter any word to he, she or they—mother, father, son, daughter or child, to suit any particular case'.[71] Most of the verses on the four-page list the firm gave to potential customers were suitable for the death of a parent or child, alongside general verses suitable for young or old. A small section of 'Verses suitable for Sudden Death' were included in this list, and variations of these could be found on personal In Memoriam cards, mass printed cards, and even in In Memoriam newspaper columns, where families could post a verse describing their grief. The verses 'He left his home in perfect health, And little thought of death so nigh' and 'Take warning from my sudden call, That you for death prepare' were particularly popular after disasters.[72]

During the First World War an increase in memorial verse literature helped families choose appropriate memorial words. The military deaths many suddenly encountered meant that the pre-existing verses used to describe sudden death, although in many cases still applicable, did not quite encompass the new circumstances the bereaved faced. At the beginning of the interwar years there was a market for memorial verses which surpassed this pre-war norm.

In the foreword of a collection of quotations suitable for monuments, memorial wreaths, and cards, published in 1918, Sheila E. Braine outlined the problems faced when choosing suitable memorial verses:

> A memorial card, too, and the flowers—bright symbols of Hope—which we send as a last token of affection, these likewise must bear a brief message from us. But what shall it be? The felicitous phrase, the well-expressed

[71] A. McCallum, 'In Memoriam Verses, Texts, &c.' (Newcastle upon Tyne, [n.d., pre-1914]), Beamish Museum, GS 20.2.92.

[72] Beamish Museum, GS 20.2.92; 1982-192.2; L.141.

> loving thought do not always 'leap to the pen'; we dimly recollect suitable quotations, but how did they really go, and in what book are they to be found?[73]

While these words were, of course, intended to increase her book's appeal to the reader, they may have been prompted by her experience of grieving for her brother, revealed in the book's dedication to 'the dear memory of Bevil, who fell at Gallipoli 1915'.[74] Although Braine was promoting her work, this is a rare glimpse into the social and personal pressure people could feel when selecting a memorial verse. It was, in this instance, a glimpse into upper-class problems in writing memorial lines that were less constrained by the printer. Although all could select from set verses, Braine's reflections are those of a woman who had more choice over the inclusion of memorial words than her working-class counterparts would have done. Working-class families could not have afforded the extra expense of printers making up blocks of type for their individual requirements, instead having to rely on individual pronouns that could easily be swapped from longer blocks of print.

Not all In Memoriam cards produced in Britain were in English, and the identity of the dead could be expressed through the choice of language the card was printed in. This linguistic fluidity is particularly apparent in Welsh cards, which could be printed wholly in Welsh, wholly in English, or a mixture of the two. During the early twentieth century there was a decrease in the number of Welsh speakers, although there were regional patterns to this. The high influx of people moving from England to industrial Wales to seek work weakened Welsh, as did trade unionism, which encouraged English as the main language of class struggle.[75] In 1901 50 per cent of the population of Wales spoke Welsh, compared to 37 per cent in 1921.[76] The family of Private W. W. Owen, 1st Battalion Welsh Guards, commissioned a memorial card in Welsh to remember him by.[77] The card included a reproduction of a portrait photograph, and details of his age, date of death, mother's details, and some memorial verses. Owen's family clearly felt that this outward expression of grief, to be shared among friends, was best expressed in Welsh. Without knowing more about his family, it is hard to say that this decision was because

[73] Sheila E. Braine, *'That's for Remembrance': A Collection of Quotations for Present-Day Use, Suitable for Monuments, Mural Tablets, Memorial Wreaths and Cards, &c.* (London, 1918), 5.

[74] Braine, *'That's for Remembrance'*, 7.

[75] Janet Davies, *The Welsh Language: A History* (Cardiff, 2014), 88–90.

[76] Davies, *The Welsh Language*, 87.

[77] First World War Poetry Digital Archive, 'In Memoriam card for William Owen', http://ww1lit.nsms.ox.ac.uk/ww1lit/gwa/item/7107 [Accessed 21.06.2020].

the family's primary language was Welsh, because it was the one spoken at home, and had special intimacy, or contained the words to express what they wanted to say in the most appropriate way. The family lived in Penygroes, Carmarthenshire, North Wales, which was, and still is, an area known for its protection of Welsh language, and local linguistic practice most likely accounted for the language of the memorial. What is significant here is that Owen died in a global conflict, as part of a regiment whose working language was English, but in his In Memoriam card, his local and civilian identity were paramount.

In Memoriam cards were not limited to men who died in war service, and the deaths of nurses who served were also marked in this way. Hilda Read's mother produced a memorial card she 'had printed for private circulation amongst my daughters many friends'.[78] Although Read died in 1920, her work during the First World War was thought of as a contributing factor to her death by her family. Deference was paid to her profession through the inclusion of poetic lines that commented on 'Her every thought for others' good, So ends her pure, unselfish life, spent in sweet Mercy's sisterhood'. Read's memorial card included also her photograph in civilian dress, with a poem which linked her to her Lancashire roots, with the starting lines 'Where Pendle lifts its lofty crest, And Ribble weaves its shining way'. Read's middle-class mother clearly paid above the standard rate for this memorial card. She reprinted the obituary she published in the *Blackburn Weekly Telegraph* in it, which would not have been cheap. Read's multiple personalities, as a nurse, daughter, and Lancastrian woman, were delicately balanced in the card, an indication of the extra money spent on the printing, which allowed Read's mother to construct her daughter's identity in a way which holistically contributed to her memory among friends.

Memorial ephemera were also produced by the families of those who died in other conflicts, following the conventions of memorial cards but adding specific details of the death in question. Memorial cards were created for those who died as part of the Easter Rising (1916) and the Irish War of Independence (1919–21) against British rule in Ireland.[79] The family of

[78] IWM, EN1/3/DEA/003/2(116).

[79] For work on the Easter Rising and the War of Independence see, as a starting point: Linda Connolly, *Women and the Irish Revolution: Feminism, Activism, Violence* (Dublin, 2020); Ciara Boylan, Sarah-Anne Buckley, and Pat Dolan, *Family Histories of the Irish Revolution* (Dublin, 2018); Richard S. Grayson and Fearghal McGarry (eds.), *Remembering 1916: The Easter Rising, the Somme and the Politics of Memory in Ireland* (Cambridge, 2016); Diarmaid Ferriter, *A Nation and Not a Rabble: The Irish Revolution 1913–1923* (London, 2015); John Horne and Edward Madigan (eds.), *Towards Commemoration: Ireland in War and Revolution 1912–1923* (Dublin, 2013); Marie Coleman,

Charles D'Arcy, a 15yearold who fought as part of the Irish Citizen Army in Dublin, created a memorial card for him when he was shot by a British sniper during the Easter Rising. The memorial card features a small image of D'Arcy, his name, address, and date of death, as well as prayers, a quotation from St Ambrose, and indulgences.[80] While this card was in memory of a boy who died fighting in the Easter Rising, it has many similarities to Catholic memorial cards for the dead of the First World War. In addition to In Memoriam cards, Catholics might also have a mass card, which mentioned that the soldier in question was killed in action, and requested that Mass was said for them. The family of Patrick O'Hare, a working-class Irish Catholic who died in 1916, created a mass card after his death, which made reference to the war he had perished in, and which has been kept in his family's archive for the past hundred years.[81]

During the First World War some families had the option of adding a halftone printed image to their In Memoriam card. In the first decade of the twentieth century it was uncommon to include a photograph of the deceased within a memorial card. For the vast majority of people the only way to do so was to have a photograph printed separately and pasted in. The family of Thomas Anderson, who perished in the West Stanley mining disaster, cut out his portrait from a small, wallet-sized, photograph, and pasted it in the upper-left-hand corner of the verso, above his memorial verse.[82] From the mid-1910s, halftone printing was used to print images of the dead. This printing technique had been in existence since the 1880s, but was generally reserved for newspaper printing until the war encouraged memorial card printers to add this to their repertoire. The family of Evan Jones, who died in 1917, included a halftone image of his head, next to the memorial verses printed on the verso.[83] These cards were not available to everyone—a prerequisite was that there had to be a photograph of the deceased to copy and a nearby printer who could transfer this image into dots, with the extra costs associated with this. Despite these barriers the ability to add a printed photograph of their loved one to an In Memoriam card was of great comfort and

The Irish Revolution, 1916–1923 (Abingdon, 2013); Keith Jeffrey, *The GPO and the Easter Rising* (Dublin, 2006).

[80] National Museum of Ireland, HE:EW.4147.

[81] BBC Northern Ireland, 'Medal collection keeps WW1 memory alive', 26 August 2014, https://www.bbc.co.uk/news/uk-northern-ireland-28898790 [Accessed 21.06.2020].

[82] Beamish Museum, 2006-58.13.

[83] First World War Poetry Digital Archive, 'Memorial Card for Evan Jones', http://ww1lit.nsms.ox.ac.uk/ww1lit/items/show/6125 [Accessed 24.07.2020].

importance. Through it the dead could be further individualized and a memorial with increased relevance for family and friends created.

Photographs could also be printed onto postcards, which could be sent to friends and family in the wake of a death. These were much rarer than traditional In Memoriam cards and could be created in addition to these more customary memorial forms. There was a commercial element to them, as a way for postcard printers to earn additional income. But they also had a more practical display element which informed their design. The family of George O. Holland, killed 'somewhere in France' in 1917, used a postcard to tell people of his death. At the head of the postcard was an image of a white cross, with the phrase 'greater love hath no man than this', the first sentence of the oft-cited biblical passage from John 15:13, widely used to commemorate the war dead.[84] A portrait photograph of Holland was framed by a laurel wreath, with a king's crown and the Union Jack above, and below were his details, his date of death, a small memorial verse, and the phrase 'till we meet again'.[85] This postcard contained all of the elements of an In Memoriam card, but was produced in a way where one could see all of the elements at once, leaving no doubt as to who was being commemorated. Burial Notices could also be printed on postcard stock. A half-printed, half-drawn Burial Notice for Private Feifal Prepstine, 39th Royal Fusiliers, buried in Ramla, Israel, shows Prepstine in his military uniform, alongside a hand-drawn image of a grave marker with his family name underneath a Star of David, and details of his burial.[86] The Burial Notice is in both Hebrew and English, with the details of his name, rank, and burial date repeated in both languages.[87] Although details of the card have been hand-drawn, the card itself was printed, for distribution to family and friends. The date on the card helped them remember the date on which to hold yahrzeit on the anniversary of Prepstine's death. These items were created for display in the home, as they could be easily framed or pasted onto a wall in a way that other, folded, mourning ephemera could not, and were a form of commemorative ephemera designed to be sent into other homes to form a focal point of displayable grief.

Despite their importance, not all families had a photograph of their loved one, or, if they did, it was not necessarily a recent one. There is a disparity

[84] The full quotation is 'Greater love hath no man than this, that a man lay down his life for his friends' (King James Bible, John 15:13).

[85] Alastair Fraser, private collection.

[86] Jewish Museum London, 'Burial Card for Pte. Feifal Prepstine'. The card has been digitized as part of the British Jews in the First World War Collection, available at https://www.jewsfww.uk/adrian-andrusier-image-collections-the-jewish-brigade-897.php [Accessed 19.06.2020].

[87] My thanks to Irena Fliter for help with translation.

between the First World War dead, who often had a photograph of themselves taken in uniform which they sent to their families, and the victims of disasters, who would not necessarily have had such a recent image. Memorial pamphlets produced after large mining disasters often included reproductions of portrait photographs of men who died in the explosions. The images included often show a proportion of the deceased as young children, taken from the only photograph of them in existence.[88] It is telling of the power of memorial photographs and their affective meanings that these images of men, shown as children, were included. The emotional power of an image of the dead, however dated, clearly held a memorial resonance for the family and the local community, who purchased the pamphlets. Through their images the names of the dead were linked to a near-tangible person, and the personhood re-given to the dead through the inclusion of their image was of great importance in the face of mass death.

Long-Form Print Memorials: Books, Pamphlets, and Letter Collections

With money came the opportunity for deeply personalized memorial forms which created a lasting legacy for the dead. During the First World War, middle-class families commissioned pamphlets detailing their loss, while upper-class families commissioned books to memorialize the lives of their deceased family members. The length of these memorial forms allowed families to construct the narrative of their loved one's life, which would, they hoped, stand the test of time. They allowed for a full picture of a personality, and of life achievements, that the types of short-form ephemera accessible to the working-class, who comprised the overwhelming majority of the First World War dead, and the entirety of the disaster dead, never would. These long-form memorials were exclusively available to a small section of British society. They were multi-layered, and, at times, highly politicized. This was implied in soft discourse surrounding First Word War soldiers and their sacrifice, but was overt in memorials to Welsh volunteers in the Spanish Civil War. Here, members of the International Brigade were commemorated

[88] See, for example, 'Wellington Pit Explosion, May 11, 1910. Portraits of Entombed Men' (W. Halton & Sons, Whitehaven, [1910]), [3–6]; Eleanor Neasham, 'Consett Chronicle Art Memento' (Consett, 1909), 36–7.

through memorial pamphlets as a form of continued resistance against fascist powers.

Pamphlets were largely commissioned by middle-class families, as a form of memorial that could include more detail than an In Memoriam card but was still relatively affordable. The family of Private Philip G. Holmes, 2/7th Battalion Manchester Regiment, created three different pamphlets to commemorate his life.[89] The pamphlets comprised a large printed account of his life, a small printed poem written by his father, T. W. Holmes, and a poem by Reverend F. I. Harrison. The pamphlets contain a sketch of Holmes's life, including details about his military service and death. While these items were reasonably commonplace in middle- and upper-middle-class houses, their production was not. Holmes's father was the owner of the South London Printing Co., and his son had worked with him for two years at the business before he signed up. Given these connections, the printing process itself became an act of memorialization within its own right. Not only were the memorial ephemera a reminder of Holmes's life and his image, with poems forming fitting memorials to his memory, but the act of producing the items took on an enhanced meaning for those who knew and worked with him.

Long-form memorial items were a way of establishing a particular memorial legacy, which ranged from the personal to the political. A specific type of pamphlet which merged these categories through personal beliefs was produced to commemorate Welsh men who fought for the British Battalion of the International Brigade during the Spanish Civil War. The memorial pamphlet was still a popular commemorative form in the 1930s, only losing memorial relevance after the Second World War. The Welsh response to the war was particularly strong, as Hywel Francis explained, because of a strong history of political activism and broad support for 'proletarian internationalism', which produced workers keen to participate in the fight against fascism.[90] Welsh volunteers viewed the Spanish Civil War as important for democracy worldwide, arguing that the thirty-three Welsh men who died did not die in vain. This was not only of comfort to the affected families, but was a necessary way of framing their deaths given the hostility shown to those whose family members were involved in the conflict. One mother who received a telegram saying her son was wounded was told by the postman who delivered it that it was 'a pity he [her son] wasn't killed'.[91]

[89] British Library, Tab.11748.aa.2.(182–4).

[90] Hywel Francis, *Miners Against Fascism: Wales and the Spanish Civil War* (London, 2012), 23.

[91] Natalie Ann Stuart, 'The Memory of the Spanish Civil War and the Families of British International Brigadiers' (Unpublished PhD, De Montfort University, 2001), 211.

The memorial material produced to commemorate the Welsh dead of the Spanish Civil War celebrated the life of the individual and their politics, fusing this with the grief of the family. The items were small folio pamphlets with an image of the dead, their age, and a small description of their life and death. Many of the mourning items for those who died in the Spanish Civil War were printed by Enoch Collins, a self-proclaimed 'Comrade in Industry and fellow trade unionist'.[92] The memorial cards labelled the dead 'working class heroes' who perished in the 'fight against fascism'.[93] To some extent this continued the cult of celebrity that had already sprung up around the volunteers, who were already generally well known for their social or political exploits.[94]

The families of the dead contributed to these pamphlets by providing letters, images, and other material which were reprinted in them, and were included to produce a particular type of memorial legacy. The memorials were decidedly political, produced in tandem with the local activist movement, and so constitute a slightly different form of memorial ephemera, which used the hallmarks of standard memorial forms but added a new layer of political meaning. The memorial card for Brazell Thomas, printed in 1938, contained all of the usual elements of a memorial pamphlet, including a photograph, his address, age, and the date of death, the words 'What greater love hath any one, Who dies that others might live' emblazoned on the front page.[95] The pamphlet also contained text which discussed the cause he died for, and a small section where his parents and wider family discussed their loss, noting that they missed him, but were proud of the actions and beliefs which led to his death. The pamphlet also reprinted a letter from Thomas to his parents. The letter read:

> Dear Mother, If you receive this letter it will mean that I will have joined in the same fate as has fallen so many of the world working class. There are thousands of the cream of our class who are paying supreme penalty in the struggle for a world fit for everybody to live in. But, for you, I am one in particular—your son. You must not grieve you must be proud.[96]

This call for his family not to be upset at his death was reprinted over ephemera throughout the twentieth century. It was reprinted in the 1970s, to garner support for a memorial to Welsh men who died in the Spanish Civil War.

[92] Richard Burton Archives, SC177/1.
[93] Such as the memorial card to Tom Howell. Richard Burton Archives, SC117.
[94] Francis, *Miners Against Fascism*, 180.
[95] Richard Burton Archives, SC177/1.
[96] South Wales Coalfield Collection, MNA/PP/35/53(12).

In his letter, Thomas appealed to both his family and the wider community. There was an element of self-constructed memorialization in this. Through this letter Thomas attempted to shape his own posthumous legacy. By sharing it on a piece of public ephemera, alongside quotations approving of his actions, his family bolstered his desire to be remembered in a particular way, allowing him agency through this self-directed memorial narrative.

Printing the words of the dead, through small letter excerpts or full books containing correspondence, was a popular form of memorialization. Printing letters after the death of a loved one was highly popular during and after the First World War. Memorial books, produced by wealthy families who wanted a more detailed memorial item to commemorate their loved ones, often included letters in their pages. This was a continuation of a popular Victorian genre, when families wrote about the dead for personal remembrance, or for circulation to family and friends.[97] Elite families during the First World War revived these Victorian conventions, writing or commissioning memorial works for their loved ones. Michael Roper suggests that this revival was due to the shocking manner of violent death, which combined with the distance from the body to compel middle and upper-class families to produce this extra memorial form.[98] Parents who had perhaps been gifted memorial books in their youth produced them for their sons as a way of expressing their grief and sharing their memories with others.

Memorial books were almost exclusively privately printed, with some available for purchase through booksellers. The *Memoir and Letters of T.I.W. Wilson, Captain Manchester Regiment* was available for 1*s* 6*d* from the publishers, Sidgwick & Jackson.[99] A particularly detailed book of remembrance was written and anonymously published by the author Marie Connor Leighton after the loss of her son Roland, most famously known as Vera Brittain's fiancé. In the foreword to the book the publishers claimed her account was 'a record exact and faithful, both in large things and in small, of the short years of a boy who willingly and even joyously gave up his life and all its brilliant promise for the sake of his country'.[100] This sort of phrase was common for the genre. Forewords were often written by a professional who knew the man well and could speak to his higher qualities. In *Harry: Schoolboy and Soldier*, the Reverend F. S. Guy Warman, Bishop of Truro, who had been

[97] Pat Jalland, *Death in the Victorian Family* (Oxford, 1996), 287–8.

[98] Michael Roper, *The Secret Battle: Emotional Survival in the Great War* (Manchester, 2009), 224.

[99] Anonymous, *Memoir and Letters of T.I.W. Wilson, M.C. Captain Manchester Regiment* (London, 1917), frontispiece.

[100] [Marie Connor Leighton], *Boy of My Heart* (London, [1916]), foreword.

asked to write the foreword, exclaimed, 'it is with real sympathy and sense of privilege that I wrote a foreword to this brief happy story of one of the many lads who gave their lives in the great struggle.'[101]

These memorial books were decidedly personal, even when they were not written by a family member. After Harry Foss Wilson's death, his memoir was ghostwritten by Lilian Howard Dalton, who wrote a range of religious books in the interwar period, including a history of the Society for Promoting Christian Knowledge. Despite the content being written by someone who was not a part of the family, Harry's father, as the sole remaining parent, was featured heavily. Dalton included letters he had written to her as part of the research for the volume, and excerpts from his letters were included. In the letters to Dalton, Harry's father commented on the bias that is usually found in memoirs, concluding that 'certainly it would be difficult to write of Harry without bias! The comfort is that the bias will unquestionably be shared by all who knew him.'[102] These lines contained a wry appreciation for the readers of the book, as well as a knowing awareness of the function of the memorial item.

Memorial books to young officers in the First World War followed a set of conventions which emphasized youth, religious devotion, and loss to the individual's community, friends, and family. Many of the memorial books discussed the deceased's Christian values, encouraging the reader to take comfort from religious ideas about the nature of death and the value of a 'good' life. Writers of the memorial books would take comfort from their subject being 'Godly'.[103] Letters from vicars were included in the collections to emphasize the deceased's exemplary Christian life. In Harry Wilson's memorial book, the local vicar from his childhood days wrote: 'He is dead, but his influence lives on in the lives and memories of those whom he influenced by his Christ-like life.'[104] These letters, which dictated that the deceased had lived a godly life, which could be attested to by religious leaders, were intended to give some comfort to the parents of the bereaved. Through these words they could receive solace by hoping for a reunion in the next life, and console themselves by reflecting that, through virtue of character and service, their sons were in good stead to receive a heavenly reward.

101 Lilian Dalton, *Harry: Schoolboy and Soldier* (London, 1919), p. v.
102 Dalton, *Harry*, 1–2.
103 See, for example, the memorial book produced by the siblings of Edmund Llewelyn Lewis. IWM, Eph.C. INMEM K.3100-K.08.
104 Dalton, *Harry*, 56.

Family members could also apply to the deceased's friends for material to include in printed memorials. The niece of S. B. Macnaughtan, a nurse who died doing war work, posted a notice in the newspaper to ask friends of her deceased aunt to loan her any letters 'which would be suitable for incorporation in the proposed book', as she 'hoped to publish an account of the war experiences…of the late Miss Macnaughtan, as narrated in her diaries and letters'.[105] This is significant because it highlights the community aspect of publishing these books. Friends and family were able to shape the memorial through the donation of letters and influence the memory of the deceased through their written and verbal reminiscences. Although family members often dictated the content, extended family and friends could subtly alter this through the inclusion or exclusion of their memories of the dead.

These memorial books illuminate inter-family dynamics, indicating which members of the family were able to speak for the dead. A niece collecting letters, as in the case of S. B. Macnaughtan, was particularly unusual. Given the demographics of the war dead who were able to afford this kind of memorial, it was often the parents of the deceased who chose and solicited letters from friends. When the parents of the man in question were deceased, siblings stepped in to fill this role. The brothers and sisters of Edmund Llewelyn Lewis published a small volume about his life and death, *Gaudeamus: Thoughts and Recollections*. They dedicated this collection to their parents, writing that Edmund's spirit, 'eager, pure, was the fruit of your own spirits'.[106] Instead of using letters sent to the family in the aftermath of his death, they instead published reflections on their own interactions with him, alongside poetry, letters exchanged with and about him, and recollections of conversations. This volume was explicitly designed as a memory-store for the siblings. In the words of his brother Gwilym, 'ever since he [Edmund] was reported missing there seems to have been such a *hole* in the family'.[107] There were no outside voices incorporated into the memorial narrative; this was a book of sibling mourning, which sought to capture their memories of their brother before they faded.

These books and pamphlets were formed by a community of the bereaved and were, in turn, received by a community of mourners. Memorial books only had very small print runs, and were explicitly intended for friends and family. Receiving one of these items marked a person as someone who was perceived to be heavily affected by loss, and helped those outside of the

[105] IWM, EN1/3/DEA/1(2). [106] IWM, Eph.C. INMEM K.3100-K.08.
[107] IWM, Eph.C. INMEM K.3100-K.08.

immediate family reminisce and grieve alongside the family members. Friends could shape memorial books by donating particular letters, and different family members could assume responsibility for directing the content of the books and pamphlets. The range of individuals who could be involved in their production sometimes made them community projects of people worked through their grief by creating memorial books. Glimpses of posthumous legacy building can be seen through letters to the family written by men who knew that they might not return home. These letters were woven with testimonies from family and friends to create connected memorial items which could speak to multiple people. Their creation was an active process which melded ways of knowing the deceased to create something that could be recognized by those who knew them.

If there was enough printed material, informal memorial scrapbooks could be created by a family at home as legacy-making objects. In the case of well-respected, usually upper-middle or upper-class families who had multiple column inches dedicated to their loved one's death, people could create scrapbooks containing the clippings. Captain W. Langdon's family pasted obituaries into a scrapbook, with each entry accompanied by a note detailing the date and place of publication.[108] Most of the obituaries featured in the scrapbook were variations on a theme. They most commonly mentioned his education and his father, who was a former president of the Manchester Chamber of Commerce. Some discussed Langdon's philanthropy, and his time working with poor children in the East End of London. Only two discussed the manner of his death. The obituaries and death notices kept and preserved in the family scrapbook all emphasized his education, profession, family ties, and his commitment to the poor. There was subtle variation between the different obituaries. His finals words were reported as 'well, men, do your best' and 'here they come; do your best' in the *Jewish Chronicle* and the *Court Journal* respectively. Two different photographs of Captain Langdon were in circulation in the press, both of him in uniform, one with a cap and one without, emphasizing the dual role he occupied. Much like printed memorial books, his family's social standing allowed them to create, through the posting of multiple obituaries, a memorial book which contained a longer, fuller, description of his life than was afforded to the majority of the war dead.

[108] Captain Langdon 'Obituary Book'.

Conclusion

The creation and dissemination of memorial ephemera was a highly significant part of family mourning. Newspaper announcements were immediate, and let others in the community, who had not been informed, know that one of their members had perished. These quasi-public announcements were targeted at different groups of people, and constituted the beginning of the memorialization process for many families. Soon after a death, families printed memorial ephemera, such as In Memoriam cards, which were disseminated to family and friends. Some families also produced memorial ephemera months, rather than weeks, after an individual's death. Middle- and upper-class families commissioned publishers to print books to memorialize their war dead, with their longer production time befitting the grander scale of the commemoration. Friends and extended family could help contribute to these long-form memorial items, and through the publication of material written by the deceased an element of posthumous legacy could be secured. While announcements in the newspaper and the creation of memorial ephemera worked to different time scales, they both functioned as a signal to those outside of the family that the deceased could and should be mourned. These forms of memorialization acted as a social cue, to be read by others, which indicated that the family was grieving, and that this grief could be shared by others.

As a fluid form of printed material, there were some changes to the types of memorial ephemera produced throughout the twentieth century. In the early 1900s, memorial postcards to the mass dead after a disaster were common, but it was only during the First World War that personal postcards to individual dead were created. In Memoriam cards were common throughout the whole of the interwar period, although printing techniques and cultural shifts meant that the design of the cards developed over the four decades. Memorial pamphlets were more common after war than disaster, although mass memorial booklets were sometimes printed for the disaster dead. The memorial book as a long-form remembrance item was revived during the First World War by parents of officers who died prematurely. The legacies that these items created were subject to class-based differences. The ephemerality of the material that working-class families used, such as death notices, and perhaps a small number of In Memoriam cards, dictated that the family member would only be remembered through this mourning ephemera by a small number of people. Upper-middle- and upper-class families who had recourse to multiple death notices, obituaries, and long-form print technology created a stronger print memory of the deceased, which contained the possibility of extending the legacy of the dead through its increased durability.

The printed afterlives of the dead in the early twentieth century were brought to life by their family members. Family members chose which memorial ephemera to create, dictated what it would look like, its memorial feel, and who to disseminate it to. While these choices were made within a certain societal framework, they allowed the families of the dead choice over the memorial presentation of their loved one. Memorial ephemera became a powerful tool which families used to cement the memory of the dead. Families began to process their own grief through these cultural customs, and created memorials to aid private remembrance in domestic settings, linking households through the ephemera of the dead.

Family Mourning After War and Disaster in Twentieth-Century Britain. Ann-Marie Foster, Oxford University Press.
 DOI: 10.1093/9780191968129.003.0004

4

Domesticating Death

Although families sought to spread their memories of the dead to extended family and friends, for those closest to the deceased, home was where they remembered them. 'Home' has a twofold meaning, it encompasses both the physical building which contains a set number of rooms and the social construction of the home as a place where people live. People brought houses into their mourning rituals, and displayed signifiers of their loss on its walls, through its windows, and in the objects and clothes it contained. The house itself could physically indicate the death of one of its members. For many working-class families, shutting the curtains of a house was a way of signalling to the outside world there had been a death in the family.[1] This chapter explores the domestic memorialization of the dead through the display of objects and ephemera, and through the performance of rituals within private spaces. It contends that both individuals and families based key memorialization practices in their domestic space. This represented an area they could, to some extent, control, and through which they could grieve. During the First World War, the fact that this home-based memorialization was essential to mourning was recognized by the government, who ran a competition to find a suitable domestic memorial item. This was not only a propaganda exercise, as the war of attrition bit and morale was waning, but an important action that recognized that domestic memorialization was of the utmost importance to families.

Private memorialization was available far more rapidly than public commemoration, if indeed the dead were formally remembered outside the home at all. As Eli Davies has emphasized, exploring conflicts through the lens of domesticity allows for individual experiences which challenge homogenous narratives to emerge.[2] After war and disaster, it could take years or decades for public memorials to be built. Locally circulated memorial pamphlets took the weight of this memorial load in the interim, locating the names and often

[1] James Stevens Curl, *The Victorian Celebration of Death* (Newton Abbot, 1972), 7; *The Evening Chronicle*, 18 February 1909, p. 5.

[2] Eli Davies, '"At least we can lock the door": Radical Domesticity in the Writing of Bernadette Devlin and Nell Mccafferty', *Journal of War & Culture Studies* 14:1 (2021), 72.

faces of the dead within a local commemorative landscape based on ephemera. Domestic remembrance allowed families to begin to memorialize the dead in a space which was significant to them long before any official public recognition was granted.

Without being overly reductive, people were primarily memorialized in the home, where family members intimately interacted and occupied a shared space. Julie-Marie Strange's work draws attention to the importance of domestic remembrance in deaths from illness or old age, through both inherited and everyday objects which could remind the bereaved of the dead.[3] Families treated the war and disaster dead in the ways they treated other family members, by remembering them in the setting they were most used to seeing them in. Physical memorialization of the dead within the home often followed quasi-public print commemoration which highlighted the tragic circumstances a loved one had died in, be it disaster or war, elevating the memorial items on display to ones which commented on the mode of death, as a stark reminder of the difficult death on display.

For many, this domestic display was designed to act as a memory point for a cross-section of family, friends, and neighbours. Throughout the early twentieth century domestic spaces were both private and quasi-public. The concept of the home as a private space became popular in the nineteenth century as a trickle-down effect of the middle-class preoccupation with delineating private space, with the parlour acting as an interstitial space in which outsiders could glimpse a heavily ordered version of the rest of the home—presupposing that one had enough room to create separate spaces.[4] Depending on who owned the house, and the number of people living there, if there were servants or lodgers, and the number of visitors to the house, there could be quite a number of people living in or passing through its doors. Rachel Hurdley notes the performativity of the house which holds 'front stage and back stage regions (although these are not necessarily spatially fixed), where different performances take place'.[5] Graham Allan and Graham Crow note the changeability of the home as a space in which privacy can be sought but also one that others can enter, at the discretion of the people who inhabit the property.[6] Allan has further explored the social boundaries which dictate the

[3] Julie-Marie Strange, *Death, Grief and Poverty in Britain, 1870–1914* (Cambridge, 2005), 213.

[4] Graham Allan, 'Insiders and Outsiders: Boundaries around the Home', in Graham Allan and Graham Crow (eds.), *Home and Family: Creating the Domestic Sphere* (Basingstoke, 1989), 149, 155; Rachel Hurdley, *Home, Materiality, Memory and Belonging* (Houndmills, 2013), 14.

[5] Hurdley, *Home, Materiality, Memory and Belonging*, 15.

[6] Graham Allan and Graham Crow, 'Introduction', in Graham Allan and Graham Crow (eds.) *Home and Family: Creating the Domestic Sphere* (Basingstoke, 1989), 4.

use of space within the home, suggesting that those allowed into the space differ between households, while authority to invite people into the home is also changeable. He argues that a 'special occasion', such as a funeral, changes the social norms within a home and permits people who would usually be excluded to enter domestic space.[7] Extending the concept of the home as a liminal space, Jane Hamlett shows that links to the outside world could be developed through interior decoration and books, as well as through visitors, which could help the family locate itself within the wider world.[8] The home was porous, and the family mediated contact with the outside world in this liminal space, which could make showcasing the dead a form of micro-community memorial.

Houses and Display

Living situations between socioeconomic groups varied wildly, and the homes of the bereaved could range from houses shared with multiple families to grand estates. Within Victorian and early twentieth-century middle-class homes a lot of weight was often placed on the parlour. The parlour was a feature of many homes in the interwar period, and it was not until after the Second World War that it was eliminated from modern homes, which meant that there was a formal space in many homes which was used only on special occasions.[9] As Thad Logan argues, examining the parlour can reveal a great deal about gender, domesticity, commerce, and aesthetics in the everyday lives of middle-class individuals.[10] Extending this, the decorations and meaningful items in the homes of all classes can be indicative of wider family values.

Not all of those affected by sudden death had the luxury of an abundance of rooms to decorate or the wealth necessary to decorate as they pleased. Homes for miners in the early twentieth century were often crowded, and family space was often shared with others who lived in the same house. This overcrowding was blamed on the false assumption that miners had too many children, yet in the 1911 census miners had just over four children on

[7] Allan, 'Insiders and Outsiders', 141–2.

[8] Jane Hamlett, *Material Relations: Domestic Interiors and Middle-Class Families in England, 1850–1910* (Manchester, 2010), 31–40.

[9] Judy Attfield, 'Bringing Modernity Home: Open Plan in the British Domestic Interior', in Irene Cieraad (ed.), *At Home: An Anthropology of Domestic Space* (New York, 1999), 77; John Benson, *The Working Class in Britain 1850–1939* (London, 2003), 103.

[10] Thad Logan, *The Victorian Parlour: A Cultural Study* (Cambridge, 2001).

average, which was not out of line with other occupational groups.[11] Instead, the crowding of miners' homes came from the common practice of taking in lodgers, which meant that it was not uncommon for families to share one or two rooms in a house. Home ownership rates among miners varied across the decades. In 1913, 20 per cent of the mining community in South Wales owned their own property. After the First World War home ownership became more commonplace, although it was still a working-class elite who were able to afford to buy their own homes.[12] Depending on the area and household income, housing varied in quality, and it is very difficult to paint a picture of common housing experiences during the period. The living conditions of the miners indicate that, as with the families of those who died in war, there was a vast difference in the types of houses and economic wealth of the various families involved with the tragedy, which dictated the memorial forms they could afford to purchase and the space available to display these items in.

Families had a choice between personalized items and mass-manufactured memorials, both of which spoke to intimate articulations of wealth and aesthetic taste. The late nineteenth and early twentieth centuries saw a change in the way the decoration of homes was understood.[13] A shift in domestic responsibility for this took place between 1880 and 1930, when men, who had previously dictated interior design, were replaced by women who became responsible for their home's domestic aesthetic.[14] Throughout the first four decades of the twentieth century men and women consumed mass-produced objects and decorations for the interiors of their homes. The middle classes were perhaps the most avid consumers, but there was a mass market for decorative objects which began to produce commemorative items during the First World War.[15] Items ranged from memorial china to mass-produced frames in which to place individual memorials. While there is more evidence for consumerism in middle-class households, the rate and type of ephemera produced indicates that, for all but the very poorest, there was some level of decoration in most houses in the early twentieth century. Memorial objects and their display were integrated into home-based decorative practices, forming poignant sites of memory within a wider domestic aesthetic.

[11] John Benson, *British Coalminers in the Nineteenth Century* (London, 1989), 121.

[12] Benson, *The Working Class in Britain 1850–1939*, 74–5.

[13] Hurdley, *Home, Materiality, Memory and Belonging*, 15.

[14] Irene Cieraad, 'Introduction: Anthropology at Home', in Irene Cieraad (ed.), *At Home: An Anthropology of Domestic Space* (New York, 1999), 2; Hurdley, *Home, Materiality, Memory and Belonging*, 46.

[15] For more on consumerism during this period see Deborah Cohen, *Household Gods: The British and their Possessions* (New Haven, 2006), ch. 2.

Households often contained items which reflected the aesthetic tastes and memory locations of family members, from photographs to ephemera. Paper ephemera in particular were used to decorate households when more expensive decorative material could not be had. Jim Bullock, a miner born in 1903, remembered that in the colliery home where he grew up, 'over the fireside downstairs there was a large, framed parchment with words written in gilt, which we were made to recite before we could eat'.[16] During the First World War 'another verse was fastened to the wall which gave us all great comfort, for my brothers were fighting in France. It simply said, "A thousand shall fall at thy side and ten thousand at thy right hand, but it shall not come nigh thee."' Bullock's was a fairly typical mining house provided by the colliery company near the pit. The house was built in the mid-nineteenth century and, when Jim was young, had as many as sixteen people living in it at one time. The type of ephemera favoured by the family were religious, but their placement, in the hub of the house, was typical of where these paper decorations would have been placed within many homes. Additional pieces were added during key events and were adapted to suit the new circumstances in which the families found themselves. Had Bullock's brothers not returned, their memorial ephemera would have joined the other pieces on the wall.

Displaying Death

Within the home, domestic objects of death tended towards the small and intimate, and formed part of the everyday life of the bereaved. These could be singular, clustered, and displayed in any part of the interior. Items retained significant memorial resonance, and families attempted to ensure that their members were able to keep a small memento, if at all possible. A common feature of home-based memorialization was the blending of different types of memorial item. Some of these items were highly personal, such as a loved one's belongings, whereas others, such as a state-sanctioned memorial plaque, were smaller echoes of wider remembrance initiatives. Nearly all forms of memorial included the name of the deceased, and some kind of individualizing feature, such as a photograph or a select verse. Memorial ephemera were often framed, or added to other larger items, sometimes forming small shrines to the deceased. Some objects were hidden from view, while others were displayed proudly on walls or mantelpieces. Some could take on religious

[16] Jim Bullock, *Bowers Row: Recollections of a Mining Village* (Wakefield, 1976), 4–5.

meanings. For Catholic families in particular, the objects of the dead could become religious relics.[17] Domestic memorialization followed some general trends, but families could pick and choose which of these to follow, marrying tangible and intangible ways of mourning to help them process their grief.

These mementos of the dead formed part of the physical and emotional shape of the house, offering spaces where family members and others could remember the dead. J. H. Armitage recalled the typical working-class parlour from the late 1910s:

> In most houses that could boast a front room or a parlour, the four walls would [be] literaly [*sic*] covered with large framed portraits of dead relatives and others who had 'Passed Away'. Also the appropriate 'Funeral Card' would be in one corner of the frame under the glass. Sometimes instead of cards, satin bookmarks would be given to the relatives. These had the same details on them as the cards had, and were usually put into either the family Bible or the family album. This latter volume contained only photographs of past generations of relatives long since departed. Any visitors calling, particularly on a Sunday afternoon, would be duly shown round family 'likenesses' with the relish of an attendant showing the works of art in a gallery to a captive audience. The frames themselves were perfect examples of the picture framers craft with either ornate mouldings (often gilded) or severely plain and sepulchrally black, all handmade and highly polished or lacquered…In the case of a back-to-back house with no front room, the family album took the place of the pictures on the wall, and was duly displayed to anyone who came to tea on Sunday. As we did have a front room, well mother kept it in the time honoured way, pictures, ornaments, aspidistra, the lot.[18]

The Armitage family parlour was most likely where they placed a photograph of George, his soldier brother, when he died in 1916.

Armitage's description, flippant in places though it is, reveals a lot about the location of memorialization in the 1910s. The ritualized way in which the dead were revealed and discussed on a Sunday allowed the bereaved a chance to talk of their loved one, but also constituted a place of memory formation, where stories of the dead could be rehearsed and remembered by younger

[17] Patrick Houlihan, *Catholicism in the Great War: Religion and Everyday Life in Germany and Austro-Hungary, 1914–1922* (Cambridge, 2015), 226.

[18] Burnett Archive, J. H. Armitage, 'Twenty Three Years or The Late Way of Life and Living by "The Exile"', 100–2.

generations who were present. It also indicates the importance of ephemera as facilitators of these memory points. Funeral cards and mourning ephemera were included in the family rituals of memorialization as much as the images of the dead. They were used as methods of showing the dead to the friends and relatives who were invited into this liminal space within the home and formed the basis of the social memory formation which took place.

Memorial ephemera were often framed, and popular places to display these items were in downstairs rooms and hallways.[19] Sometimes, this took the form of a shrine, as in the case of a pair of sisters who both lost their fiancés in the First World War, and created 'a little shrine in the corner of their flat devoted to these two men'.[20] Rare examples of items kept in bedrooms and more intimate areas of the house can occasionally be glimpsed. A woman whose husband won a Military Cross, and died in 1929 as a result of the effects of gas, kept his framed citation in her bedroom until at least 1974, when she moved into a nursing home.[21] This is not to say that memorial items in private rooms were uncommon, but the intimate nature of the bedroom and the regulation of people who entered and recorded this space within the home mean that this is a particularly challenging space to explore.

Ephemeral items could echo wider public memorial responses to war, making explicit connections between public forms of commemoration which showcased the blood sacrifice made by families. The Disabled Soldiers & Sailors Handicrafts Association produced a 'Family Roll of Service and Sacrifice in the Great War', a single-sheet, illustrated paper document in which one could record the rank, name, 'sphere of action', 'theatre of war service', relation to the family member recording the information, and other details about family members and their war. The roll was illustrated and contained small spaces around the outside for photographs of family members to be pasted. The Brown family completed one such family roll of honour, recording that one son was killed, another was wounded in France, and the rest of the family had been involved in various kinds of war work.[22] These items were completed by the family and framed as a domestic memorial to their war work, which they could elaborate on when friends visited.

[19] Lisa Maynard, '"I pass them when I walk in the house and I pass them when I walk out of the house": Fraternal Curations of Wartime Loss', The Senses and Spaces of Death, Dying and Remembering, Leeds, 28 March 2018.

[20] Mass Observation, Autumn 2014 R.1025.

[21] Durham Light Infantry Collection, Museum Donor Files, 4090.

[22] British Library, Tab.11748.aa.2(165).

Their inclusion in household displays of war ephemera, mimicking common memorials, marked the family as particularly patriotic.

Families were highly inventive, and used objects already in their possession, or which were cheaply available, to create bespoke memorial items with a sense of longevity about them. These items were designed to be physical reminders of the dead, holding a tangible weight that complemented ephemeral memory items. In North-East England 'disaster glasses' were a popular memorial form from the 1880s until the First World War. These were small, ordinary glasses, which engravers would customize for the families of the dead.[23] They were often created after mining disasters, but were also engraved after deaths at sea, or in memory of individuals. One such disaster glass was created 'In Memory of Richard Kirk who lost his life in Benwell Colliery Explosion March 19 1907 age 55 years'.[24] Some engravers worked out of workshops, but others were itinerant, and simply engraved glasses that families had at home.[25] These glasses could be created to memorialize all the dead, or a member of a community who died in a wider disaster, and were a way for family and friends to possess a tangible memorial, of which they could dictate the content.

After mining disasters local artists might also produce personal memorial plates. These objects feature in disaster collections in South Wales, although, due to their fragile nature, the practice may have been more geographically widespread than this. Memorial plates could be created by a variety of family members and were usually painted items, although, as seen in the next paragraph, on rare occasions they featured newspaper clippings. After the 1913 Senghenydd mining disaster a painted plate 'In Loving Memory of my Dear Brother Phillip Lower' was made or commissioned by a sibling.[26] The plate mirrored an In Memoriam card, with details of the accident and a memorial verse painted on it and was clearly designed to be displayed in the home as a personal memorial item.

A particularly detailed memorial plate was created for Gwilym M. Rees, who died in the 1913 Senghenydd disaster, which married public memorial information with private to make a family memorial object. The memorial plate features newspaper cuttings of memorial verses pasted either side of a photograph of Rees pasted in the centre of the plate (see Fig. 6).

[23] John Brooks and William Cowan, *An Alarming Accident: Or Every Glass Tells a Story* (Newcastle upon Tyne, 2008), 7, 59.

[24] William Cowan, 'Look Back in Wonder: Disaster Glasses Revisited: A Catalogue of Known Engravings within the "Northeastern Disaster Glass" Genre' ([Beamish], 2013), 60.

[25] Cowan, 'Look Back in Wonder', 69.

[26] Big Pit National Coal Museum, 2003.189.

Fig. 6. Commemorative Plate for Gwilym M. Rees. Courtesy of National Museum Wales, NMGW F87.329.

Red roses with dark green stems were painted either side of the photograph, and 'In Loving Memory of Gwilym M. Rees who lost his life in the Senghenydd Explosion Oct 14th 1913' was painted at the bottom of the plate.[27] This plate is a beautiful example of public and private family-directed commemoration meeting through a memorial object. The photograph of Rees was cut from a newspaper reproduction of a photograph that was, as usual, supplied to publications by the family of the deceased. This photograph was cut out and pasted onto the plate, alongside memorial verses cut from the newspaper that may well have been the original verses selected by the family for his public memorial. The creation of this item represented the culmination of the memorial

[27] National Museum Wales, F78.329.

forms that the family could use to commemorate the dead. It was inventive, personal, and linked different family memorializations in a holistic way.

After war and disaster, photographs of the dead became focal points of mourning. This was also common after deaths from illness or old age, but the image of someone who died suddenly was particularly freighted with emotion. Images of the dead had the power to console, to wound, and to shape the memoryscape of the family. The anthropologist Fiona Parrott stresses that using photographs to remember the dead invoked 'embodied memories of domestic spaces and narratives that could not be read from the content of the picture'.[28] Catherine Moriarty has also drawn attention to the importance of portrait photographs in the construction of memorialization after the First World War. She argues that portrait photographs were seen as highly important by families, who used them as points of mourning in the aftermath of the war.[29] This was also true of other conflicts, and letters sent by men in the Spanish Civil War asked their wives for photographs of their families, and sent images in return, which became points of memory if they did not survive the fighting.[30]

In 1997, Beverley Tinson interviewed Blodwen Bryan, the 96-year-old widow of a miner who died in the 1934 Gresford disaster. Tinson noted that Bryan called her attention to a particular portrait: 'There's a good likeness of my husband in a photograph on the wall in the other room . . . a very good picture of him. Many a one would've taken it down and put it away somewhere.'[31] Her husband's photograph, in a downstairs room of the house, was on her wall for over sixty years as an aide-mémoire. Her comment about its continued existence upon her wall is somewhat telling: Bryan called attention to her long-standing commitment to her husband and, through it, the presence his memory maintained within their home.

After mining disasters, photographs of the deceased were framed and displayed in the household, and pre-existing framed photographs took on a new and special meaning for the family, becoming permanent reminders of the dead. Part of the appeal of the photographs lay in the fact that they were already present within the household, and so were instantly accessible as a

[28] Fiona R. Parrott, 'Bringing Home the Dead: Photographs, Family Imaginaries and Mortal Remains', in Mikkel Bille, Frida Hastrup, and Tim Flohr (eds.), *An Anthropology of Absence: Materialisations of Transcendence and Loss* (London, 2010), 135.

[29] Catherine Moriarty, '"Though in a picture only": Photographs and Commemoration', in Gail Braybon (ed.), *Evidence, History and the Great War* (New York, 2008), 36.

[30] Hywel Frances, *Miners against Fascism: Wales and the Spanish Civil War* (London, 2012), 277.

[31] Beverley Tinson, *The Gresford Letters: Aftermath of a Disaster* (Gwespyr, 2009), 52.

point of mourning. One journalist, visiting families after the 1909 West Stanley mining disaster, reported that he knocked at a door, which was

> answered by a homely-looking woman, who invited me into the kitchen, where there were four women, including one wearing a white bandage around her head. It was no difficult matter to distinguish the widow. She was a slightly built person; her blanched, pallid face, clearly indicated the effect of the terrible shock she had been called upon to undergo. She was overcome with grief, and threw her hands into the air and wept aloud. Suddenly she ceased. A kind neighbour was tenderly nursing her young child, meanwhile looking piteously at the bereaved and comfortless widow. Just as I was turning to leave, thoroughly overwhelmed by the awful scene, the bereaved one gave a low, frightened, shudder, turned to the corner of the room, and gazed passionately at a portrait for a few moments. Then she sank into a chair, and burst into tears anew.[32]

This piece of journalism reveals the striking way in which 'portraits', most likely a photograph, became focal points of family grief. It also emphasizes the community that surrounded and supported the bereaved in the immediacy of their grief. In this scene, an image of the deceased served as a poignant reminder of loss, and a fresh source of pain, although one which would change as time passed.

Photographs were significant, not only as a memorial form in and of themselves, but as a way of communicating about the dead in the early stages of loss. Photographs could be used to communicate memorial messages. During the First World War, Private Leonardi used the reverse of photographs of his wife and child to send messages to them posthumously. On the reverse of a photograph of his wife he wrote, 'If anything should happen please will the finder of these photos send them to [wife's address] and oblige Pte. E. Leonardi 10655'; the message on the back of the photograph of his daughter simply read, 'I love you Gracy Darling with all my hearts content'.[33] Photographs of the dead could also be of importance to the survivors of disasters, who used them to ease their trauma. Walter Reinhold Storch, a survivor of the 1915 *Lusitania* disaster, wrote to the sister of a woman who had drowned, saying that he had tried to help her but could not. He wrote, 'I must confess that I cannot get this awful sight [of her drowning] from my mind' and asked for a

[32] *Durham Chronicle*, 26 February 1909, p. 4.
[33] Harry Taylor, private collection, Pte E. Leonardi effects.

photograph of the woman he could not save, to help him with his trauma.[34] While this was an unusual request, the significance of the photograph in helping the living to come to terms with death was highly significant.

Photographs of deceased family and friends also appeared on mantelpieces alongside other memorial items. In 1918 the Reverend Prebendary H. T. Dixon of Christ Church, Clifton, wrote to the father of Harry Wilson, who died in action in 1918, revealing, 'His photograph looks down upon me from my mantelpiece. I often stay to look into his strong but gentle face. Visitors ask with admiration—"Who is this?" I reply, "It is the photograph of one whom I am proud to have known."'[35]

These items were displayed in homes throughout the interwar period. Showcasing how resilient memorial items were, the 1937 Mass Observation mantelpiece directive asked all new observers to document 'in order from left to right, all the objects on your mantelpiece, mentioning what is in the middle'.[36] There are some well-known methodological issues with using Mass Observation, as volunteers tended to be a self-selecting portion of the lower middle class.[37] With this in mind, the answers to this directive suggest that displaying photographs of the dead on mantelpieces was not uncommon in middle-class homes in the late 1930s. Overall, 7 per cent of Mass Observation responders reported that an image of a deceased family member or friend was displayed on their mantelpiece.[38] There were also broader reminders of the war peppered throughout responses to various directives: in ashtrays from Ypres, boxes of old regimental badges, and trench art.[39] Additional Mass Observation calls which asked people to describe mantelpieces, written by schoolboys, suggest that First World War mementos were present in many households in the interwar period, prompting comments such as, 'one lifts [the candlestick] with a shock, discovering it to be very light in weight as it is made in the form of a shell'.[40] First World War items were explicitly mentioned by 8 per cent of the total number of respondents to the mantelpiece questions, a not insignificant number given that nearly twenty years had passed since the end of the war, and especially given that

[34] National Maritime Museum, AGC/S/27.

[35] Lilian Dalton, *Harry: Schoolboy and Soldier* (London, 1919), 54–6.

[36] MO, 'Mass-Observation Directive to New Observers' [June, 1937], 1. The Mass Observation Archive holds ninety-one responses to the June mantelpiece directive from day survey volunteers along with approximately thirty more respondents.

[37] Penny Summerfield, 'Mass-Observation: Social Research or Social Movement?', *Journal of Contemporary History* 20:3 (1985), 441–2.

[38] MO, June 1937, Day Survey.

[39] MO, SXMOA1/3/7/3 Misc Directives, No Name; Folder 2/6; Schoolboy Directives.

[40] MO, SXMOA1/3/7/3 Folder 2/6.

there may have also been non-military remembrances of the dead which were not noted by the volunteers.

By the late 1930s the mantelpiece display of photographs of those who died in war service was predominantly visually associated with the First World War. Images showed soldiers in uniform and frames were accessorized with poppies. One Mass Observation volunteer wrote about the sitting room of an unmarried woman, approximately 50 years of age, on whose mantelpiece was 'a photograph of a soldier in uniform (probably brother killed in war)'.[41] In another woman's home, the drawing-room mantelpiece featured a 'photo of son of a friend, who was killed at 18 in the war, in gold frame'.[42] One woman reported that in the house of 'middle class people, old, well off' she found a silver frame with a photograph of a soldier 'with a poppy fastened to it' and a separate 'small wooden cross with poppy fastened to it' next to a newspaper cutting.[43] It is a likely that the cutting was a Death Notice or In Memoriam post, taken from the newspaper to be used in this domestic memorial tableau. In the family's bedroom the same woman found two photographs of soldiers framed upon the mantelpiece.[44]

These adapted photograph frames, which merge personal photographs with public commemorative poppies, emphasize the porosity between private and public mourning practices. The poppies, made by disabled soldiers and sailors from 1926 onwards, became a focal point of November remembrance practices. By 1938, at a conservative estimate, two million poppies were sold annually.[45] In the case of the photo frame with the poppy fastened to it, it was likely a poppy saved from at least the previous November, eight months before the directive, which gives some indication of the time-frames involved in this ornamented memorialization. Here, popular remembrance practices and intimate family memorials intersected within the home to create a personal memorial which was in dialogue with public remembrance practices. There may have also been an element of performativity to this, through the marriage of these memorial forms, which would have drawn on well-established national memorial practices by the late 1930s.

The longevity of some of these memorial items, from the frames which hung in family homes, to photographs of the dead which were displayed on the mantelpiece until at least the late 1930s, indicates the everyday presence the memory of the dead could have within the home. These objects were not

[41] MO, SXMOA1/3/7/3 Folder 3/6.
[42] MO, SXMOA1/3/7/3 Folder 3/6.
[43] MO, SXMOA1/3/7/3 Folder 3/6.
[44] MO, SXMOA1/3/7/3 Folder 3/6.
[45] Adrian Gregory, *The Silence of Memory* (London, 1994), 108.

simply items to hang for a short period and remove as the sudden shock of immediate grief dulled, but long-term physical reminders of the dead. These mementos were treasured and displayed in family rooms for both members of the household to see and for outsiders to observe when they were invited into the home. This quasi-public form of memorial display allowed invited outsiders to observe the curated memorial space of the family and allowed visitors to participate by remembering the dead in an intangible way, by reminiscing about the deceased.

Embodying Death

Running alongside the objects of display were the emotions that the bereaved lived with. In the aftermath of war and disaster people lived with their bereavement and they were left with their feelings of loss and the desire to memorialize their loved one. While many of the remaining traces of family memorialization can be found in objects, the feelings and intangible actions of the bereaved also contained everyday traces of mourning. Grief can be found in snippets of conversation, such as a war widow who mentioned to her friend that 'it was always the worst coming home to nothing'.[46] They can also be found in physical and embodied commemorative actions. One teenager who was very close to his uncles was very affected when they died in the First World War. In later life his daughter recalled that 'he always marched proudly on Remembrance Sunday'.[47] Memorialization in the home did not rest solely with objects, but with discussions, rituals, and everyday flashes of memory.

Many memorial actions developed a commemorative rhythm, which fell along yearly, monthly, and daily lines. Rachel Buchanan, the last surviving victim of the 1915 Quintinshill railway disaster, who was only 3 years old when the accident happened, woke up on the date of the crash, 22 May, at the time of the crash, every year.[48] After the death of her fiancé Roland Leighton, Vera Brittain created a personal memorial to him: 'Always at 11 p.m. on the 23rd day of the month I mean to pause in whatever I am doing & let my spirit go out to his.'[49] Every month on the anniversary of his death she reread his

[46] C. S. Peel, *How we Lived Then 1914–1918: A Sketch of Social and Domestic Life in England during the War* (London, 1929), 50.

[47] MO, Autumn 2014, R1227.

[48] Rachel Buchanan, quoted in Jack Richards and Adrian Searle, *The Quintinshill Conspiracy* (Barnsley, 2013), 239.

[49] Vera Brittain, *Chronicle of Youth* (London, 1981), 387.

letters, 'crying bitterly', and leaning out of the window to 'pray to Him [Leighton]' at the time of his death.[50] Everyday activities could also come to symbolize loss. After the Gresford disaster, the widow of a miner whose body was entombed continued to prepare his meals and warm his clothes for a considerable amount of time after his death.[51] These personal memorials became ritualized through their repetition, giving the bereaved the space and time to remember the dead. These regular remembrances were personal, and could be private, but provided a memorial rhythm. This internal clock became the time that other memorial acts were measured by, entering into the historical record in tiny moments of grief.

Social rituals, such as donning mourning, were complemented by private ones, like reading letters or remembering the deceased at a particular time. These formalized rituals of loss ran alongside everyday bereavement: the return to the empty house or the passing of a memorial plate displayed on the wall. Individuals reacted to death in their own ways. Sometimes this was socially mediated, and worked in harmony with outward expressions of grief, such as the display of memorial material, but in each case, individual grief and mourning were inherently personal.

At times memorials could be quite literally incorporated in a body and inked directly into the skin. A 1917 photograph of a munitions worker shows a woman staring directly at the camera, her arms crossed to reveal a tattoo of her sweetheart's name above a cross. After he died, fighting in the First World War, she had the memorial cross inked underneath his name.[52] Tattooing was not widespread until the latter half of the twentieth century, and even then women were less commonly tattooed than men.[53] This woman was unusual in her use of tattoos to mark a loss, but she represents a small subculture of people who might permanently memorialize the dead on their skin. This highly personal memorial form relied on other cultural norms, through the naming of her sweetheart and the memorial cross, but transformed these ubiquitous markers of loss into a poignant symbol of their shared life which she now physically embodied.

Personal items were important points of memory building, and owning items which belonged to the deceased could be of great comfort to family

[50] Brittain, *Chronicle of Youth*, 408.

[51] Michael Pollard, *The Hardest Work Under Heaven: The Life and Death of the British Coal Miner* (London, 1984), 179.

[52] Imperial War Museum, HU 82199.

[53] Beverly Yuen Thompson, *Covered in Ink: Tattoos, Women and the Politics of the Body* (New York, 2015), 17. Also see Jane Caplan (ed.), *Written on the Body: The Tattoo in European and American History* (Princeton, 2000).

members. For families who owned many domestic items, bequeathed objects, which were then used in other households, could provide some emotional comfort. Jane Hamlett has noted the core role of the will as a way of distributing household items after the death of their owner as an important memorial practice in peacetime.[54] Similarly, Linda Maynard has shown that middle and upper-class brothers in the First World War bequeathed furniture to their siblings, which was highly valued as a physical memento within their household.[55] Outside of bequeathment, family members informally distributed items among themselves, which would allow individuals to negotiate for items which had particular memorial resonance for them.

During the First World War, whenever possible, the War Office returned a deceased soldier's items to the family. The return of items could lead to some tension between family members as they negotiated who received which object. A particularly detailed example of what this meant to different members of the family was recounted by the upper-middle-class Vera Brittain. Upon his death, Roland Leighton's parents allowed his fiancée, Brittain, to keep some of the personal effects returned to them. Brittain recovered the letters she had sent to him, as well as a pipe and a fountain pen she had previously sent him, and a copy of Rupert Brooke's poems.[56] Yet she was barred from taking the item most dear to her, Leighton's exercise book full of poems, so she copied them into a small book of her own.[57] Brittain was allowed to reclaim the objects that she had given Leighton but was not allowed any of the other items returned to the family. It was Leighton's mother who was allowed to edit and publish his poems, as the person with the perceived closest and longest relationship with Roland, despite their significance to Brittain.[58] While less documented, it is almost certain that these same discussions over who inherited which keepsake took place in the homes of the disaster dead.

In addition to the objects returned to Brittain she took a small regimental coat badge from his clothes and made it into a necklace 'so that I can have it always around my neck'.[59] This action is highly reminiscent of the wearing of sweetheart brooches produced in wartime. Sweetheart brooches, worn as a brooch or a necklace, were small talismans of the regimental badge, smaller,

[54] Hamlett, *Material Relations*, 188–94.

[55] Linda Maynard, *Brothers in the Great War: Siblings, Masculinity and Emotion* (Manchester, 2020), 250.

[56] Vera Brittain, in Alan Bishop and Mark Bostridge (eds.), *Letters from a Lost Generation* (London, 2004), 214–15.

[57] Brittain, *Letters from a Lost Generation*, 213–14.

[58] Brittain, *Letters from a Lost Generation*, 215.

[59] Brittain, *Letters from a Lost Generation*, 215.

more decorative, and mass produced by manufacturers and jewellers, that were often gifted to women before soldiers went to war. When a sweetheart died, these badges could become poignant symbols of loss. Penny Streeter's authoritative work on the brooches found that one woman whose husband died at the Somme wore her sweetheart brooch until her own death.[60] Brittain created a posthumous version of a sweetheart brooch which reminded her of Leighton. She felt an affinity with this type of sentimental symbol but, without Leighton giving her one before his passing, fashioned one herself as a signifier of her loss and the public symbol this entitled her to take.

These wartime possessions were not received without problems: the items themselves could be in a state of disintegration, might be deemed unhygienic and inadvisable to return, were returned in an incomplete state, or could add to the grief already felt by the family. The return of personal effects, as well as having a positive emotional effect on the family, also had the potential to disrupt grieving processes. Some did not receive the full personal effects of their loved one and attempted to express their feelings about this oversight to those involved. H. C. McBeath wrote to complain about the 'few paltry things' returned to him after the death of his son, Harry, in 1915. In the letter he explained that he 'almost felt it an insult to send such [few items] to me'. He went on to explain that 'amongst other things taken from his body before burial were a gold Ring, Wrist Watch, silver Cigarette Case & Field glasses besides articles of lesser value', commenting that 'it was not their value that concerned me so much, but I and his family would liked to have had them as a memento of one who died for his King & Country'.[61]

Mourning clothes, popular in many working-class areas until the 1930s, were another way to signal domestic grief. Mourning dress was used as a way of showing the outside world the stage of grief an immediate family member was in. It was worn for strictly defined time periods, which depended on the closeness of the bereaved to the deceased and their gender. It was wildly popular between 1840 and 1860, when clothes in expensive crape were purchased by middle and upper-class families, but had calmed by the 1880s to include lower-cost materials.[62] Wearing mourning garments was a highly symbolic gesture: it signified to the outside world that one was recently bereaved and that it should be taken into consideration in social situations.

[60] Penny Streeter, 'Symbolic Jewels: The Military Sweetheart Brooch in Wartime Britain' (Unpublished PhD, University of Sussex, 2018), 203.

[61] Harry Taylor, private collection, letter from H. C. McBeath to the Officer in charge of No 2 Records [1915].

[62] Pat Jalland, *Death in the Victorian Family* (Oxford, 1996), 300–5.

Although the First World War changed the way that middle- and upper-class women used mourning dress, with it decreasing in popularity throughout the war, it nonetheless remained an important ritual for many women as a means of expressing their grief.[63] Simpler forms of mourning were also donned by men. Black armbands were worn by bereaved soldiers and it was possible for them to cover a top button in black crape to signify that a loved one had died.[64] Brittain documented people's initial reactions to her mourning attire, commenting in her diary that the crowd in Brighton 'showed their vulgarity by gazing inquisitively at my mourning as I went by'.[65] That Brittain felt she could don full mourning, which was usually reserved for close family and wives only, signifies the public role that she, as his fiancée, took for herself. In this instance she assumed the same mantle as a wife.

While it is thought that the war accelerated changes to middle- and upper-class attitudes towards mourning, by making mourning periods shorter and dress less elaborate, working-class death rituals incorporated mourning clothes until the Second World War. In Lancashire, for example, the family would wear black for a year after the death of a loved one, well into the 1930s.[66] After the 1916 Woodhorn mining disaster, Alice, James, William, Robert, and Ernie Howard, children of Ralph, who died in the explosion, were photographed wearing mourning clothes on the day of their father's funeral, which they would presumably wear for some time afterwards.[67] Mourning clothes would sometimes be those the family had to hand, and new clothes were sometimes bought with this in mind. Others bought new clothes in the event of a death, selling them on afterwards. J. H. Armitage suggested that 'very often, the black mourning clothes (especially mens [*sic*] suits) were in pawn at the "Pop Shop" before they were paid for through a clothing club on the "Weekly"!'[68] Men, in particular, were not expected to wear mourning for an extended period of time. In some communities mourning clothes were expected well into the interwar years, and families went to some lengths to ensure that they performed this significant social ritual.

While clothes could comfort the bereaved, and give a visible marker of the pain felt, they could also be the cause of emotional pain. While, for some,

[63] Lucie Whitmore, '"A matter of individual opinion and feeling": The Changing Culture of Mourning Dress in the First World War', *Women's History Review* 27:4 (2018), 580.

[64] There are some images of soldiers with crape-covered buttons which suggest that this could be used as an alternative.

[65] Brittain, *Chronicle of Youth*, 377.

[66] Elizabeth Roberts, 'The Lancashire Way of Death', in Ralph Houlbrooke (ed.), *Death, Ritual, and Bereavement* (London, 1989), 205.

[67] Woodhorn Archives, NRO 11096/1.

[68] Armitage, 'Twenty Three Years', 101.

the return of belongings could be cathartic others had a very strong negative association with their return. As officers had paid for their uniform it was felt that this, along with their other items, should be returned to the family. Emily Brayshaw has posited that clothes were 'perhaps the most abject, traumatising *signs* for absent bodies'.[69] These clothes were still soiled and stained, and often bore marks of their owner's death. Vera Brittain arrived at the house of her deceased fiancé's parents just as his belongings did, writing: 'it was terrible . . . all the sepulchres and catacombs of Rome could not make me realise mortality & corruption as vividly as did the smell of these clothes.'[70] The returned clothes could prompt a visceral traumatic response in the individuals who beheld them, especially if they were torn or bloodied.

Brittain was barred, although perhaps not deliberately, from the burial ceremony of Leighton's clothes. Claire Leighton, Roland's younger sister, recalled the moment that she and her father buried his 'blood-stained and bullet-riddled' tunic.[71] It was January, she was holding a pail of hot water to thaw the frosty ground, and both of them kept furtively glancing around for signs of Roland's mother, who had not seen the coat since the bundle of Roland's belongings had arrived.[72] This was an intimate act of two family members obscuring the painful object from the eyes of a third. As an intimate family ritual this burial of the tunic became a small symbol of Leighton's death: in many ways it served as a symbolic burial of Leighton's body. Yet, unlike a burial which customarily contained rituals and the attendance of family and friends, this was a painful, small burial with no extraneous ritual attached to it. The item was hurriedly hidden from sight in order to protect Leighton's mother from its abhorrent presence within the home, while it offered some small sense of closure to Leighton's father and sister.

Official Death

The importance of domestic memorialization to the general public, and to those who lost a loved one in war, was clearly recognized by the government, who, from 1917, created objects of remembrance to send to the bereaved.

[69] Emily Brayshaw, 'Remembering Roland Leighton: Uniforms as the Materials of Memory and Mourning in World War I', in Zahra Newby and Ruth E. Toulson (eds.), *The Materiality of Mourning: Cross-Disciplinary Perspectives* (Milton, 2018), 51.

[70] Brittain, *Chronicle of Youth*, 382.

[71] Claire Leighton, 'Foreword', in Brittain, *Chronicle of Youth*, 9.

[72] Leighton, 'Foreword', in Brittain, *Chronicle of Youth*, 10; Brittain, *Letters from a Lost Generation*, 212.

Letters, scrolls, and Next of Kin Memorial Plaques were sent to the families of the British Armed Forces. During the early years of the war the War Office sent bereaved families a message with a facsimile signature from the Secretary of State for War, which read: 'The King commands me to assure you of the true sympathy of His Majesty and The Queen in your sorrow.' In late 1917 the phrasing of the letter was changed, due to an increasing concern that the bereaved needed to be handled carefully in light of French mutinies and the Russian Revolution.[73] The message was sent in weighty envelopes, and special care was taken over the quality of paper.[74] This attention to detail recognized the material role that these letters would play in domestic constructions of death. State-sanctioned letters, which emphasized the King's sympathy, were the beginning of a much longer memorial relationship between state and family.

A key object which was often a part of household remembrance practices was the Next of Kin Memorial Plaque. In October 1916 the War Cabinet began to explore the possibility of creating memorials for the bereaved. The advisory committee for the scheme was formed of representatives from the War Office, Colonial Office, India Office, Army, and Admiralty, assisted by an artistic committee of the Directors of the Victoria & Albert Museum, the National Gallery, and the Keeper of the Coins and Medals at the British Museum. The committee decided that the memorial would comprise a bronze plaque, and opened a competition for its design. The Next of Kin Memorial Plaque was sent to Dominion and Imperial soldiers, and both the imagery and wording, helped by the Imperialist Rudyard Kipling, were designed to link subject to state.

In August 1917 *The Times* announced the competition to decide the design of a new memorial plaque to be sent to the family of the deceased. The criteria stated that the designer had to be born a British subject, and stipulated that enough room should be left for the dead person's name, and that the words 'he died for freedom and honour' had to be included somewhere in the design.[75] In order to fairly judge the competition results, the committee requested that each design was marked with a pseudonym, which was placed on the front of a sealed envelope containing the artist's real name.

[73] Anne-Marie Hughes, 'Death, Service and Citizenship in Britain in the First World War' (Unpublished PhD, University of Manchester, 2009), 46–7. The new wording read: 'The King commands me to assure you of the true sympathy of His Majesty and the Queen in your sorrow. He whose loss you mourn died in the noblest of causes. His Country will be ever grateful to him for the sacrifice he has made for Freedom and Justice.'

[74] Hughes, 'Death, Service and Citizenship', 52.

[75] *The Times*, 13 August 1917, p. 9.

The competition was so popular that at its close in December 1917 over 800 entries had been sent from around the globe.

The winning design, by Edward Carter Preston, showed the figure of Britannia holding a trident and a laurel wreath, a lion prowling by her side, and, in the background, a dolphin jumping from the sea (a reference to the Navy). At the very bottom of the plaque, an eagle (representing Imperial Germany) was held in the jaws of a lion. Individual names were impressed onto the plaque. The plaque design was not immediately well received by King George V, who wondered 'what the fish were doing floating about in an irresponsible manner round the middle'.[76] Given the confusion of the monarch, there is some question of how well the symbolism was understood by the wider public.[77] While the nation and armed forces were represented on the plaque, this may not have been understood by all, although whether this affected the memorial resonance of the plaque within homes is unclear.

The plaques were sent alongside a King George Scroll, which read:

> He whom this scroll commemorates was numbered among those who, at the call of King and Country, left all that was dear to them, endured hardness, faced danger, and finally passed out of the sight of men by the path of duty and self-sacrifice, giving up their own lives that others might live in freedom. Let those who come after see to it that his name not be forgotten.

The deceased's name was written at the foot of the scroll. Taken together the plaque and scroll formed powerful memorial items. The plaques were designed to dull with age, symbolizing the dulling of grief as time progressed, although many families polished them regularly and so they retained their brightness. These plaques became a state-sanctioned form of personal memorial: they were produced en masse, but their size, portability, and personalization meant that they breached the public–private memorial divide.

In theory, every family whose loved one died on active service was to receive a plaque, but it is unclear whether this was the case in practice. Somewhere between 800,000 and 1,150,000 plaques were produced over a two-year period, with 600 produced for nurses who died through war service, with the wording changed to 'she died for freedom and honour'.[78] Those who were killed while working in manual labour for the war effort, such as

[76] Quoted in Hughes, 'Death, Service and Citizenship', 65.

[77] Giles Penman's MPhil research promises to be fruitful on this point.

[78] Philip Dutton, '"The Dead Man's Penny": A History of the Next of Kin Memorial Plaque', *Imperial War Museum Review* 3 (1988), 66.

munitions factory workers, were not awarded a Next of Kin Memorial Plaque. The plaques represent a memorial which was designed to engage the Empire, and the soldiers who fought for it. They were sent abroad, and the families of the approximately 200,000 deceased who fought for Dominion armies received one, forming an Imperial memorial network through these mass-produced memory objects. The classical allusions in the plaque, combined with the royal concern of the scroll, offered a sanitized and Imperial narrative of war which deliberately showcased the nobility of sacrifice. The 'blood price' families paid was rewarded with rhetoric meant to soothe, while emphasizing the military role of the dead.

These government-commissioned objects were not immediately available to the family and, as a memorial form, did not appear in the first flush of grief. Next of Kin Memorial Plaques were nearly all disseminated to families between 1919 and 1920, and so the family of a serviceman or servicewoman who died in 1914 could wait three years to know that there would be an official memorial created, and five years after the death before this official memorial was received. The Next of Kin Memorial Plaques and medals were not instantly shipped to the family, and they could wait a considerable amount of time before these items arrived in their household. The delay in these items arriving, and their official nature, meant that they were unlikely to be the only form of memorial used by the family. It also meant that their place in the household and the way that they were to be presented in the space could be planned in advance. A frame could be sourced or created, and ideas about an appropriate place to put it could be discussed before the item arrived within the home. Instead of forming the nexus of family mourning, the plaques supplemented existing memorialization practices.

While the plaques were generally accepted, some families strongly disliked these state-sanctioned memorials. Private Joseph Alfred Pearson's mother refused to accept his Next of Kin Memorial Plaque, although his father accepted his medals.[79] There were also stories in the press about extreme reactions to receiving these items. In 1921 an upsetting report circulated that a grieving mother, whose son was killed in 1918, died by suicide after receiving his memorial plaque. Emmeline Mantz, aged 65 at the time of her death, was reported to have felt her son's loss 'very keenly' and that 'the receipt of a memorial plaque revived the trouble'.[80] While this is an unusual and

[79] Lives of the First World War, 'Joseph's Memorial Plaque and Medals', https://livesofthefirstworldwar.iwm.org.uk/story/18946 [Accessed 17.05.2021].

[80] *Birmingham Gazette*, 17 March 1921, p. 7; *The Daily News*, 17 March 1921, p. 5. My thanks to Giles Penman for bringing this case to my attention.

particularly sad example, not all families were pleased to receive the Next of Kin Memorial Plaque. At the very least its delivery provoked renewed feelings of loss, and, although Mantz's case was extreme, it was widely accepted that the reception of a memorial plaque brought with it difficult emotions.

These items were displayed in homes, and were often framed alongside medal sets in the interwar period. Nearly every British soldier who fought in the First World War was awarded a British War and a Victory medal, with others awarded if they had been involved in specific campaigns or had enlisted before conscription was introduced in 1916.[81] British war medals were unusual in that they had the name and regimental number of each soldier impressed onto the rim of each medal, which made them both easily identifiable and increased their value to the families because of this personalization. A soldier's next of kin could apply to the War Office for these medals in the event of their untimely death, and many families chose to claim their loved one's medals in this way in the years immediately following the war. On rare occasions families incorporated sets of medals where both father and son perished, one in the Second Anglo-Boer War and the other in the First World War.[82] These items, the medals and the Next of Kin Memorial Plaques, were often framed and displayed, sometimes alongside images of the deceased or postcards they had sent home, and were part of a booming memorial framing trade after the First World War.

A large choice of frames was available to house the medals, Next of Kin Memorial Plaques, and King George Scrolls. Handmade frames, mass-manufactured offerings, and customized hangings were all reasonably common throughout the interwar years and catered to a variety of aesthetic tastes and price points. The free-market approach to the manufacture of frames was not without criticism. George Francis Hill, a member of the committee for the design of the Next of Kin Memorial Plaque, infamously commented, 'As to the frames, anyone who pleases can put [them] on the market...Of course if we had a proper "Committee of Taste" such things could not happen.'[83] The proliferation of frame manufacture in the interwar period reflected the need for people with varying levels of income to grieve in a culturally mediated way. Some people decided to bypass the framing process or reuse holes drilled

[81] The British War Medal was awarded to anyone who served abroad between 5 August 1914 and 11 November 1918, extended to include service in Russia and mine clearing at sea until 1920. The Victory Medal was issued for service in an active theatre of war between 5 August 1914 and 11 November 1918.

[82] Harry Taylor, private collection.

[83] George Francis Hill, quoted in Dutton, '"The Dead Man's Penny"', 66.

to attach the plaque to a frame, such as John Mawson's plaque, which was hung by a simple chain.[84] Families displayed their state-sanctioned mementos of death in a common way that was controlled by the manufacture of standardized frames and which allowed them to signify to any visitors to the house who entered the rooms that a family member had died in service.

Harry Taylor, an expert in framed medal sets belonging to casualties of the First World War, has identified four particularly common types of frame: plain rectangular oak frames, black lacquered frames, leather tooled frames (common among the families of officers), and mirrors which were transformed into frames.[85] Common manufactured frames were typically plain and edged with black lacquer or oak panelling. The majority of people in the interwar period used local framers, such as Nielsen's of Hartlepool or T. Rushworth and Sons in Durham, or even a larger framing company with offices in the town where they lived, such as Boots the Chemist or the Co-Operative Society. These framing companies could generally accommodate special framing requests, such as using a mirror frame. All types of frame were common within homes in the 1920s and 1930s, and the quality of the frame chosen, although not always the style, generally reflected the socioeconomic status of the family.

Custom made Next of Kin Memorial Plaque frames were widely advertised in local newspapers. In 1921 the *Perthshire Advertiser* advertised that the '"Wright" War Memorial Plaque Holder' was available for sale by A. F. Dalgleish, jeweller and silversmith. The frame, in the shape of a Victoria Cross, was sold in oxidized copper for 7*s* 6*d*, or in oxidized copper with oxidized silver accents for 10*s*. The frames were advertised as 'Simple, Beautiful, Symbolical, and in keeping with the sacredness of the subject'.[86] These frames were reasonably common, affordable, and sold throughout Britain. The family of Private Robert Willis Dawson, of the Durham Light Infantry, purchased a 10*s* Wright memorial frame, with a silver wreath decorated with leaves and ribbons displaying the years 1914 to 1918 wrapped around the cardinal points.

People of all classes could commission appropriate plaque frames or make them by hand. The Next of Kin Memorial Plaque and medals of Arthur Edward Peters were encased in a frame carved in the shape of a Royal Artilleries crest. This example was particularly intricate, and suggests some labour of love on behalf of the carver. Pre-carved handmade frames could also be purchased. On occasion, German prisoners of war carved frames for

[84] Durham Light Infantry Collection, 2567/2; also see 2149/1 where a metal hook was welded to the back of Francis William Blake's Next of Kin Memorial Plaque.

[85] Interview with Harry Taylor, 24 July 2018.

[86] *Perthshire Advertiser*, 18 June 1921, p. 6.

the local populace to buy. One frame for a North-East soldier who died in the First World War was carved by local prisoners of war. The poor quality of the wood, and its similarity to other pieces produced by prisoners of war in Northumberland, suggest that this frame was sold for a small amount.[87]

Upper-class families could purchase pre-made frames with high-quality materials or create bespoke items. Spink and Son of London was a popular framer used by wealthy families, which produced well-crafted frames for officers' medals to reside in. They were not the only company to offer bespoke services. In 1920, the Arnold family commissioned a solid silver frame for their son's medals from Mappin & Webb, a silversmith company, which cost £21.[88] Occasionally, custom orders were made, such as the triptych memorial for William Hislop, which was inlaid with ivory, mother of pearl, and decorated with several different kinds of wood.[89] The triptych design made it easy to hide the Next of Kin Memorial Plaque when the family so desired.

Families of all classes often liked to have the option of keeping their plaque safe and out of sight, and popular frames allowed the owner to hide or display the memorial as appropriate. The families of officers often created a memorial book-frame with the Next of Kin Memorial Plaque and medals behind glass or leather, and a small compartment to keep the Scroll safe. These book-like memorials allowed the family privacy to view the Next of Kin Memorial Plaque when they wanted to, and hide the loss of the officer from the outside world, through the opening and closing of a hinged lid. Instead of displaying the plaques, they could be hidden away, and other types of memorial form, such as a photograph, or the published letters of the man in question, could take the principal form of memorialization within the home. These types of frame, where the item could be hidden or revealed, suggest that, for the families who could afford it, the option of privacy was important. Families of the deceased seemingly wanted to be able to both present their loved one's death, and to hide and protect these public signifiers of loss, especially in houses that could see a considerable amount of footfall. This choice was rather different from the ones made by poorer families, who had to remove the memorial from the wall or mount it in a different room. One family sewed a special memorial pouch for their memorial plaque to be kept in, which allowed it to be hidden if desired.[90] This type of framing allowed families much finer

[87] Harry Taylor, private collection. Also see IWM, EPH 546. See Northumberland Fusiliers 'Wooden Carvings', https://www.northumberlandfusiliers.org.uk/about/museum/wooden-carvings/ [Accessed 31.09.2018] for items carved in a similar style.

[88] Harry Taylor, private collection. Receipt from Mappin & Webb, 19 July 1922.

[89] Harry Taylor, private collection.

[90] Durham Light Infantry Collection, 2013.10.1+2.

control over who could observe how they remembered the dead in a private space and indicates memorial cultures that were sensitive to waves of grief.

These state-sanctioned memorial objects were married with other, civilian, forms of domestic commemoration. Hannah Campbell McKay, the wife of Private Alexander McKay, Scottish Rifles, created a particularly touching collection of memorial items. The family lived in a tenement building in the Gorbals in Glasgow, and spent a great deal of their limited income on memorial items. One frame housed his Next of Kin Memorial Plaque, with the words 'lest we forget' carved underneath, and with a small, plain, wooden cross at the top of the frame. This was complemented by a separate frame in an art nouveau style, which displayed a photograph of McKay alongside his medals. His King George Scroll is held in a solid wood frame with a gilt edge, and a separate glass memorial the size of a brick and covered in gilt was also created. McKay's family requested that his Imperial War Graves Commission (IWGC) headstone was inscribed 'too dearly loved to be forgotten', which was rather fitting given the attention they gave his memorial items.[91]

The McKay family also kept small objects which were clearly of some importance to them: a set of charms, McKay's eating implements stamped with his regimental number, and a small pendant.[92] Some of these items were intended to be worn on the body. The pendant includes two images of McKay, constituting a highly personal item, one which was presumably worn by his wife. One of the photographs included in the pendant was been reproduced from the military photograph displayed in the ornate frame. The image in the pendant had been reproduced in halftone print, which was only used to print images in newspapers, indicating that a family member allowed his image to appear in a newspaper, cut it out, and placed it in the pendant. The porosity of these items is striking—externally produced items which relied on domestic items were reincorporated into domestic settings. Here the photograph was used in the home, reproduced outside of the home, and then brought back in to produce a personal piece of memorial material.

Domesticating Cemeteries

Families of the war dead in particular could attempt to create relationships between the home and the grave of their loved one. Those who were able to

[91] Commonwealth War Graves Commission website, Alexander Shearer McKay, https://www.cwgc.org/find-war-dead/casualty/92925/mckay,-alexander-shearer/ [Accessed 30.06.2018].

[92] Harry Taylor, private collection.

visit graves might place personalized items on them, or ask the IWGC to help facilitate this. Hanna Smyth's work has shown the porosity of the boundaries between the home and the grave for families of Dotminion war dead. She shows that people could personalize their loved one's grave by sending items, such as seeds, to be placed in IWGC cemeteries.[93] While these additions to the grave were not always permitted, it is clear that there was a rich commemorative culture which took advantage of the porosity of the grave space, although this was highly regulated by the IWGC.

The families of British soldiers often left significant items on the graves of the dead, or asked for yearly floral tributes to be placed on their graves. H. A. Landsdown's father was granted permission to place a carving of a gun and carriage made by his comrades on his son's grave. This remained on Landsdown's grave until the 1930s, when it disintegrated due to weather damage.[94] Other families arranged for poppy wreaths to be laid on the grave at pertinent points, such as Armistice Day or Christmas, linking the deceased to significant commemorative and family days.[95] Sometimes graveside visitors brought back souvenirs which became domestic points of remembrance. In 1937 the widow of Private J. Greenwood visited his grave in Marseilles. She brought back a cutting of a rose bush from her husband's grave and planted it in her garden, 'to remind my children of their father'.[96]

Families could maintain close connections with overseas graves in the interwar period. Pilgrimages were popular immediately after the war, followed by a brief hiatus in the mid-1920s, becoming popular again in the 1930s.[97] Families continued to visit war graves after the Second World War, including some that were newly discovered. When Minnie Windebank's husband Percy's grave was discovered in 1955 she wrote to the IWGC, the body in charge of burying and maintaining cemeteries of the war dead, exclaiming, 'what a shock it gave me, after 38 years'.[98] In later years, these discoveries made the local news. In 1955 *The Irish Independent* published an account of Belfast-born Alexander Graham, whose mother Jeannie was 81 when she was told her son's body had been found.[99] Families who had lost, or never received,

[93] Hanna Smyth, 'The Material Culture of Remembrance and Identity: South Africa, India, Canada & Australia's Imperial War Graves Commission Sites on the First World War's Western Front' (Unpublished PhD, University of Oxford, 2019), 244-47.

[94] CWGC, efile, CWGC/8/1/4/1/1/64 (AA32590).

[95] CWGC, efile, CWGC/8/1/4/1/1/58[1–2] (AA31431).

[96] CWGC, efile, SL16341.

[97] David W. Lloyd, *Battlefield Tourism: Pilgrimage and the Commemoration of the Great War in Britain, Australia and Canada, 1919–1939* (Oxford, 1998), 217–18.

[98] CWGC, efile, CWGC/8/1/4/1/3/170.

[99] CWGC, efile, CWGC/8/1/4/1/3/169.

details of their loved one's war grave could spend years trying to find where they were buried. One man whose father had died in the war 'spent years tracking down his grave' and visited with his wife and siblings, although his mother, the deceased's widow, was too old to travel.[100]

Gravesites can also tell us something of relationships between sweethearts and their lover's family. Sweethearts and fiancées took part in continued remembrance practices and formed an important part of the family memory of the war, showing a long-lasting and connected family grief. While sweethearts remembered their former fiancés in personal ways, through looking at photographs and other private remembrance practices, some joined with wider family practices. In 1919 Mabel Landsdown asked the IWGC to tell her how she, her mother, and the mother and father of her sweetheart could visit the graves of her brother and her sweetheart, both killed in 1917.[101] That she was visiting the grave of her sweetheart with his parents, two years after his death, is a testimony to the relationship that she had with her partner's family. Sweethearts could be included in broader family remembrance for some time after their loved one had passed away and were clearly treated as a part of the family by other members. One woman recalled visiting her uncle's fiancée while her family were on holiday in the Isle of Man in the mid-1940s. Her uncle was killed at Passchendaele in 1917 and initially declared 'missing, presumed killed'. His mother 'for years cherished the hope that he might return'.[102] His fiancée never married and kept in touch with the family for decades.

Family attempts to cement their history in public could fail, leaving state-led memory in its place. In 1947 Margaret Matherson asked the IWGC if it would be possible to inter her mother's ashes in the grave of her father, Sergeant A. H. Lister, buried in Bucquoy Road British Cemetery, Ficheux, France. After some internal consultation, the Commission decided that they would allow it if she managed the particulars. While they allowed the request, in their correspondence they added that, 'The Commission would also request that as this request is somewhat unusual no publicity should be given to the arrangement and that no reference to the internment is made on the headstone already erected over the grave.'[103] The uniformity of IWGC graves was of the utmost importance to the IWGC, and trumped any familial concern that may have arisen about Matherson's mother being buried in an

[100] Mass Observation, Autumn 2014, M3202.
[101] CWGC, efile, CWGC/8/1/4/1/1/64 (AA32590).
[102] MO, Autumn 2014, H2637.
[103] CWGC, efile, CWGC/8/1/4/1/1/69 (AA3712).

unmarked grave. This obfuscation of individual graves which turned into family sites of mourning is important, as it erased family relationships with the grave, with male military deaths elevated above all other considerations. It reduced family connections to the grave and the men buried there to their military role, instead of the complex roles they assumed in life, as husbands and fathers. Although by the early 1960s the Commission occasionally replaced headstones with additional inscriptions to the memory of the spouse of the dead (although it is not clear whether they were buried in the same grave), irregularities in bureaucratic processes meant that for others the familial importance of the grave was obscured.[104] By refusing to place Lister's name on the gravestone, her relationship to her husband was hidden from the public eye, and the additional importance of the site for the family veiled.

Conclusion

On the first anniversary of Leighton's death, Brittain reflected: 'it is absurd to say time makes one forget; I miss Him as much now as ever I did. One recovers from the shock…but one never gets over the loss, for one is never the same after it.'[105] Families who suffered a sudden death had to navigate their new realities, and work commemoration of the dead into their everyday existence. Memorialization began in the home, and families used mementos of the dead, combined with rituals of remembrance, to try to make sense of their loss. Some hid their objects from view, signalling the privacy of their grief. Others placed memorial items in the parlour, the room where guests would traditionally be invited in to sit on Sunday afternoons, to be shown in social rituals.

Loss and grief were, and still are, difficult feelings to work through. Running alongside formal memorialization was informal memory work, noticing absences, missing the deceased, and remembering everyday interactions. This worked alongside formal memory, such as the display of In Memoriam cards, or the centring of a photograph in a communal room. These types of memorialization intersected with highly formalized state-commissioned memory pieces. Some families valued this official recognition

[104] In 1961 Rose Masding's name was added to that of her husband's on his CWGC grave. Her daughter was charged for the additional inscription. CWGC, efile, CWGC/8/1/4/1/2/155.
[105] Brittain, *Chronicle of Youth*, 423.

of loss, some did not. Domestic memory making had already begun, so these official objects were integrated into pre-existing memorial displays. These domesticated displays of death formed the basis of long-term family memorialization, which was to continually re-imbue these objects with commemorative meaning.

Family Mourning After War and Disaster in Twentieth-Century Britain. Ann-Marie Foster, Oxford University Press.
 DOI: 10.1093/9780191968129.003.0005

5
Building Legacy

Uniquely in the period between the First and Second World Wars, families donated the memorial ephemera and objects they created in the aftermath of a loved one's death to national collections. Museums offered a safe place to guard these memorial objects, and the memory of the individual attached to it, as well as the opportunity to mark individual loss in a society beset by the facelessness of mass death. Most commonly, people donated copies of the memorial items created for friends and family to institutional repositories. These acts should be seen as deliberate attempts by families to mark their individual loss in nationally recognized, long-lasting institutions. The institutional support for such legacy building activities was uneven, and while the families of First World War dead were encouraged to donate items while the war was still ongoing, the families of those who died in disasters had to wait decades to be included in this type of memorial activity. There were no national memorials to the disaster dead until the National Mining Memorial for the dead of Welsh mining disasters was unveiled in 2013. While there are personal memorials to the mining dead in museums and archives up and down the United Kingdom, there was no national call for this material in the same way that there was for the war dead.

This chapter focuses on the Imperial War Museum's (IWM) attempt to collect family items during and immediately following the First World War through the Bond of Sacrifice and Women's Work collections. Both initiatives drew on family archives to populate their collections, relying on donations from the public to create mass memorials to the dead. These collections were highly significant for donor families, who saw the donation of objects as a memorial act. They were especially significant for working-class families, who were suddenly invited to donate items to a national space, and develop collections in a hitherto unprecedented way.

Museums that depict war have a difficult task in accessing and retaining socially acceptable narratives of past events. As Sue Malvern notes, although museums are often seen as 'monuments to cultural achievement' a museum dedicated to war can be interpreted as an institution that 'celebrates the uncelebratable'.[1] Andrew Whitmarsh argues that military museums traditionally focus on two types of individuals: those who have won awards for bravery, and those who have achieved a high rank.[2] The portrayal of individual soldiers as heroic martyrs has the power to imbue war museums with a reverential air. Jay Winter has argued that war museums should be interpreted as 'sacred sites' which transcend traditional understandings of museums as sites which store and display objects.[3] The inclusion of personal objects indicates that for those who donated this could well be the case—however, the unequal display of the photographs of the dead, and family reactions to that, suggest that at the outset the IWM had not come into its commemorative own. War museums present a particularly tricky institution to profile—they are monuments to death, but in which the individual death can be remembered, and at times even glamorized. After 1918, war museums were still negotiating their identity, and the families of the war dead certainly hoped that by donating objects they might shape these nascent institutions, although ultimately little came of their wishes.

The two collections focused on here, Bond of Sacrifice and the Women's Work collections, are unusual because of the amount of administrative paperwork that was retained by the IWM. Due to a general lack of administrative record keeping, very little is known about the majority of donations to museums at the turn of the century.[4] The IWM's administrative archive, however, reveals a wealth of letters from individuals who donated memorial items to the museum. These letters range from perfunctory descriptions of the material to ones which express considerable emotion. They also reveal remarkable amounts of memorial agency. The Bond of Sacrifice collection in particular contains items from working-class families who were not sure that their donations would be well received but who nonetheless sent them to the museum to be held in a national collection. Given the financial cost of sending a memorial photograph for the collection, which for some was too high,

[1] Sue Malvern, 'War, Memory and Museums: Art and Artefact in the Imperial War Museum', *History Workshop Journal* 49 (Spring, 2000), 178.

[2] Andrew Whitmarsh, '"We will remember them": Memory and Commemoration in War Museums', *Journal of Conservation and Museum Studies* 7 (2001), 8.

[3] Jay Winter, 'Museums and the Representation of War', in Wolfgang Muchitsch (ed.), *Does War Belong in Museums? The Representation of Violence in Exhibitions* (Bielefeld, 2013), 22.

[4] Some scholars have managed to work around this using inventive methodologies: see Kate Hill, *Women and Museums 1850–1914* (Manchester, 2016), 48–9, 76–102; also see Felicity Bodenstein, 'A Show of Generosity: Donations and the Intimacy of Display in the "Cabinet des médailles et antiques" in Paris from 1830 to 1930', in Kate Hill (ed.), *Museums and Biographies: Stories, Objects, Identities* (Woodbridge, 2014), 13–27.

these letters form an archive of grief in and of themselves. They tell a story of families who highly valued these collections and saw them as a way of commemorating the individual dead in a way not possible in other large-scale commemorative events.

Objects can, and do, have a powerful effect on society through their collection and display in museums, but the donation of items can also have a powerful effect on the donor. As Kate Hill argues in her study of pre-First World War relationships between women and museums, women in the late nineteenth and early twentieth centuries extended their domestic space into the public through museum donations of objects that had belonged to a deceased family member. Hill suggests that this was an elite phenomenon, as they treated municipal museums as extensions of the home, with museums assuming the role of a quasi-public drawing room or study.[5] While the collections discussed here are slightly different, being family donations to a national institution, the picture that Hill paints of a middle-class awareness of how to interact with museums is borne out in the donations to the IWM. Because of personal reactions to the death of a loved one, these donations also have the potential to be highly political. As Elizabeth Crooke has shown for twenty-first-century museums, the display of private items of grief in memorial museums can be deliberate political acts which form part of wider campaigns for social justice.[6] Donation could generate a multitude of competing emotions of which people's letters barely scratch the surface. The donation of items to museums unveils the ways that people attempted, with varying degrees of success, to shape the museum's focus and reveals how curators related to the public.

Collecting War

In the early years of the war, officials and curators recognized that they should document the conflict, and during the latter half of the war in particular there was a frenzy of collecting. For British and Dominion troops, much of this official wartime collection drive was centred on London. The Canadian War Records Office, founded in 1916, collected regimental war accounts, film, paintings, photographs, and memorabilia in its London offices.[7]

[5] Hill, *Women and Museums*, 59–60.

[6] Elizabeth Crooke, 'Memory Politics and Material Culture: Display in the Memorial Museum', *Memory Studies* 12:6 (2019), 617–29.

[7] Gaynor Kavanagh, *Museums and the First World War: A Social History* (London, 1994), 120–1.

These large-scale efforts were mirrored by a passion for collection among smaller institutions and the public. Individual servicepeople collected items from the battlefields, and surrounding area, alongside official attempts to collect items of special significance to the war effort. As Jennifer Wellington notes, war relics, defined as items which had been in close proximity to the war, were particularly popular items to collect as they provided people with a perceived authentic experience.[8] Public exhibitions could be bolstered with the addition of captured war material and were designed to boost morale.[9] This proliferation of collecting items of war was indicative of a society which needed to understand its experiences through physical objects. The value of these objects was in their role as witnesses to war, and they offered a shorthand for people's experiences, which the collectors imagined could be understood by others who had experienced the war differently. Collections of war material could increase empathy and understanding of war experiences boost morale, and constituted an important pastime for troops.

Concerted efforts to collect wartime items were also made outside of London. The Cambridge University Librarian, Francis Jenkinson, who was approaching retirement when the war broke out, was instrumental in creating the War Reserve Collection at the university. From 1915, Jenkinson dedicated a significant portion of his time to collecting First World War ephemera for the Library.[10] Jenkinson wrote to various people, including public offices, men on fighting fronts, and sympathetic neutrals around the globe, asking them to send printed items. He pursued announcements and letters in the press which might lead to an interesting donation of ephemera. In 1916 he wrote to Colonel J. H. Collett, 1/5th Battalion Gloucester Rifles:

> I see in the *Morning Post* reference to the *Fifth Gloucester Gazette*, and your name is mentioned...I am making great efforts to get together a War Collection for this Library...I have a certain number of trench magazines, etc., but I have *not* this. Can you help me get a set?...So many of these publications will disappear after the War that copies ought to be housed in a few safe places.[11]

[8] Jennifer Wellington, *Exhibiting War: The Great War, Museums, and Memory in Britain, Canada, and Australia* (Cambridge, 2017), 16.

[9] Paul Cornish, '"Just a Boyish Habit...?" British and Commonwealth War Trophies and the First World War', in Nicholas J. Saunders and Paul Cornish (eds.), *Contested Objects: Material Memories of the Great War* (Abingdon, 2009), 12.

[10] David McKitterick, 'Jenkinson, Francis John Henry (1853–1923)', *Oxford Dictionary of National Biography.*

[11] Letter from Francis Jenkinson to Col J. H. Collett, reprinted in H. F. Stewart, *Francis Jenkinson, Fellow of Trinity College Cambridge and University Librarian: A Memoir* (Cambridge, 1926), 77.

So keen was he to grow the collection that Jenkinson befriended many of the men training for a commission at Trinity College, Cambridge, 'eager to interest them' in his wartime collection.[12] His was an unusual passion. Accounts stress his determination to create a meaningful collection and his doggedness in pursuing relevant material, although his staff also contributed to this endeavour. Jenkinson relied on networks of informants, as well as his status at the university, to complete his collection. The institutional weight of the university, as well as people's links to it, undoubtedly influenced the decisions of potential donors.

In 1917, the government began to consolidate its involvement in collecting, primarily through agreeing to establish the National War Museum, which was renamed the Imperial War Museum later that year. The idea of a national war museum grew from a range of individual initiatives; most notably led by Charles ffoulkes, Curator of the Tower Armouries, and the Conservative MP Ian Malcolm.[13] The scheme rapidly progressed with the support of Sir Alfred Mond, and the War Cabinet approved both the plan and a small grant for acquisitions, in addition to paying for secretarial work, on 5 March 1917.[14] Wellington argues that this consolidation came from government needs and popular demand. By 1917 war weariness meant that the government increasingly controlled the war narrative, in line with other propagandistic endeavours.[15] There were also practical reasons for the national museum to begin in wartime. As one member of the committee argued, items would be far easier to acquire while the war was ongoing than after it had ended.[16]

The Museum directorate attempted to establish representative and widespread collections before items were lost in the war. To direct collection efforts, specialist subcommittees—Admiralty, Munitions, War Office, Records and Literature, and Women's Work—were initially formed, swiftly followed by Air Services, Dominions, and Loan Exhibition.[17] Between these groups, the museum collected a wide range of material, although weaponry was often a priority. The founding trio of the IWM, Alfred Mond (Minister for Works), Martin Conway (MP and Museum Director), and Charles ffoulkes (Curator and Museum Secretary), were strongly influenced by late-Victorian

[12] Stewart, *Francis Jenkinson*, 76.

[13] Gaynor Kavanagh, 'Museum as Memorial: The Origins of the Imperial War Museum', *Journal of Contemporary History* 23:1 (1988), 80.

[14] Kavanagh, 'Museum as Memorial', 81.

[15] Wellington, *Exhibiting War*, 37.

[16] Paul Cornish, '"Sacred Relics": Objects in the Imperial War Museum, 1917–1939', in Nicholas J. Saunders (ed.), *Matters of Conflict: Material Culture, Memory and the First World War* (Abingdon, 2004), 36.

[17] Kavanagh, 'Museum as Memorial', 82. There was briefly a Red Cross subcommittee, but this was dropped after a few months.

gentleman-scholar museums which sought to amass large collections of discretely categorized items.[18] ffoulkes, former Curator of the Tower Armoury, was particularly insistent on collecting weaponry, to showcase the scientific improvements in machinery throughout the war.

Although the War Reserve Collection and the IWM were the major institutional collectors during the war, other organizations also collected items of significance. The British Museum Library acquired a range of ephemera during and after the First World War through legal deposit. Following a 1662 law, a copy of all printed material published in Britain was required to be deposited in the British Museum Library.[19] As such, material received during the First World War was, for the most part, treated as a legal deposit rather than a donation by the Museum.[20] These legal deposits were requested through Army Units and wider campaigns to raise awareness about this legal obligation. Article 1933 of the King's Regulations stated: 'C.Os. are invited to send copies of all historical records and regimental magazines and newspapers which may be privately printed, to the principal librarian of the British Museum.'[21] In 1917 the War Office issued a General Routine Order to all units requesting that ephemeral material be sent to the British Museum Library.[22]

These requests were married with a campaign to raise awareness of the British Museum Library's interest in the material. In December 1915, newspapers advertised that the library was welcoming donations of trench journals, and, as early as January 1916, wider regimental magazines were including this information for their troops.[23] Although by 1917 the IWM was actively collecting, items in the British Museum Library's collection of wartime ephemera were overwhelmingly published in 1917, suggesting that the IWM was not initially seen as the natural home of wartime ephemera.[24]

[18] Wellington, *Exhibiting War*, 48.

[19] See the Department for Culture Media & Sport, 'Guidance on the Legal Deposit Libraries (Non-Print Works) Regulations 2013' (2013) for a precis of the history of legal deposit.

[20] In regards to printed ephemera, often accessioned into the library during the war, the line between 'legal deposit' and 'donated material' was often blurred because of the nature of small print runs and editions of trench journals printed outside of the country.

[21] HMSO, 'The King's Regulations and Order for the Army 1912 Reprinted with Amendments Published in Army Orders up to 1st August 1914' (London, 1914), 399. In 1919 an amendment was added, asking that copies were sent to both the British Museum Library and to the War Office. See HMSO, 'Various Amendments and Reprints of Amendments to the King's Regulations Published Between 1916 and 1921' (London, 1920), 26. My thanks to Alison Bailey on this point.

[22] John Pegum, 'British Army Trench Journals and a Geography of Identity', in M. Hammond and S. Towhead (eds.), *Publishing in the First World War: Essays in Book History* (Basingstoke, 2007), 131.

[23] Alison Bailey, '"Curious and characteristic literature": First World War Trench Journals and Posters', *electronic British Library Journal* (Forthcoming, 2024), [2].

[24] Ann-Marie Foster, '"I am sending herewith"—First World War Ephemera at the British Library', *electronic British Library Journal* (2017), 4.

In the latter half of the war, troops sent increasing amounts of ephemeral material to the British Museum Library, bolstering their collections of trench journals and other items, and creating a wide-ranging wartime collection. Occasionally the British Museum Library and the IWM attempted to collect the same items, which were later merged with or siphoned into other national collections. The British Museum Library began collecting war posters in the early years of the war, but ceased when it became apparent that the IWM was doing the same. Some posters the British Museum Library had collected were later moved to the Victoria & Albert Museum.[25]

Memorial objects and ephemera to individuals who died in the war occasionally appeared in all of these national collections, although it was only specific collection drives that increased donations of this material to various institutions. While collection drives by the large institutions attempted to focus on different aspects of the war, the War Reserve Collection and the British Museum Library collection often overlapped, and, when individuals began donating memorial ephemera, there could be some confusion over where to send them. Publishers who printed memorial material seem to have, at times—although not always—followed legal deposit conventions and sent items to the British Museum Library. Private Philip G. Holmes's family, who owned the South London Printing Co., and were clearly au fait with the legal deposit rules, sent memorial items they had created to the British Museum Library to be held in perpetuity. However, there was not a widespread consensus that memorial material would be welcomed into these wartime collection drives, nor an awareness that memorial items might be of interest to librarians. Although not seemingly discouraged, the donation of memorial ephemera was not actively encouraged during the First World War or in its immediate aftermath. Despite these donations by individual printing companies, the majority of personal memorial material seems to have been donated to the IWM, held in the Bond of Sacrifice and Women's Work collections. These two collection drives, although utilizing different tactics, formed the largest contemporary collection of memorabilia of the dead.

Collecting the Personal at the Imperial War Museum

The Bond of Sacrifice and Women's Work collections were contemporary collection drives which encouraged the families of the dead to submit

[25] Bailey, '"Curious and characteristic literature"', [4].

photographs of the deceased, accompanied by short biographies, to the IWM. The Bond of Sacrifice focused on men's experiences of war, with a relatively narrow definition of war work, but the Women's Work collection encompassed the broader experiences of women in war, including nurses, munition workers, and others who aided the war effort. The two collections were advertised differently, and while the Bond of Sacrifice donors were generally self-selecting, the Women's Work collection benefited from the work of women who tracked down families of those who died: the collection is a testament to their tenacity. Because of the sheer number of men who died, the Bond of Sacrifice collection was advertised in newspapers. It was only in the case of prominent figures that curators at the museum wrote to individuals to request a photograph, unlike the Women's Work curators, who wrote to the families of all the women who died as a result of war work.

Both collections were established in 1917, and within three months of the IWM's approval of the Bond of Sacrifice collection there were notices in the newspapers requesting donations of soldiers' photographs. Between 1917 and 1921 the Bond of Sacrifice amassed a public response of 15,000 images accompanied by 3,000 letters.[26] Collection began in 1917 and continued into the early 1920s, with one of the last donations to the collection sent in January 1922.[27] The Women's Work subcommittee was formed in 1917. It was chaired by Lady Florence Priscilla Norman CBE, and included Lady Dorothy Maud Haig and Lady Ellen Askwith CBE, as well as Agnes Ethel Conway, the daughter of the IWM's Director-General, who became their Honourable Secretary. Their aim was to create a record of women's war work, and to collect items which could later be exhibited by the museum. They took their memorial duty seriously and in 1918 began to gather images of women who had lost their lives.

While both of these collections recorded the images and names of the dead, at no point was there any suggestion that they should be merged, and gendered experiences of death were considered as separate issues by the museum. Women's Work was a separate collection within the wider umbrella of the museum, of which the memorial photographs were only a small part, and it was never merged with the wider collection or given adequate display space. Despite this, the Women's Work memorial collection attempted to place women's loss on a par with men's. As Deborah Thom argues, the objects

[26] Catherine Long, 'Memory of the First World War: The Dichotomy of Individual Reflection and National Remembrance' (Unpublished MA Thesis, University of Birmingham, 2015), 2.

[27] Imperial War Museum, EN1/1/PHO/047(78).

and ephemera that women donated to museums, as well as the curatorial decisions about them, were deliberate attempts by women to shape national narratives.[28]

While the Women's Work subcommittee gathered considerable amounts of material relating to women in war, including a complete Women's Roll of Honour, the same significance was not afforded to women as it was to men who had aided in the war effort. Madelyn Walker, the artist who decorated the Roll of Honour, commented that 'it seems to me a pity that the official record of these honoured women should be on a less impressive scale than those of the men which are now being prepared'.[29] Alison Fell argues that memorials which were exclusively dedicated to, or included, women were 'vehicles for public messages about women and their contribution to the war', which varied from the significance of certain professional groups to the sacrifices made by women as representative of women's claims to full citizenship.[30] Public memorials to women who had died, particularly nurses, created and unveiled in the 1920s, elevated their status to that of 'supreme sacrifice' which ideologically aligned their deaths with those of servicemen.[31] Munitions workers were not given the same level of prestige, but women who died in factory explosions were sometimes added to rolls of honour and were locally treated as having died on war service, even if they were not officially recognized as such.[32] Although both groups were, at various times, discussed in terms of sacrifice, the reality was an uneven approach to placing women within wider memorial culture in the interwar years.

This difficulty in positioning women's deaths within a wider landscape of commemoration can be seen in discussions about how to label the war dead. Despite women receiving a Roll of Honour, as well as the Women's Work collection of memorial photographs, there was tension when trying to word how women's deaths should be interpreted, and the definition of women's deaths in war subtly altered over time. In mid-1917, a letter sent to the Ministry of Munitions asked if women would be included in the list of munitions workers who died as a result of work that the Department was preparing for the IWM. The letter requested that they send a duplicate of the list to the subcommittee so they could include it in an exhibition to women 'who have died

[28] Deborah Thom, 'Making Spectaculars: Museums and how we Remember Gender in Wartime', in Gail Braybon (ed.), *Evidence, History and the Great War* (New York, 2008), 51.

[29] IWM, EN1/3/DEA/1(12).

[30] Alison S. Fell, *Women as Veterans in Britain and France after the First World War* (Cambridge, 2018), 39.

[31] Fell, *Women as Veterans*, 22, 46–50.

[32] Fell, *Women as Veterans*, 194–5.

for through their war-work'.[33] At this stage, describing women's deaths as for their country was clearly too bold to be contemplated, a position which remained constant throughout the war.

In April 1918, a letter sent by Agnes Conway subtly changed the tone of the representation of women's deaths, by describing that they had 'lost their lives as a result of their war work', which made the wording softer and more euphemistic.[34] It was only when the Women's Work subcommittee sent letters to the families of the deceased, between 1919 and 1920, that the idea of deliberate sacrifice entered into the rhetoric, with women having 'laid down their lives while working for their country'.[35] This subtle shift in commemorative language, from the couching of the deaths as ones encountered in the workplace, to emphasizing that, although the deaths happened in the workplace, they had nonetheless 'laid down their lives', deliberately invoked the socially recognized language of sacrifice. It was only a male Red Cross worker who felt bold enough to declare in an active voice that one of his staff, Marjorie Edwards, 'gave her life for her Country'.[36] This change in position follows the gradual shifts of public discourse about women war dead and places the IWM's collection at the forefront of these discussions. As a memorial collection, the blood sacrifice of the women whose images they were collecting was plain to the subcommittee. Through their exhibitions they attempted to shape the public narrative about war deaths.

The Bond of Sacrifice was, in part, shaped by public perceptions of what the IWM should be collecting. It was originally intended to commemorate all soldiers who fought, dead or alive, but the focus of the collection rapidly shifted from recording the images of all soldiers to providing a repository of information about those who did not survive the war as people increasingly sent images of the dead. Initially, the Bond of Sacrifice curators wrote letters to individuals asking for specific officers' images, but notices in newspapers quickly became their preferred mode of contact with families—although they also occasionally wrote to photography studios directly to ask for photographs of officers to be sent for the collection.[37]

Newspaper announcements focused on the need for individuals to donate items in order for the collection to be successful. In July 1917 the *Daily Mail* posted an article about the 'Roll for Heroes', stating the collection's intent:

[33] IWM, EN1/3/DEA/020(4). [34] IWM, EN1/3/DEA/020(13).
[35] IWM, EN1/3/DEA/003/1(54). [36] IWM, EN1/3/DEA/1(30).
[37] For letters indicating their policy of collection see IWM, EPH/1/PHO/013(03); for letters indicating word of mouth see IWM, EN1/1/PHO/032(40); also Long, 'Memory of the First World War', 14.

> The name of every man killed in the war will appear on bronze tablets in the National War Museum...Photographs of every officer, decorated or killed, are being sought, and will be included in the collections.[38]

In 1918 appeals in the press focused on the role of the family in helping with this effort, with Martin Conway urging individuals that 'it is only by the co-operation of relatives that our end can be attained'.[39] Although the scope of the collection had been widened from its initial focus on officers, the extent to which it was ever fully egalitarian is questionable. By 1918, the IWM was accepting portraits from all soldiers who perished, but in 1919 a special announcement emphasized a desire to obtain 'a portrait of every British officer who has lost his life'.[40] As Catherine Long notes, whenever the wording of the announcements strayed into elitist territory complaints were made by the families of privates.[41] In a similar collection bias, although the call was for all soldiers in the Commonwealth, the overwhelming majority of portraits contained within the collection were of British soldiers.[42]

Both collections were originally intended to be displayed for the public once the museum opened; however, only the Women's Work memorial collection was to achieve this aim. By the time the IWM first opened its doors in its temporary home of the Crystal Palace in 1920 it was obvious, to the curators at least, that the Bond of Sacrifice images would never be shown—there were simply too many. They explained this in letters sent to those who enquired why the items were not on view. Families were told that:

> Owing to the enormous number of photographs received it was found impossible to show them to the public. They are at present carefully filed and catalogued so that any individual copy can be shown if required. By this means a more or less permanent record can be kept, as if the photographs were exposed to the light they would rapidly deteriorate.[43]

The curators occasionally offered hope that the collection would one day be on display. In 1920 a letter blamed the temporary accommodation, claiming 'it has been found impossible to exhibit even a small proportion of the large

[38] *Daily Mail*, 21 July 1917.

[39] IWM, EN1/1/PHO/025(15).

[40] *Daily Mail*, 10 March 1919. For examples of general appeals for men and officers see *The Times*, 30 May 1918; *Daily Mail*, 31 May 1918.

[41] Long, 'Memory of the First World War', 18.

[42] There were, of course, exceptions to this. See, for example, the family of Captain Anthony Wilding: IWM, EN1/1/PHO/047(42).

[43] IWM, EN1/1/PHO/047(47).

number of portraits that we have. I hope in course of time that this question will be considered, but at present moment there is very little available wall space in the Crystal Palace.'[44] This came as a great shock to the donors. Some parents had offered forthright explanations of what the display of their son's photograph would mean for them. In 1919 H. Quibell wrote: 'Amidst the turmoil these little things go a considerable way towards driving the dark clouds away & I am proud to know that our "Sonny" has a little corner of his own in the Museum.'[45]

This dismay was most obviously manifested in letters of complaint to the curators of the collection. Donors visited the museum to see their photographs on display, and were perplexed when this did not happen. After visiting the Crystal Palace, L. Green informed the curators that she was 'disappointed to find, when visiting the war museum, that there were no photos of any of the soldiers who had given their lives or any mementoes of them individually. I understood there were lots shown, & my own son's photograph sent for that purpose.'[46] E. A. Tickle wrote a rather scathing letter to the curators, explaining:

> I do not want to feel he is just put on one side. I am sure you will quite understand my meaning. It's a mothers sacred love for her dear one. I should like to feel I can tell my friends that he is there with all his comrades He was only a boy but God love him he well did his duty.[47]

Some contributors were sympathetic when curators explained that there were simply too many photographs to display. E. Murphy wrote a reasoned reply to an explanatory letter from the curators of the collection, consoling them that 'I can quite understand that they cannot all be on show at once, as you have photos of so many dead ones & that sad people and unhappy homes th[i]s war [h]as made.'[48] Murphy's letter hints at a secondary reason for refusing to display the photographs once the museum had moved to more suitable premises. Such a vast reminder of loss was not how the museum decided to honour the war dead. The individuality of the images, combined with the sheer scale of them, meant that not only was it impractical to display them, regardless of the venue, but that this graphic reminder of mass loss was too overwhelming to display. Ultimately the curators fell back on curatorial excuses to explain

44 IWM, EN1/1/PHO/047(49).
45 IWM, EN1/1/PHO/027(36).
46 IWM, EN1/1/PHO/047(50).
47 IWM, EN1/1/PHO/047(53).
48 IWM, EN1/1/PHO/027(56).

their decision to the public. Any enquiry about the display of photographs was, from 1920, met with a standardized reply which emphasized the enormous size of the collection and their archival status.

Although the Bond of Sacrifice photographs were never publicly shown, those collected for the Women's Work collection were placed on public display. In 1918 images of the dead were featured as part of a women's work exhibition hosted by the Whitechapel Art Gallery. The Women's Work subcommittee displayed their material in the lower gallery, and the Minister of Labour provided the top gallery with material related to women's services.[49] The shrine was almost altar-like in appearance, with candles flanking a central memorial, and the British flag above the centrepiece, flanked on both sides by the photographs of the dead.[50] While this display method was deemed adequate for the Whitechapel exhibition, the exhibits were to be displayed differently in the Crystal Palace.

When the IWM was opened at Crystal Palace it contained a small memorial shrine, with custom-made books containing the images collected by the Women's Work subcommittee. The books were kept in the shrine, which had the words 'they lost their lovely youth facing the rough cloud of war' over the entrance.[51] They contained 400 images of the women who died, with a short description of each more photographs were added as the popularity of the shrine grew.[52] On the opening of the Women's Section at the Museum, the books were described as 'a great attraction'.[53] They proved so popular that many of the images of the deceased became soiled, and Agnes Conway wrote to many families who had already donated a photograph asking them to provide another. Far from a hidden memorial, the Women's Work display was well used and clearly popular with visitors to the museum.

The display of the Women's Work photographs in Crystal Palace may have contributed to the unrest felt when relatives of the male war dead could not find their image on display. E. A. Tickle wrote a reproachful letter to the Bond of Sacrifice collection saying that she 'thought they might perhaps have been put in Large Books for folks to see'.[54] It is not impossible that on a visit to the museum Tickle saw the Women's Work memorial books and hoped that the same would be created for the Bond of Sacrifice. Some of the families of the dead wrote letters indicating that they understood why the collection could

[49] IWM, 'A Closer Look at the Women's Work Collection', https://www.iwm.org.uk/history/a--closer-look-at-the-womens-work-collection [Accessed 25.01.2021].

[50] IWM, Q31113.

[51] Cornish, 'Sacred Relics', 46.

[52] IWM, EN1/3/DEA/1(45); IWM, EN1/3/DEA/020(28).

[53] IWM, EN1/3/DEA/1(44).

[54] IWM, EN1/1/PHO/047(51).

not be shown. However, an unspoken bond between museum and public, in which citizens tried to understand what a museum should be, and what it should show, was broken by this lack of display.

Family Reactions to the Collections

These collections of photographs did considerable emotional work: the curators and subcommittee members tried to emotionally negotiate the interwar landscape, but the collection also helped families come to terms with feelings of grief. The collections were inherently personal and placed individuals at the heart of national commemoration. As Catherine Moriarty writes, the photographic form was integral to this: while public memorials located loss within national and international frameworks, 'the photograph was acute in its specificity, a direct trace of one who had died'.[55] Although these images are by their very nature personalized, there was still a uniformity to the collection, and sparse details of a life attached to the photographs, such as a name and regiment, are reminders that, for all that, these soldiers' faces are different. The things that families remembered them for, their character, foibles, and experiences, were not translated to this national collection. Families did, however, try to inject some of this personal information into the collection when donating their images of the dead. Family members tried to ensure that the character of their loved one was understood, such as Joseph Sullivan, who wrote that his son was an

> exceptionally good and wise Boy and our only child liked and Respected By all who knew him then early and in childhood he gave indications of a Remarkable Disposition and talent that astonished me his father. But I attribute that to his mothers side for she certainly looked after him assiduously.[56]

The letters which accompanied the photographs reveal why people chose to donate these personal items, and allow a glimpse into family grief. When people wrote to the museum they offered their memories of the deceased. While individual motivations for donation were different, these collections

[55] Catherine Moriarty, '"Though in a picture only": Photographs and Commemoration', in Gail Braybon (ed.), *Evidence, History and the Great War* (New York, 2008), 43.

[56] IWM, EN1/1/PHO/047(30).

not only show the scope of contemporary collections of the ephemera of the dead, but the wider resonance that these collections had with the public.

Family members were those who were most likely to donate a picture of a soldier to the Bond of Sacrifice, although people from extended kin networks sometimes donated photographs of their loved ones. While parents were the most common donors, wives, siblings, and friends also sent photographs of the deceased to the collection. H. M. Waithman sent her younger brother's portrait to the IWM, reflecting: 'I feel I should like him to be among the rest.'[57] The mother of a soldier who lived in New Zealand asked a relative to write to the museum to ask if a photograph of her son had already been donated by one of his friends, so she would not duplicate it.[58] Bessie Smith donated the photographs of two unrelated soldiers together, explaining, 'it is the wish of B. S. M. Wests family & mine that these photos should be placed together if possible, & we would consider it a very great favour if you could see to this for us, as they were both very old friends & were both killed near Arras & buried near each other.'[59] Sometimes friends assumed an explicitly parental role for the friends of their sons. A. W. Hunt explained: 'enclosed find photos of our dear son Pte. E.A.J. Hunt, likewise, one of a most intimate friend, likewise Killed in Action whose mother & father having passed away before having forwarded photo of their dear boy on to you.'[60] It is clear that people talked about the collection, with one woman writing that a 'friend of mine who sent her husbands [photograph]' was her reason for sending one of her own.[61]

Almost all of the memorial material contained within the Women's Work collection was requested from the families of those who died. Agnes Conway wrote to individual families asking for photographs of the dead, 'printed in carbon or platinotype to ensure permanence', to add to the collection.[62] Many of the respondents were mothers, but fathers, siblings, and (very rarely, given the usual ages of the deceased) children replied to Conway's requests. The standard letter sent to the next of kin emphasized the women's sacrifice, mirroring language used about their male counterparts:

> The Committee of the Imperial War Museum is anxious adequately to commemorate the splendid service rendered by women during the war, and with this end in view is hoping to form a complete collection of portraits of women who have laid down their lives while working for their country.

[57] IWM, EN1/1/PHO/037(4).
[58] IWM, EN1/1/PHO/047(42).
[59] IWM, EN1/1/PHO/032(35).
[60] IWM, EN1/1/PHO/047(20).
[61] IWM, EN1/1/PHO/032(40).
[62] IWM, EN1/3/DEA/003/1(52).

> The Committee would greatly appreciate the gift of a portrait of.......to place in this collection. It will be kept for all time in the Imperial War Museum and should preferably be cabinet size, unmounted, and printed by some permanent process. The photograph should bear the name, date, and manner of death on the back.[63]

The collection of the manner of death was significant. Through collecting information about the myriad ways women died supporting the nation the subcommittee was able to build this into the memorial landscape they were creating. In pluralizing the manner of death the Women's Work subcommittee sought to go beyond collecting memorials for nurses, and included munitions workers, land army workers, and women in other voluntary and paid roles.

Families involved in the Women's Work collection were highly gratified by Conway's attempt to collect the photographs of the dead. One mother wrote to Conway, expressing her thanks for requesting a photograph of her daughter, Florence Buckley: 'I am glad that her portrait will be among those noble women who gave their lives for their country.'[64] Another mother wrote that they had visited the Museum, and sent their 'warmest thanks' to 'those who have arranged the Women's Section with such care and sympathy'.[65] Harry Butler, a widower, wrote to Conway expressing his thanks for requesting a photograph of his wife, commenting, 'I take it as a great compliment in your wishing for one.'[66] A letter from B. Smith framed the collection in a slightly different light, couching it as a recognizable service performed for bereaved families, and one which the museum, as a place of national memory, could perform, writing: 'Our beautiful girls with their merry, helpful ways are such a miss from the homes that greatly appreciate (as mothers) this much compensation for our loss.'[67]

When families could not be reached, Conway wrote to the deceased's employer, to ask if they had a photograph of the woman they could donate to the collection. In 1919 the Commandant of Thorncombe Hospital sent a photograph of Dorothy Ede, a VAD worker who died in 1915.[68] At times, Conway went as far as to ask for details of individuals she read about in the newspaper. In 1917 she sent a letter to H. C. Gates, HM Coroner for Cheshire, saying that her attention had been drawn to a cutting in the *Daily Mail* about the inquest of Florence Gleave, who died of TNT poisoning. This high-profile

[63] IWM, EN1/3/DEA/003/1(54).
[64] IWM, EN1/3/DEA/003/1(23).
[65] IWM, EN1/3/DEA/003/1(7).
[66] IWM, EN1/3/DEA/003/1(33).
[67] IWM, EN1/3/DEA/003/2(91).
[68] IWM, EN1/3/DEA/003/1(47).

death led to a range of newspaper articles about her, and the unfortunate circumstances of her death. The coroner sent a newspaper clipping with further information about 'the proceedings at the Inquest held by me on the body of the poor Girl Florence Gleave', offering to answer any questions that Conway had about the case.[69] In 1918 Conway attempted to trace the next of kin of Mrs Lomas, who worked in Morecambe. She sent a letter to Mrs Woodhouse asking for help with her enquiries, and received a reply from R. N. Ashworth, on behalf of Mrs Woodhouse. He wrote:

> I am sorry to say no one here knows anything about the next of kin of the late Mrs Lomas beyond the fact of her dying and leaving a boy in the care of Mrs Woodhouse who after the internment of Mrs Lomas took the boy to Manchester and gave him in charge of his Grandfather, the grandfather let the boy kiss Mrs Woodhouse and then took the boy away not looking over-pleased leaving the goodhearted woman on the Victoria Station without thanks. Should the boy ever come to see Mrs Woodhouse she will inform him of your request.[70]

Conway replied, asking Mrs Woodhouse to forward a letter asking for a photograph to the grandfather.[71] It is largely through Conway's tenacity that the Women's Work memorial section is remarkably complete. The number of deceased women was much smaller than that of men, but this targeted collection strategy was extremely successful and resulted in a high number of photographs being donated.

Families often took images from pre-existent ephemera to fulfil Conway's requests. M. Arnold sent a photograph of her sister, who died of meningitis while working as a nurse. In the letter she apologized for the quality of the enclosed photograph, writing, 'I am afraid it is not a good one—as it had to be taken from a [photo]'.[72] Another wrote to Conway saying that she needed to request a reprint from a negative held by the photographer who took the original.[73] Some photographers were happy to release a negative to be stored in the Museum, although others were either reluctant to part with it, had gone out of business, or had been called up to active service and could not be contacted.[74] These photographs were carefully selected by the family.

[69] IWM, EN1/3/DEA/020(64).

[70] IWM, EN1/3/DEA/020(37).

[71] IWM, EN1/3/DEA/020(38).

[72] IWM, EN1/3/DEA/003/1(3).

[73] IWM, EN1/3/DEA/003/1(19).

[74] For examples of photographers releasing negatives see IWM, EN1/3/DEA/003/1(26); EN1/3/DEA/003/1(39).

As V. Meads explained her choice, 'has been specially done from a small picture & is considered the best existing likeness of her.'[75]

Some families were so gratified that the IWM was collecting photographs of the dead that they also donated other memorial items. A. G. Fowler sent the Bond of Sacrifice curators an edited collection of letters written by his deceased son, explaining; 'I printed a few for family purposes. I hope you will personally read them…It is a splendid idea to set apart a place for such Books.'[76] F. R. Coulson explained he had 'melancholy pleasure in sending you the enclosed little book of poems by my late son'.[77] Donors were supposed to enclose biographical details about the man in the photograph submitted and some donors sent a printed memorial booklet in lieu of written biographical information.[78] A. Goodchild provided no printed biography, but instead pasted a small obituary the family had commissioned, alongside an In Memoriam post.[79] This use of ephemeral material reinforced the important role that it played in consolidating the memory of the dead beyond the family home. Far from simply providing a vehicle for family and friends to remember the dead, these items also became the basis of the transfer of memory of the dead from the family to a national institution.

The types of ephemera requested by the IWM reveal the limitations of family collections. These gaps in family memorabilia are most noticeable in the Women's Work collection because of Conway's direct approach. Families wrote to Conway apologizing that they did not own better photographs of the deceased to send. Mrs Brooker wrote to Conway apologizing because 'I have not got a better photo of my sister', who died of TNT poisoning at a munitions factory in Burry Port, Wales.[80] Some families only had a single photograph of their loved one, such as Mary E. Eddy, who sent the only photograph of her daughter that she owned.[81] A man who had been widowed while on active duty in France and 'got home to [*sic*] late to see her alive' forwarded his only two photographs of his wife, asking Conway to pick which she would like him to have reproduced for the exhibition.[82] Some families struggled to provide a suitable photograph at all. In 1918 A. Gates wrote: 'I am sorry I cannot send you a Photo of my Daughter as she as [*sic*] not been took since she was 3 years old or I should have been only to pleased to have sent you one.'[83] Following Conway's encouragement, Gates sent the only photograph she had, writing,

75 IWM, EN1/3/DEA/1(32).
76 IWM, EN1/1/PHO/025(34).
77 IWM, EN1/1/PHO/025(22).
78 IWM, EN1/1/PHO/025(23).
79 IWM, EN1/1/PHO/037(36).
80 IWM, EN1/3/DEA/020(3).
81 IWM, EN1/3/DEA/020(23).
82 IWM, EN1/3/DEA/020(40).
83 IWM, EN1/3/DEA/020(46).

'it is only very small and was took when she went to school but if it will be of any use, I shall be pleased for you to keep it. I only wish I had a larger one of her.'[84] One husband sent the only photograph of his wife that he had left, 'which is the last that was taken of her'.[85] The lack of photographs of the dead, or the family only having unsuitable images, will have also been the case for the families of servicemen who died, and indicates the difference in class assumptions about the type of memorial material available and the willingness of families to contribute to this collection.

These instances of individuals being unable to supply a suitable photograph affected the families of munitions workers far more than the families of nurses or volunteers, and the class basis of these differences is stark. While many working-class families had photographs of their loved ones, they were not necessarily plentiful, nor were they recent. Some mentioned the direct costs incurred by even the request for the photographs. Mrs Silcock wrote: 'Enclosed you will find a photo of my daughter it is the only one I have and I cant afford to get a bigger one as I only get 7/6 a week.'[86] Another mother wrote: 'I went a fortnight ago to see the photographer the price will be 10/6 the kind you require. I have not been able to pay for it yet as we are not in very good circumstances but I will get it as soon as I possibly can & send it on. My poor little girls death was a great loss to me financially & otherwise.'[87] Yet another family gently reproached Agnes Conway for requesting second copies as the first had become soiled from overuse, chiding, 'I hope this copy may not be so soon spoilt as they come very expensive to replace.'[88] While in some cases original photographs sent by the families were reproduced by the IWM for display, this was not a consistent policy, and was only offered, upon occasion, from late 1920. Before that, and for the original collection of photographs, families were expected to pay to produce the photographs of the dead they sent. For families who may well have been relying on wages from the woman who lost her life, the cost of contributing to her public memorial could be more than they were able to afford.

The socioeconomic issues which were alluded to in the Women's Work letters were also mirrored in the Bond of Sacrifice collection. Within the collection there is a seemingly middle-class bias. Many donors were employed in professional occupations, such as nursing and the Civil Service, indicating the rough socioeconomic status of their family more broadly. There was also some attempt to collect photographs of notable individuals, and curators

[84] IWM, EN1/3/DEA/020(45).
[85] IWM, EN1/3/DEA/020(66).
[86] IWM, EN1/3/DEA/020(54).
[87] IWM, EN1/3/DEA/020(62).
[88] IWM, EN1/3/DEA/003/2(83).

of the collection used personal networks to obtain these.[89] Because of this innate class bias, perpetuated through the newspaper advertisements for the collection, individuals could be nervous when approaching the museum. Harry Quibell donated a photograph of his son, writing, 'we are only ordinary people, but I should be pleased to see his name amongst our Heros. He did his best poor lad.'[90] This self-definition did not stop Quibell from approaching the museum, but did frame the way he offered his donation, which showed a keen awareness of the institutional weight the museum represented.

While some donors only supplied the items requested by the museum, others wrote personal notes which hinted at how they had been emotionally affected by the death of a family member. Ethel Murphy sent a photograph of her husband, writing:

> He was a good man and the best of Husbands their for [*sic*] I want to do all I can so that he shall not be forgotten. I can quite understand that they cannot all be on show at once, as you have photos of so many dead ones & that sad people and unhappy homes this war as made. I have a baby girl year and two months which is a great comfort to me, but nothing can take the place of one so dear as my Husband.[91]

While not dwelling on the circumstances of his death, and the undoubtedly difficult position it left her in, Murphy conveyed her love and loss in a succinct manner, personalizing the correspondence and conveying her grief. E. B. H. Bigland described herself as a 'very proud but sorrow stricken mother who lost her All (her only Son and child)'.[92] J. Sullivan went so far as to write that he heard his son's voice, explaining, 'I am greatly comforted when I hear his angel voice calling Regularly in my right ear the one mono sillible Dadda it tells me all I want to know, namely Gods goodness and wondrous power.'[93] How literally this was taken by the writer is unclear, but it indicates that the donors felt comfortable revealing these personal thoughts to curatorial staff, both to reinforce the poignancy of their donation and share the very human emotions that they were grappling with in their private lives.

Some donors hinted at these emotions in their correspondence. M. A. Gearing, who lost a brother in active service and her husband during an air raid, wrote to the museum explaining why she was so slow to donate

[89] Long, 'Memory of the First World War', 17.
[90] IWM, EN1/1/PHO/037(18).
[91] IWM, EN1/1/PHO/027(56).
[92] IWM, EN1/1/PHO/027(38).
[93] IWM, EN1/1/PHO/047(30).

her brother's image to the Bond of Sacrifice collection: 'i am sorry to have to tell you that Pt JR Howitt was killed in action on the 27 of June 1918 & just before my poor husband died through one air raid so that i have not felt like writing before.'[94] Without delving into her feelings, the telling phrase 'I have not felt like writing before' speaks to a year of grief. This, combined with the economic impact of widowhood and the end of the war, with all that came with it for the families of those whose loved ones did not come home, was conveyed to the curators, who, it was assumed, would understand the hard war Gearing had experienced.

The emotional impact of women's deaths on the family can also be glimpsed through their letters to Agnes Conway. The raw emotion of donors was generally less than those in the Bond of Sacrifice collection, perhaps because they had been asked for photographs through letters which acknowledged their grief. However, the bittersweet sadness at being asked to provide a photograph of the deceased was often mentioned. A particularly emotive letter was sent by Mrs Caswell, whose daughter died while working in a munitions factory. She wrote:

> I shall be very pleased to send you a photo of my dear little daughter that laid down her precious young life for her King and beloved Country she was so proud to be able to serve both and she was one of the best excuse me writing like this but I cant help it I loved her so and my I am missing her cheery letters so and it does seem so hard to think I will never see her in this world again.[95]

This stream of consciousness gives voice to the very deep emotions that were at play in many of the families who lost a loved one in the First World War. Deaths in factories were especially tragic. Although they were known to be dangerous places, the fresh hazards presented by handling chemicals and explosives resulted in new types of death which were, for the most part, not the kind people had envisaged women suffering and came as an unexpected shock. As Dinah Bamber, a bereaved mother, explained, 'we have 4 Sons serving their (King) and Country not having a thought our youngest daughter should be taken first.'[96]

In an extremely rare instance of a widower expressing his feelings on the loss of his wife through war work, Harry Robinson wrote that women had

[94] IWM, EN1/1/PHO/032(10).
[95] IWM, EN1/3/DEA/020(15).
[96] IWM, EN1/3/DEA/020(68).

'given their lives for the safety of humanity, and particularly of our own Country'.[97] His family was a military one, and the photograph of his wife sent to the museum was enlarged from a family photograph, taken when his sons were home on leave. Not only did Robinson attempt to understand his wife's loss in military terms, he infused it with ideas of domesticity and service, explaining:

> Although many of the women may not have actually been serving on the battlefields abroad they have been doing equal service in various spheres at home and have thus formed a kind of second casualty list along with those broken by grief.[98]

Robinson was particularly pleased 'to hear that the public are much interested in the collection' and was highly gratified to send a photograph of his 'dear wife'.[99] While he did not write explicitly of his personal grief, he was clearly proud of his wife's war work, and understood her death as in keeping with the family's wider war service.

Some portraits were sent to the Bond of Sacrifice at poignant times of the year, and were clearly engaged with as part of wider family remembrance practices on intimate anniversaries. F. J. Gould sent his son's photograph on a particularly significant date, explaining: 'today is the anniversary of our son's death near Arras (1917) and we have sad pleasure in giving his pictures to those who can appreciate.'[100] Some families sent a photograph of their dead soldier on Armistice Day, highlighting the bitter toll of the war, and an emotionally freighted moment to join familial memory to national remembrance practices. A. Goodchild sent a photograph of her son and two clippings, one of his death notice and another of an In Memoriam posting for him, to the IWM on 11 November 1918.[101] These donations marked a moment in time when significant moments for the family were projected through the donation of a photograph of their loved one. They were a way of aligning personal and national commemoration, whether through the inclusion of national commemoration in the personal, as with Gould's donation, or the folding of personal memorial acts into national ones, as Goodchild did.

It is clear that families tried to control how they donated items to the Bond of Sacrifice, and correspondence from the Women's Work collection could disrupt family mourning. Not all requests from the collection were welcome,

97 IWM, EN1/3/DEA/003/3(125).
98 IWM, EN1/3/DEA/003/3(125).
99 IWM, EN1/3/DEA/003/3(125).
100 IWM, EN1/1/PHO/025(4).
101 IWM, EN1/1/PHO/037(36).

and requests for photographs of the deceased could be highly upsetting for the family. Olive A. Turton, sister of a nurse who died in Egypt, wrote to Agnes Conway on her family's behalf. She requested:

> Would you kindly acknowledge, or send any correspondence necessary to my business address, 21, Thurlow Road, Hampstead, as above, as mother has never been the same since her death, and as she is still very ill, I do not wish her to see any correspondence relating to my sister's death, it would be sure to make her worse.

The extreme grief which could accompany sudden death did not necessarily welcome reminders and letters. Far from being a healing balm, correspondence from the museum could be an intrusive reminder of loss. These outside intrusions into the memorial rhythm that families had created in their homes could jar and disrupt personal understandings of memorial time.

Women who wrote to Agnes Conway were not only keen on elaborating on their own experience of loss, but were also aware of the weight of cumulative deaths, and showed empathy towards other suffering families. M. Knights sent a photograph of her 'Dear Daughter' to Conway, asking where she could view it, commenting, 'I should much like to see them for myself as it must be very interesting allso [*sic*] very sad for those who have lost perhaps their all. War widows do not have much to spend on outings.'[102] Another parent highlighted how pleased they were that their daughter's portrait was in the collection, 'to commemorate the work she did in the War & the supreme sacrifice which she made as so many others did as well.'[103] B. Smith Lee, who was corresponding with Conway about her daughter's photograph, told her about a nurse who served alongside her daughter, who died by suicide. Smith Lee clearly attributed her daughter's friend's death to the war, closing her letter with the lament 'Oh! when shall we hear of the last lass in this great struggle?'[104]

Those who donated an image of a loved one to the IWM entered into a dialogue with the curators of the collection. Donors received a thank-you letter as standard, which emphasized the sincerity of the museum's thanks for building their collection, and reiterated the respect their donation would be treated with.[105] The only time that the Keeper of Photographs lapsed in his otherwise aloof and professional responses to Bond of Sacrifice donors was

[102] IWM, EN1/3/DEA/020(35).
[103] IWM, EN1/3/DEA/003/1(30).
[104] IWM, EN1/3/DEA/003/2(90).
[105] St Fagans National Museum of History, 46.316.12.

immediately after the declaration of peace. In a letter dated 11 November 1918, he wrote a letter to a Captain F. H. Peyton, who had donated his son's photograph:

> I am writing this with the bells of Victory just starting to ring, and I cannot help saying how deeply I feel for the parents of the heroic men, to whose efforts we owe the glorious termination of the awful war. Like yourself, I have had two sons fighting, one in the M.G.C., and one in the R.N.V.R. I have not heard of or from the latter for a month, but trust that he is safe.[106]

In the days after peace was declared letters written by curators became far less guarded, so much so that some of the letters were immediately marked 'not for publication' as they contained decidedly xenophobic comments.[107] On the whole, correspondence was respectful, and emphasized how important people's donations were to the museum, while following a relatively standard blueprint.

This correspondence was seemingly more personal in the Women's Work collection, in letters to Conway which offered thoughts on the subcommittee's work. One family wrote that they had been to visit the IWM '& our warmest thanks are due to those who have arranged the Women's Section with such care and sympathy'.[108] Other families made a pilgrimage to see their loved one's image displayed in the Museum. In 1920 the sister of W. H. Burtenshaw sent a photograph of her, writing, 'I should be so grateful if you could at some time or other let me know when & where the photos can be seen as I should like to bring my Mother to see them.'[109] Sometimes letters to Conway contained mild reproach. One mother wrote enclosing a second photograph of her daughter, asking where they could be seen. As she explained, 'several of our friends when visiting the IWM have been unable to find it.'[110] These personal responses from the curators of both collections was clearly of some importance to the family. Through this correspondence they felt their losses were seen, and understood, by the representatives of this national institution.

Families who wrote to the IWM entered into a dialogue with the institution. Some families were keen to emphasize the emotional meaning of the collection, and document their sadness, but others sent a bare minimum of information, and were happy with standardized replies. What is clear is that individuals were overwhelmingly pleased that their family member was to be commemorated in a national setting. For families of women who died, being

[106] IWM, EN1/1/PHO/037(8).
[107] Long, 'Memory of the First World War', 22–3.
[108] IWM, EN1/3/DEA/003/1(7).
[109] IWM, EN1/3/DEA/003/1(29).
[110] IWM, EN1/3/DEA/003/1(35).

able to see the image of their loved one on display was of great importance, and was meaningful to many. The act of donation was important to those who chose to send their loved one's image to the Bond of Sacrifice collection, particularly on significant memorial days, and, although some people were upset that the images were not on display, they seem to have felt that there was comfort to be gained through their place in a national collection. In many ways, the IWM complemented other national commemorations, and allowed individuals a more intimate point of contact than could be achieved by other state-level initiatives.

Conclusion

The IWM's collection of photographs of the dead during and after the war was, in many ways, a remarkable undertaking. The two photograph collections were, as is perhaps to be expected, plagued with class bias, but working-class families had their photographs accepted alongside middle- and upper-class ones. Families used these opportunities to transfer traces of their loss into national collections through the donation of family photographs. These active transfer processes speak to individuals who wanted national recognition for their loss. As the reaction to the Bond of Sacrifice collection not being displayed indicates, there was genuine upset when it was felt that this unspoken contract between donor and museum had been broken. There was a strong desire among certain families to remember the individual dead on a national stage, which was offered through these collections. The facelessness of national memorials, epitomized by the Tomb of the Unknown Warrior, stood in stark contrast to these highly personalized memorial forms.

These collections were also significant as women were remembered in the same museum as men. The Women's Work display areas were far from ideal, and spatially suggested that women's sacrifice was less than that of their male counterparts. The popularity of the Women's Work memorial books, however, indicates the very real interest that members of the public had in remembering women war dead. Through them, families of the dead created strong legacies which consolidated the memory of women on a national stage, although, without a permanent display for the women who died, the effectiveness of this as a way of forging national memory is questionable.

Although those who died in war were memorialized through these collections, mining deaths were to have no similar collection drive. The three major UK mining museums, the Big Pit in South Wales (1980), the National Mining

Museum Scotland (1984), and the National Mining Museum in Yorkshire (1988), were all opened within ten years of each other. All were based at former mining sites that had recently been closed as part of the long tail of deindustrialization in mining communities at the end of the twentieth century. As mining communities banded together to try to fight attacks on local collieries, the simultaneous reopening of the pits as heritage sites helped contribute to the historicization of an occupation which was still extant. There were no equivalent calls for family donations to these national memorials to mining. Instead, the initial focus of these museums was the impact of mining on the landscape itself, shown by pit engines and industrial machinery. This formed a different memorial to the dead, one in which the death of industry was presented to the nation, while miners simultaneously fought to save their jobs. While those who died in mining disasters were not forgotten, it was only at the end of the twentieth century that they again became a focus for the national memory of mining.

Those who donated photographs to the IWM made a significant attempt to place their family narrative within a national one, humanizing the collections in their grief and individualizing the collective face of mass death. The collections emphasized loss in wartime in a remarkable way, and there was no national equivalent for those who died at work in peacetime. Writing about the Bond of Sacrifice collection, Moriarty suggests that it encourages us to 'imagine the many thousands of photographs that remain in family albums, cherished or forgotten, and those that have been destroyed over the years, or those that have come unstuck from their familial associations and now emerge at postcard dealers and market stalls'.[111] It is to the lifespan of these photographs and objects that we next turn. Families sent duplicate photographic copies to the IWM, while the original image stayed in the home, forming part of the family legacy that developed and evolved over time.

Family Mourning After War and Disaster in Twentieth-Century Britain. Ann-Marie Foster, Oxford University Press.
 DOI: 10.1093/9780191968129.003.0006

[111] Moriarty, '"Though in a picture only"', 44.

6

Extending Legacy

The centenary of the First World War in Britain highlighted, in a rather stark way, the split between public and private memorial practices. There was an extreme interest in family histories of the war throughout the centenary and, at the start of the four-year period, historians of the First World War predicted that family memories of the conflict would fuel British national engagement with wider public centenary initiatives. As Keith Jeffery suggested in 2015, a combination of micro-histories, 'communal memories and family narratives…[will] sustain the extraordinary public interest in the war'.[1] The importance of family narratives of war was recognized by international enterprises, such as Europeana's '1914–1918', and national ones, such as Imperial War Museum's 'Lives of the First World War'.[2] These online platforms of remembrance revealed a plethora of objects and ephemera which still remain in family archives and form the spine of many people's First World War memorial practices. These family objects have the potential to contain a deep emotional resonance for their custodians across decades. This was reflected in public broadcasts, and in the lead up to the 2018 Armistice Day celebrations, when BBC radio programmes featured family objects which individual members of the public used to remember their dead.[3] Yet, nationally, Remembrance Sunday in 2018 was characterized by a mass memorial service at the Cenotaph, a service in Westminster Abbey, and artistic memorialization such as Pages of the Sea. While the centenary period has witnessed a heavy focus on collecting family memorial objects, on Armistice Day itself they were largely absent from national commemorations.

Although family history has the serious power to disrupt, when it is funnelled through national and institutional platforms this possibility is taken

[1] Keith Jeffery, 'Commemoration in the United Kingdom: A Multitude of Memories', *Australian Journal of Political Science* 50:3 (2015), 566.

[2] Bart Ziino, 'Introduction: Remembering the First World War Today', in Bart Ziino (ed.) *Remembering the First World War* (London, 2015), 9; also see James Wallis '"Great-grandfather, what did *you* do in the Great War?" The Phenomenon of Conducting First World War Family History Research', in Bart Ziino (ed.), *Remembering the First World War* (London, 2015), 31–4.

[3] For example, the Today Show, Radio 4, 10 November 2018. Thanks to James McConnel for bringing this to my attention.

away from families, who preserve their fragmented family histories both away from and within these institutions. The cultural memory of the First World War in particular is one which has dominated people's ideas of what it meant for their ancestors to participate in conflict. It can be very hard for people to dissociate their ancestor's experiences from this wider understanding of war. In their work on the 2014–18 centenary of the war, Lucy Noakes and James Wallis found that the strong cultural memory which lauded soldiers as victims effectively blocked diverse and nuanced understandings of the conflict which sought to change public understanding.[4] Although individual narratives of people's ancestors can and do disrupt our historical knowledge, there is a danger of homogeneity when family histories meld with national and institutional ones. This chapter focuses on people who feel a pull to share their family histories of traumatic events in a multitude of ways: familial, institutional, and online.

The chapter traces how family memory of the First World War and early twentieth-century disasters changed and developed from the 1970s. By the 1970s the cultural memory of the war was a tragic one which focused on male experiences of fighting on the Western Front. This genesis of the memory of the First World War as white, male, tragic, and trench-based lay in the war poets of the 1930s. In this understanding of war, as Correlli Bartlett claimed, 'trench reminiscences told much the same story: of idealism turning into sour disillusionment, of the futility of fighting, of the obscenity of death and mutilation, and the terrors of the battle'.[5] This negative view of war was consolidated in the 1960s through cultural outputs such as the publication of Alan Clark's *The Donkeys* (1961), the play *Oh! What a Lovely War* (1963), and the broadcast of the BBC's *The Great War* (1964), which focused on fighting centred on the Western Front and articulated the futility of war.[6] Dan Todman posits that the BBC television show *The Great War* (1964) was particularly important in developing family understandings of the conflict, as it encouraged groups to 'rehearse family myths about the war without challenging their underlying preconceptions'.[7] By the 1990s, the television show *Blackadder Goes Forth* (1989) and novels such as Pat Barker's *Regeneration* trilogy (1991–5) and Sebastian Faulk's *Birdsong* (1993) showed the pervasiveness of

[4] Lucy Noakes and James Wallis, 'The People's Centenary? Public History, Remembering and Forgetting in Britain's First World War Centenary', *The Public Historian* 44:2 (2022), 58–9.

[5] Correlli Bartlett, *The Collapse of British Power* (Gloucester, 1987), 429.

[6] Jay Winter and Antoine Prost, *The Great War in History* (Cambridge, 2006), 19; Derek Paget, 'Popularising Popular History: "Oh What a Lovely War" and the Sixties', *Critical Survey* 2:2 (1990), 119.

[7] Dan Todman, *The Great War: Myth and Memory* (London, 2005), 35.

this war memory. As Helen McCartney explains, by the 2000s the figure of the white victim soldier fighting in a mud-bound futile war was the pervasive cultural memory of the worldwide multi-ethnic conflict.[8]

In mining communities, individual deaths in small accidents, not large-scale disasters, dominated cultural memory until the late twentieth century. David Selway's research into the South Wales coalfields found that the collective memory of disaster did not feature prominently in cultural memories of coal until the mines were closed, when immediate danger to the workers was gone. It was only then, he argues, that big pit disasters began to attract wider remembrance in the coalfields.[9] This prominence of disaster representing the difficult working conditions for miners had been solidified by the early 2000s, when it became a shorthand for the tragic nature of loss in the mining community.[10] By the turn of the millennium war and disaster were both fixed cultural points of mass loss in deeply distressing circumstances.

Alongside these cultural memory developments there were family members who passed on objects and histories of the people who died. Following the death of a loved one, siblings, children, nieces, and nephews continued to memorialize the dead, but their memories of the deceased were increasingly mixed with cultural memories, particularly of war, that had begun to circulate. Moments of memory began to crystallize around anniversaries, be they personal ones, such as the anniversary of an individual death, or national ones, such as a centenary. The first two-thirds of this book traced the largely similar experiences of war and disaster dead: their families memorialized them through ephemera, objects, and rituals within domestic settings. Yet it is in long-term memory trends that we can see a distinct split, with significant differences in the way that war and disaster memories were influenced by cultural memory. Due to the national privileging of war narratives, the memory of war has remained more pervasive than that of disaster. Individuals turned to cultural understandings to contextualize their family histories. The centenaries and anniversaries of war and disaster have offered families a chance to show their connection to the dead on an (inter)national stage, through websites designed to memorialize the war dead and news stories which focus on family

[8] Helen B. McCartney, 'The First World War Soldier and his Contemporary Image in Britain', *International Affairs* 90:2 (2014), 299. Meghan Tinsley's work on the commemoration of Muslim soldiers in the First World War centenary offers a nuanced telling of how the public memory of war was contested in national memorial spaces. See Meghan Tinsley, *Commemorating Muslims in the First World War Centenary: Making Melancholia* (Abingdon, 2022).

[9] David Selway, 'Death Underground: Mining Accidents and Memory in South Wales, 1913–1974', *Labour History Review* 81:3 (2016), 196–209.

[10] Douglas Davies, *Mors Britannica* (Oxford, 2015), 91.

memory of tragic events. But, for many families, these platforms presented as much of an opportunity to rediscover their dead, and reclaim family connection in an online space, as it did to celebrate known connections.

Families, Material Culture, and Cultural Memory

While family memory of the dead remained strong throughout the 1920s, the 1930s and 1940s saw a weakening of the ways that some families remembered the dead, making memory objects less visible and, therefore, less likely to be remembered in the long term. Working-class families were particularly affected by their memorial objects being taken away, destroyed, or sold for the high price of silver. Memory building through objects is, in this period, also a history of disposal and loss. This was not universal, and, as we have seen already, many families kept their memorial items; however, others were tempted or forced to destroy family memorial objects. Other families lost theirs when the people who owned the objects died, and they were disposed of rather than being passed down through ancestral lines.

Local slum clearances particularly affected paper-based ephemera associated with disaster. Colin McCourt suggests that much memorial material relating to the 1910 Wellington colliery disaster was lost in the 1930s. He suspects that many of those who lived in houses rented from the Wellington pit owners lost memorial material in the slum clearances around that time. Before items were allowed into their new homes they had to be disinfected in 'the bug van', which destroyed paper-based memorial items.[11] As memorial ephemera were the main way that many families remembered the dead this represents a considerable loss, and much material that would have survived in family homes was taken away from families in the name of sanitization.

The 1930s also saw the destruction of many First World War medals. Due to the high price of silver, many cash-strapped families sold their British War Medals for scrap, as they had a relatively high silver count. The sale of medals was not exclusive to soldiers who fought in the First World War, and a man who grew up in London recalled seeing barrels of medals from the Second Anglo-Boer War on sale for one shilling apiece in the late 1940s.[12]

[11] Colin McCourt, *Newhouses Revisited: The Story of a Whitehaven Mining Community* ([Unknown], 2008), 170.

[12] Mike Wood, recounted in Matthew Richardson, 'Medals, Memory and Meaning', in Nicholas Saunders and Paul Cornish (eds.), *Contested Objects: Material Memories of the Great War* (Abingdon, 2009), 112.

Families were often forced, or encouraged, to get rid of mementos of those who died in war or disaster in the early twentieth century, which significantly weakened memory practices within the wider family. While some families may have genuinely not cared about the fate of their memorial items, for others their destruction would have been the cause of severe distress.

Families also disposed of memorial items when one of their number died, which went some way to obscuring Victorian mourning traditions associated with the dead. One woman remembered that her grandfather, who lost a brother in the war,

> acted in accordance to Victorian values. There were certain subjects that had a memorial in their house, and was surrounded by black silk or black netting with gold thread and handmade pearl buttons. Black memorial papers and stationary were kept in a pine drawer and were padlocked with a piece of ageing silk coverning [*sic*] it... I was told by my 'father', as Grandma addressed him, in front of me; that the subject of the first world war was private and that 'children' (referring to me), were not given 'permission' to think or talk about it... when my English grandparents died, these commemorative objects were quietly and discreetly packed in boxes of many sizes and mailed somewhere. I do not know where and nobody ever told me.[13]

In this instance, the family not only refused to discuss the war with their granddaughter, eliminating oral family memory processes, but continued to mourn the dead through material items in the home. The Victorian tradition of swathing memorial items with black cloth, in this family at least, continued throughout the interwar period and, perhaps, into the postwar years. Shattered familial attitudes towards a First World War death in the family ensured that their granddaughter had no meaningful way of connecting to her family's wartime past.

The effects of this loss of material markers of loss, when accompanied by the loss of living memory of the deceased, resulted in a considerably weakened family memory. People who had known the dead as adults were no longer there to reminisce, discuss, and actively remember. Instead the job of continued memorialization fell onto those who may not have had as strong a memory of the dead, such as siblings, who may have been young when their brother or sister died—although many kept a version of their memory alive

[13] Mass Observation, Autumn 2014, H1470.

until their own deaths in the 1960s and 1970s. These memory changes in the 1940s and 1950s did not wholly destroy family understandings of their ancestors, but began to test family memory, as the people and memorial items which acted as memory prompts were lost. If these memories became diluted before the Second World War, by the 1960s and 1970s, as veterans of the war became elderly, and those whose loved ones died in early twentieth-century disasters were similarly ageing, cultural ideas of war and disaster could dominate, and family memories fused with these external ways of understanding the past.

The 1970s and 1980s marked a particularly important moment for family memory of the First World War because it was during these decades that the brothers and sisters of those who died also began to pass away. During these decades a powerful memory transmission took place as those with a lived memory of the events passed away, leaving the next generation to continue family memory practices. The siblings of those who died in mining disasters were also ageing, and it was largely only those who had lost a loved one in a later mining disaster, such as Gresford in 1934, who survived beyond the 1980s. What this meant in practice was that throughout the last three decades of the twentieth century family memories of the war and disaster met with cultural memory. People who remembered the events first-hand passed away, leaving broader understandings in their stead. Yet, running alongside these culturally constructed memories were family ones, which interacted with and were influenced by larger narratives, particularly surrounding the myth of war.

Wary of the pitfalls of these memory changes, some families and individuals tried to place their loved one's First World War mementos in museum collections, to bolster their public memory and cement it in the cultural sphere.[14] These items could reveal countercultural testimony from family members which fought against the dominant memory of the war as tragic. In the 1980s a woman donated some of her brother's objects to the Durham Light Infantry Museum. He had died during the Battle of the Somme and she wanted to donate his objects to an institution she felt would honour his memory. She explained to the curator of the collection that she had the option to donate his memorabilia to a technical college a few years previously, but had declined because 'so many of these lecturers are against war for any cause and use any records to denigrate bravery and talk about jingoism that I did not respond'. She explained that her brother's 'one desire was to go to the front

[14] Ann-Marie Foster, '"We decided the museum was the best place for them": Veterans, Families and Mementoes of the First World War', *History & Memory* 31:1 (2019), 87–117.

and fight for freedom, like so many of his generation'.[15] However, while people placed these objects in repositories that they thought would keep the individual memory of the dead alive, without family histories of the individual attached, a homogenous view of the war dead began to emerge, and individual understandings of family histories were subsumed by the emerging cultural memory of war.

When trying to understand how family and cultural memories work in tandem, Susan Hill's 1989 preface to a reprint of her 1971 novel *Strange Meeting* is particularly useful. Hill provides an articulate discussion of her motivation for writing a novel about the First World War, offering an illuminating example of how the two memory types meet:

> When I was a small child, we used to visit my maternal grandmother and her sister, a Great Aunt, who lived in another time. They had come from a large family, and used to talk about it to me sometimes. There were eight sisters altogether, including one named Elizabeth, who came to a terrible end, burned to death when her nightdress caught fire as she lit the range early one morning. That story became engraved upon my memory. It still is.
>
> But there was another one, too, which had almost as great an impact. The eight sisters had just one brother, cherished and idolised by them all, of course. When he was eighteen, he went to war—the Great War, as they called it, the 1914–1918 War. On his nineteenth birthday, he was killed, like so many thousands of other young men, at the Battle of the Somme.
>
> I don't think the family was ever the same again, nor so many families like it. He was a young man from a whole generation which was, quite simply, wiped out.
>
> They had a photograph of him in his uniform, and I used to take it down and look at it. He had such a young face, even I could see that, as a child, he was not much more than a child himself. His ears stuck out, I remember, and his hair was cut very, very short under his cap. His Christian name was Sidney, and the family surname was Owen. It is a coincidence, of course, but the long arm of *that*, as they say, is a long one, and I am a believer in these small signs and symbols, as important parts of one's life.[16]

Although the death of the sister was the one that most emotionally affected Hill, it was the death of the soldier that imparted such a compelling desire to

[15] Durham Light Infantry Collection Donor Files: Letter to DLI, 23.01.1987. Unknown Acc No.
[16] Susan Hill, *Strange Meeting* (Harlow, 1989), pp. vi–vii.

tell the story of others who experienced the war—rather than the many lives lost through flannelette fires. Here, the cultural weight of the war far exceeded the social history of women's domestic deaths.

Hill went on to describe the research she undertook to write the novel, explaining that she read

> row upon row of memoirs, diaries, and letters by soldiers of the First World War, many of them privately printed by relatives, after the deaths of their young authors. I read volumes of autobiography, like Robert Graves's *Goodbye to All That*, and those of Siegfried Sassoon and Guy Chapman. I read the poets major and minor, I read long official histories and biographies of the Kaiser and General Haig, I read one novel only, Remarque's *All Quiet on the Western Front*.[17]

In this retelling of her research methods Hill unwittingly fell into the trap of the cultural memory of war. The cultural memory of war as pathos-laden was built on the backs of the war poets, Wilfred Owen, Siegfried Sassoon, Rupert Brooke, whose work has assumed a hefty cultural weight in the decades since it was first written.[18] By focusing on upper and middle-class accounts which centred the tragic male experience of war, Hill perpetuated a narrative which focused on the irony of war. Through reading about these experiences on the Western Front, she decided to write about soldiers, 'in the trenches, not anywhere else. For it was the trenches that were the real, black heart of that war.'[19] Given the cultural memory of the war that had solidified by the time she was researching her novel, it is hardly surprising that this is the conclusion that she reached.

Hill's description of her writing process belies the fusion of the great war narrative with family memory. The overarching cultural memories narrated by Hill as heavily focused on the Western Front, with a link to the Battle of the Somme, and to her great-uncle, who, by virtue of a name, was associated with the war poet Wilfred Owen, are the hallmarks of the pathos-laden narrative of the war. Yet this wider narrative is linked to both ephemera and family memory. Hill recalled Owen's photograph, the image of the dead kept in the family home, and recounts the idolization of the brother by his sisters,

[17] Hill, *Strange Meeting*, p. viii.

[18] Santanu Das, 'Reframing First World War Poetry', in Santanu Das (ed.), *The Cambridge Companion to the Poetry of the First World War* (Cambridge, 2013), 3–34.

[19] Hill, *Strange Meeting*, p. viii.

implicitly passed down to Hill by recalled tales and discussions of both him and his death.

If the culture of war was highly distinctive, what were the characteristics associated with the memory of disaster? Unlike war, which has a strong popular narrative developed through state response and cultural outputs, the memory of disaster was less officially guided. Memories of individual disasters stay strong, but disasters as a general workplace hazard which ended in tragedy, rather than the result of a series of decisions made by management, married with unsafe working practices, are all that are remembered of dangerous professions. Roger Laidlaw has charted the cultural memory of the Gresford disaster, arguing that it transformed from a bitter argument over how the disaster began, where management were shown to have forged safety documents after the disaster, to a memory which glossed over this important part of workplace history.[20] At the disaster's inquiry Stafford Cripps, a former barrister turned Labour MP, delivered such a resounding closing statement blaming managers for preventable deaths that it was published by The Miner's Federation.[21] Despite this contemporary recognition that the Gresford deaths were avoidable, this anger at managers was lost in the intervening years, and by the 1990s the disaster was remembered as a tragic loss of life, and not as a workplace injustice.

Mining disasters were brought into wider memorial practice through attempts to recognize these losses in a similar way to wartime deaths. At the Durham Miners' Gala, an annual celebration of the mining community, a special service to memorialize those who died in workplace accidents is still held.[22] Significantly, since the 1940s war and mining were commemorated together in certain religious spaces. The Miners' Memorial in Durham Cathedral, unveiled in 1947, included a book of names of miners killed at work. The mining memorial shares space with a First World War chapel, which has its own Roll of Honour on public display. In this culturally significant space for miners, the memory of their profession directly assumed similar forms to war memorials, drawing visual memorial links between mining and war and using similar memorial forms to elevate mining deaths to sit alongside wartime ones. To some extent this worked, as mining heritage was increasingly celebrated and looked to as a way of understanding community,

[20] Roger Laidlaw, 'The Gresford Disaster in Popular Memory', *Llafur* 6 (1995), 124–6.

[21] Mineworkers' Federation of Great Britain, 'Gresford Disaster: Report of the Speech by Sir Stafford Cripps, K.C. at the Government Inquiry into the Causes of the Disaster, April 15th, 16th and 17th, 1936' (London, 1936).

[22] Davies, *Mors Britannica*, 89.

particularly after the industry was privatized in the 1980s and 1990s. Amidst this backdrop of nascent cultural memory, the families of people who died in a disaster still relied on oral histories and objects to pass on their histories down the family line.

This destruction of family material and loss of living memory prompted remaining family members to found associations to remember people who died in war or disaster. The Western Front Association was founded in 1980 by the descendants of those who fought in order to keep the memory of the war alive.[23] Remembrance groups were also created by people whose families were involved in disasters, and form part of the wider heritage boom which began in the 1980s and remained strong throughout the next couple of decades. The Belfast Titanic Society, for instance, was established in 1992 by people whose family members worked on the ship, and by those whose family members did not survive.[24] Some of the most impressive grassroots memorial sites are run by those remembering mining disasters. The Aber Valley Heritage Group, established in 2008, created a museum which contains memorial items to the Senghenydd disasters, donated by family members, alongside a Facebook community which offers members a digital space to commemorate the dead.

Modern memorials to the dead of disasters were also commissioned and unveiled in the 1990s and early 2000s, often fuelled by family members who pushed for recognition for their ancestors. An early forerunner of this was the Gresford disaster memorial, constructed in 1982, which was created after a grassroots campaign led by Margaret Clapper, whose brother John died in the disaster. In the 1990s, examples include the 1909 West Stanley disaster memorial, unveiled in 1995, and the 1918 Stanrigg mining disaster memorial, constructed in 1998. Many of these memorials were only made possible by the closing of mines in the locality, which offered mining communities a space to commemorate the past dangers their professional forebearers experienced.

National commemoration of the war has, since the early 2000s, focused on family connections to the conflict, which has been felt in full force during centenary commemorations.[25] McCartney posits that family memory of the First World War has been dominated by a minority of families whose soldier ancestor met a tragic end, and for many families, 'finding a connection to the

[23] Brian Bond, *The Unquiet Western Front* (Cambridge, 2002), 90.

[24] Belfast Titanic Society, 'About Us', https://www.belfast-titanic.com/pages/index.asp?title=About_the_Belfast_Titanic_Society_ [Accessed 07.04.2021].

[25] See Todman, 'The Ninetieth Anniversary', 30–2, for a discussion of family memory being called upon in the 2006 Somme commemorations.

First World War is a rediscovery'.[26] These memories are not personal ones, and instead form a part of Marianne Hirsch's 'postmemory', which is 'distinguished from memory by generational distance and from history by deep personal connection'.[27] Hirsch uses the term to describe those who grew up surrounded by older family members whose lives were dominated by traumatic experiences.[28] Those whose families were deeply impacted by the loss of a loved one in war or disaster may well experience an intense family memory influenced by these tragic events, which has influenced the forms of memory passed down through generations.

Encountering Family Histories during the Centenary

The centenary of the First World War in Britain heightened the cult of the dead soldier and ritualized remembrance in a highly specific way. In 2012 David Cameron set the tone for the centenary commemorations that were to follow two years later, suggesting that the war was male and military service based, and arguing that the scale of sacrifice, the legacy for international relations, and the emotional and family connections meant that the war was worthy of national commemoration.[29] The tension within British commemoration of the war was particularly drawn out through school centenary projects. Schoolchildren were introduced to the war through literary texts, which, as Ann-Marie Einhaus has argued, are 'better suited to fostering a sense of national unity than the celebration of a victory that not everyone will feel equally able to share'.[30] Catriona Pennell's work has shown how battlefield tours aimed at schoolchildren were remarkably militarized, although she argues that youths on such tours reacted to this in complex ways.[31] Amidst a national understanding of the war dead as both sacrificial and tragic, families continued to remember their dead in private, while being given opportunities to share their histories on a national stage.

[26] McCartney, 'The First World War Soldier', 305.

[27] Marianne Hirsch, *Family Frames: Photography, Narrative, and Postmemory* (Cambridge, 2002), 22; Aline Cordonnier, Valérie Rousoux, Anne-Sophie Gijs, and Oliver Luminet, 'Collective Memory: An Hourglass between the Collective and the Individual', *Memory, Mind & Media* 1 (2022), 4.

[28] Hirsch, *Family Frames*, 23.

[29] Lucy Noakes, 'Centenary (United Kingdom)', in Ute Daniel, Peter Gatrell, Oliver Janz, Heather Jones, Jennifer Keene, Alan Kramer, and Bill Nasson (eds.), *1914–1918 Online: International Encyclopedia of the First World War* (2019), DOI: 10.15463/ie1418.11369.

[30] Ann-Marie Einhaus, 'Cultural Memory, Teaching and Contemporary Writing about the First World War', *Literature & History* 25:2 (2015), 190.

[31] Catriona Pennell, '"Remembrance isn't working": First World War Battlefield Tours and the Militarisation of British Youth during the Centenary', *Childhood* 27:3 (2020), 383–98.

The material culture of memorialization continued to be paramount to family remembrance, which was very often based around memorial objects handed down through generations. Modern sociological studies have shown that the objects that retain an importance to people are ones that remind them of other people.[32] Family members often want memories to stay attached to their objects, and passing selected items down through generational lines can be a strong way of creating feelings of family continuity.[33] One archaeologist, presented with his grandfather's diary, suggested that it was of such importance to him because 'the object stands for a family member I never met'.[34] These objects were accompanied by tales of their original owner, and family members were often concerned that these memories would be lost to time. When memories are retained, however, memorial objects become a visible way of accessing intergenerational family memory. They can be photographed, shared, and offer a shorthand for family members to explain a tragic event to subsequent generations. While family memory is not contained within objects, they are a useful tool for helping people to explain their family past, especially now, when online collections and 'antiques roadshow' style show-and-tell events ask people to bring their objects to be digitized. Because families created these items after war and disaster deaths, the memory of the individual they commemorate has been passed down through family lines. As has been shown elsewhere in this book, this process started as soon as a loved one died, but, as this chapter emphasizes, these memorial legacies could be powerful reminders of the dead long after their immediate family passed away, and now form a bridge between family and cultural understandings of war.

The most common way of remembering a loved one, through discussion and reminiscing, often based around objects, is traceable through the histories that families told about the dead, which have remained in the families to the present day. These anecdotal memories of the dead could be very detailed, but more often than not are now oft-told accounts of key moments in family history. In 2014 *The Chronicle* newspaper created online galleries of family memories and objects which showed that many families only knew the basics of their ancestor's war service and death. Some were able to comment on their

[32] Helen Holmes, 'Material Affinities: "Doing" Family through the Practices of Passing on', *Sociology* 53:1 (2019), 174–91; Mihaly Csikszentmihalyi, 'Why We Need Things', in S. Lubar and W. D. Kingery (eds.), *History from Things: Essays in Material Culture* (London, 1993), 27.

[33] Anna Woodham, Laura King, Liz Gloyn, Vicky Crewe, and Fiona Blair, 'We Are What We Keep: The "Family Archive", Identity and Public/Private Heritage', *Heritage & Society* 10:3 (2017), 207, 213–14.

[34] John Schofield, 'Message and Materiality in Mesopotamia, 1916–1917: My Grandfather's Diary, Social Commemoration and the Experience of the War', in Nicholas Saunders and Paul Cornish (eds.), *Contested Objects: Material Memories of the Great War* (London, 2009), 203.

legacy for the family, such as Samuel Pipe's unnamed fiancée, who never remarried and who was remembered as a great-aunt who 'was single for the rest of her life and often spoke lovingly of her Sam'.[35]

Objects were often at the heart of long-term family memory practices, and small items which were on display in family homes in the immediate aftermath of war and disaster were the ones that were kept by the family. One woman reflected that the only photograph of her grandfather she knew of was him in his army uniform, and not one with his wife and children, commenting, 'I think there is nothing sadder.'[36] Another woman noted that she placed a photograph of her great-uncle Alfred, who died at the Somme, on the mantelpiece for the centenary, and that she had commemorated him by giving her son the same second name as her ancestor.[37] Items which are easy to display and which hold personal meaning have been the ones which have extended through time, linking the past and the present within family homes.

Family objects have also proved a way of connecting to a particularly intricate memory of the First World War in Northern Ireland. The centenary commemorations on the island of Ireland were fraught with competing versions of the past, and official commemorations have emphasized plural histories which have stressed shared understandings of a politically freighted past.[38] What this difficult past means is that for many families simply admitting that they had family members who fought in the First World War, the Easter Rising, Irish War of Independence, or Civil War, or other key moments of national memory in this period, is a politically charged experience. Although many families on the island of Ireland have histories which contain Irish Republican Army volunteers and British Army members, these complex family histories can be hard to access, or can be caught in volatile political spaces.[39]

Where First World War memories are present, particularly in Northern Ireland, they are generally kept within the family. The playwright Brenda Winter-Palmer remembered seeing a framed Next of Kin Memorial Plaque in her childhood home, given to her mother by her father because

[35] Catherine Arthur, 'Your World War One Heroes: see our eight gallery of readers' family stories and pictures', *Chronicle Live*, 10 November 2014 (https://www.chroniclelive.co.uk/lifestyle/nostalgia/your-world-war-one-heroes-8049391).

[36] MO, Autumn 2014, 03436ab. [37] MO, Autumn 2014, A3434.

[38] Department of Tourism, Culture, Arts, Gaeltacht, Sport and Media, 'About Us—Decade of Centenaries', https://www.decadeofcentenaries.com/about/ [Accessed 12.03.2021].

[39] See, for example, Brian Hanley, 'Charley Bourne, Jack Ford and the Green Fields of France', in Horne and Madigan (eds.), *Towards Commemoration*, 105–13. For a discussion of how different family memories are present on the island of Ireland see Ciara Boylan, Sarah-Anne Buckley, and Pat Dolan (eds.), *Family Histories of the Irish Revolution* (Dublin, 2017).

> in all of the Kerr family of twelve children she was the one who polished it. No one in the family had talked much about him. Indeed in the 1970s in West Belfast not very many people talked freely about family connections with the British Army.[40]

Her uncle, a Catholic from West Belfast, chose to join the predominantly Unionist 36th Ulster Division, and was the subject of a play that Winter-Palmer wrote for the Living Legacies 1914–18 project as a way to reclaim her family history. Cross-community initiatives such as this, which explore families whose ancestors had members fighting in both wars, have led to some understanding of how families in the past interacted with different conflicts in varied ways.

Others have found the mention of a family member in the First World War a shock, as it was not spoken about in any meaningful way in their household.[41] Asif Shakoor has written about how he learned of his grandfather's war service from correspondence kept by his grandmother, which was only found in 2011.[42] This discovery led to deep family research, including trying to find Mahomed Gama's medals, which were sent to Britain as proof of service and never returned. For Shakoor, as with many others, a chance finding has led to a rediscovery of their family history.

For many, these family rediscoveries, even when unrelated to the serviceperson in question, have led to individuals holding the family archive. After one family admitted to their relatives that they were going to dispose of photographs of ancestors who died in the First World War a distant relative claimed them, unable to let them be destroyed or lost.[43] Even in families that have some idea of their ancestor's experiences they can be disconnected to the modern family. In one family home in Stockport the portrait of an officer with his family is prominently displayed, and the family attach a poppy to the frame, despite nobody knowing how he is related to them.[44] By the time families are two or more generations away from the dead, different people can easily adopt family responsibility for them, forging an emotional connection

[40] Brenda Walker-Palmer, 'Living Legacies 1914–18: A Note from the Director', http://www.livinglegacies1914-18.ac.uk/Old-Site/www.qub.ac.uk/sites/LivingLegacies1914-18/HostedSites/MedalintheDrawer/DirectorsNote/index.html [Accessed 12.03.2021].

[41] For a discussion of how silence has impacted the memory of the war see Jay Winter, *War Beyond Words* (Cambridge, 2017).

[42] Asif Shakoor, 'BAME Seafarers in the First World War: The Story of Mahomed Gama', Port Towns & Urban Cultures, 15 February 2018. Available http://porttowns.port.ac.uk/bame_ww1_mahomed-gama/ [Accessed 02.08.2021].

[43] MO, Autumn 2014, M2986.

[44] MO, Autumn 2014, N5545.

to a distant relative and assuming control of their memorial objects. Yet some people have found these rediscoveries of family narratives distasteful, with one Mass Observation writer commenting that they had 'noticed (only in the media admittedly) the sentimental adoption by people of a forebearer who died in the conflict as a kind of First World War mascot'.[45]

Families who kept their memorial items in the family could, by the time of the centenary of the First World War, be disconnected from their original owner. While some families treasured their objects, new generations did not necessarily share these sentiments. The great-grandson of a man who was killed in the war was given his medals in a commemorative box for Christmas by his grandparents. In 2014 he reflected:

> I was rather unimpressed as they didn't mean much to me. I think it was because I knew so little about my great-grandfather. I can't even remember a picture of him. Since my grandparents have no [*sic*] both died I think the medals are very important to my father and his brother…I wonder what will happen to them [the medals]. My cousins and I might take them, I suppose they will go to the great-great-great grandchildren of their original owner.[46]

Another man, who kept an image of a family member who won a Victoria Cross on their study wall, commented that, contrary to the placement of objects in his home, 'we do not attach much import to these mementoes'.[47]

Wary of this loss of meaning in families, some attempted to guard their objects against this memory degradation. One woman placed a note inside a filigree box that had been bought for her by her dead brother so that the meaning of the item would not be lost to time.[48] These ambivalent owners were, in some respects, the lucky ones. In 2014 a blog on Ancestry.com estimated that 7.5 million Britons were 'in the dark about their family connection' to the First World War.[49] The centenary brought with it some panic about whether families had connections to the war or not. For many, this has not been a straightforward question to answer.

Similar levels of knowledge about the dead of mining disasters can be found in family accounts, and single stories about their death or its effect on the family come to dominate family narratives of the dead. One man recalled that his father, whose own father died in the blast, remembered the 1916

[45] MO, Autumn 2014, B3227.
[46] MO, Autumn 2014, L5604.
[47] MO, Autumn 2014, W4925.
[48] MO, Autumn 2014, R1227.
[49] Ancestry.com, 'One Million World War I Heroes Forgotten by Descendants', 29 July 2014 (https://blogs.ancestry.co.uk/ancestry/2014/07/29/one-million-world-war-i-heroes-forgotten-by-descendants/).

Woodhorn colliery disaster because nobody wished him a happy birthday the day after, his fourteenth birthday.[50] On the centenary of the West Stanley mining disaster the family of Thomas Killingbrake told a local newspaper of their understanding of their ancestor's death: that he survived for some time after the disaster in a pocket of air, but went back to look for his brother-in-law, which is how he died.[51] During the same centenary another family expressed shock that their grandfather's family had been involved in an explosion at all. Their grandfather, Lewis Smith, had been injured a couple of days before the explosion, so his brother went to work in his stead, a not uncommon practice at the time. His brother died in the explosion. Reflecting on it a century later, a family member said:

> it was a long time before any of us even knew about the mining disaster. Maybe Lewis, my grandfather, felt awful because John went to work and it should have been him. We will never know because he never talked about it, so we do not know the effect it had on the family.[52]

Although Lewis's granddaughter did not know the effect it had on her grandfather, by rediscovering this family history she could reflect on how his silence influenced the family, including the surprise about it being hidden for so long.

For many, airing family histories during centenaries was a way of claiming public recognition for an ancestor's actions. In an interview for the 'War Widows' Stories' project Maggie Goren offered a lucid discussion of the effect her grandfather's death had on the family. It especially impacted her father, Herbert Evans, who was 6 when his father died. The death of Evans's father brought out particularly strong emotions throughout his adolescence. An event that was passed through the family was the receipt of her grandfather's war medal, which so upset her father that as a child he 'took this medal out of the box, he threw it across the room, and he stamped on the box'.[53] Goren attributes this to anger felt at receiving this medal as the only token of family loss sent by the government. His family should have received at least two other medals for his war service, and a Next of Kin Memorial Plaque, but these items do not seem to have been remembered, if indeed they were ever received.

[50] *Chronicle Live*, 'How the Woodhorn Colliery disaster 100 years ago changed a community', 13 August 2016.

[51] *Northern Echo*, 9 February 2009. [52] *Northern Echo*, 13 February 2009.

[53] Interview with Maggie Goren, in Nadine Muller and Ailbhe McDaid, *War Widows' Stories: A Collection of Oral History Interviews* ([Liverpool], 2017), 147–8.

Reflecting on her father's experience Goren suggests that 'he was really deeply affected by the loss of his father':

> it had an effect on the way he thought and behaved and that trickled down to our generation really. He was a man who found it very difficult to express his emotions. But he was a man of great principle and there were times in family history where things went wrong and he was always there. But he wasn't a man who could express his emotions and you wonder if that goes back to the time of losing his father...and his mother, perhaps how she dealt with it...my father said it was the only time he ever saw her weep, shortly before she died [in 1948]. So...there were many, many years of not weeping.[54]

Goren recalled that when her grandmother died she thought, 'that lady hasn't had a life...It bothered me. I thought how could she manage four children, four sons. How did she bring them up? I don't know. And my parents never talked about it.'[55] Goren's fascination with her grandmother reflects tentative studies into broader trends about modern family memory, where family narratives focus on the personality traits and endurance of ancestral family members in coping with unexpected events.[56] For Goren, much of her family story revolved around unspoken difficulties and suffering, alongside a fascination with resilience, which pivoted around her father's reluctance to talk about his experience. Goren's account throws up interesting questions of interpretation. We should bear in mind Roper's warning about the difficulties in understanding other people's life histories. In interpreting one woman's life history he reflected that although he saw the First World War as having stifled her opportunities, she interpreted her life as well-lived.[57] Goren's family history may have been difficult, but how her ancestors felt about it is missing from the conversation.

Goren was frank about her reasons for wanting to donate her family history to this public project. She contacted the 'War Widows' Stories' project to talk about her grandmother's experiences. After hearing about the project on the BBC Radio 4 programme 'Women's Hour' she 'wanted my grandmother's

[54] Interview with Goren, *War Widows' Stories*, 148.
[55] Interview with Goren, *War Widows' Stories*, 149.
[56] Green, 'Intergenerational Family Stories', 396.
[57] Michael Roper, 'Little Ruby's Hard: Young Women and the Emotional Experience of Caregiving in Britain after the First World War', in Claire Langhammer, Lucy Noakes, and Claudia Siebrecht, *Total War: An Emotional History* (Oxford, 2020), 76.

story told for my father's sake...I thought it would be nice...to get in touch and offer what I knew about my grandmother...as a sort of plea to for goodness sakes stop this fighting gentlemen.'[58] Her own pacifist feelings, which she attributed to her upbringing and her husband's experiences in the Israeli Army, fed into her desire to talk about the effects of war which reverberated down her family line in a public project. This is a rare example of someone publicly articulating why they want to place their family memory in the public sphere. A strong political viewpoint helped to prompt this decision, and Goren's family memory was strong enough that she felt compelled to tell it at such a historical remove.

Modern Memory and the Digital Turn

This presentation of family experience as a witness to history, as seen in Goren's account, is similarly present in digital spaces, and internet-based memorialization now calls attention to individual lives and deaths. Digital sites are of immense importance in allowing the families of the dead ownership of their ancestors' experiences and publicly remembering them through commemorative spaces. These spaces are both formal and informal. The memories of mining disaster victims are often supported through Facebook groups, or even through comments underneath news stories published on the anniversaries of prominent disasters. First World War families also share similar spaces, but, since the late 2000s, have also been offered a more formalized way of recording their memories through institutional websites and 'antiques roadshow' style collection drives. First World War digital memories are therefore being led by top-down memory actors (museums, archives, libraries, and universities) in a way that disaster memories are not. Digital memories of war have continued to be remembered through formalized spaces, whereas the digital memory of disaster is still largely based in community sites. Through this digital commemoration a new form of engaged e-memorialization is emerging, which will likely feed back into family remembrance practices for decades to come.

By the late 2010s, families of the war and disaster dead were on the cusp of losing their personal family memories to cultural ones. This follows the natural pace of commemorative lifecycles. Aleida Assmann suggests that anecdotes from a person's past can be transmitted in the form of communicative

[58] Interview with Goren, *War Widows' Stories*, 155.

memory, which means that these tales last between eighty to a hundred years.[59] As such, the war and disaster dead should have mostly passed out of this communicative memory transfer by now. The memories of the war and disaster dead are now cultural memory forms, characterized by visual cues, institutions of learning, and commemoration rites.[60] But the internet has changed this, and families are now able to remember the dead in online spaces. Anecdotal memory can now be digitally preserved, lengthening and extending the reach of family history in public. Not every family has enough information about their ancestors to share this, nor the resources or inclination to do so, but for those who do engage in this form of commemoration, internet spaces of historical remembrance offer a way of extending family memory of the dead.

Over the past twenty years the family history boom has made people interact with their digital family past in new and inventive ways, which often revolve around the emotional connection forged through family history research. It is clear that people who were not involved in historical events can hold an emotional connection to them, especially when it comes to the memory of war.[61] This emotionality is a positive in many ways—it engages people with history and can allow for radical reinterpretations of the past.[62] Where it can be complicated, however, is when the emotionality of commemoration gets swept up in emotional understandings of the family. The centenary of the First World War in particular has brought into sharp relief the contours of family memory and its limitations.

It is in the modern memory of the conflict, here used as a shorthand for the first two decades of the twenty-first century, that we can see how the legacies constructed across the previous hundred years have influenced family commemoration. It is highly contingent. Family memory of war and disaster sometimes passed through generational lines, and sometimes did not. The ones that did not have, in some cases, been resurrected by families in the past two decades. While much detail has been lost, with the advent of the internet and the popularity of family research much is also rediscovered, and families

[59] Aleida Assmann, 'Memory, Individual and Collective', in Robert E Gooding and Charles Tilly (eds.), *The Oxford Handbook of Contextual Political Analysis* (Oxford, 2006), 210–24; Aleida Assmann, 'Transformations between History and Memory', *Social Research* 75:1 (2008), 213–14.

[60] Assmann, 'Transformations between History and Memory', 55–6; Jan Assmann, *Religion and Cultural Memory: Ten Studies*, translated by Rodney Livingstone (Stanford, 2006), 24.

[61] Dan Todman, 'The Ninetieth Anniversary of the Battle of the Somme', in Michael Keren and Holger H. Herwig (eds.), *War Memory and Popular Culture: Essays on Modes of Remembrance and Commemoration* (London, 2009), 27.

[62] Evans, 'How Do Family Historians Work with Memory?', 93.

have, in some cases, placed absent family members back in their genealogical narrative. When these family memories are placed on the internet, a new kind of family memory emerges, which runs alongside and forms part of the cultural memory of war. This 'rediscovery' interrupts easy understandings of memory following a set course, and, since the centenary of the First World War, family and cultural history now run alongside each other in the digital sphere in an unprecedented way.

Informal family memory can be traced through social media and community initiatives. Local history groups on Facebook often post items remembering disasters which attract people who have lost family members. For example, the group 'Stanley's History', a local history group in County Durham, posted a 2015 Facebook post about the footballer Kevin Keegan, whose grandfather survived the West Stanley disaster, unveiling the memorial to the dead of the explosion. Underneath people posted that 'some of my family were in the disaster', with one commenter linking his family's experience in a different part of the Durham coalfield, saying that 'my grandad died at a one at sacriston pit disaster'.[63] These sorts of comments are not uncommon, and those with an interest in local and family history often comment on their relationships with historical events through family connections. This link to wider histories through ancestry is integral to wider remembrance practices. In former mining communities family blood ties to mining disasters are still emphasized in memorial work. On the hundredth anniversary of the Woodhorn colliery disaster, children who were related to the men lost, or who had connections with Woodhorn, laid roses for the deceased.[64] Physical sites of mining memory are still popular and have a strong community presence, although these are mirrored in online spaces.

It is in online spaces which appeal to people with a familial connection to the First World War that we can clearly see where family memory and cultural memory merge. In 2018, a report from the 'London Jews in the First World War: We Were There Too' project, which documented the experience of Jewish communities in wartime, found that there was a particular urgency to completing it, as 'first-generation descendants and holders of the memorabilia

[63] Stanley's History, 12 January 2015, https://www.facebook.com/stanleyshistory/posts/kevin-keegan-opening-the-memorial-statue-the-west-stanley-pit-disaster-also-know/592810334196500/ [Accessed 28.04.2021].

[64] '100 years on from the Woodhorn pit disaster, the painful memories still linger', *Chronicle Live*, 13 August 2016, https://www.chroniclelive.co.uk/news/north-east-news/100-years-woodhorn-pit-disaster-11745164#comments-section [Accessed 28.04.2021].

were themselves now very elderly'.[65] Reflecting further, the report explained that the coordinators 'did not anticipate the volume of material, very often of significant importance and rarity, that lie in private hands'.[66] This project, which digitized items of family history relating to the war, was one of a series of similar projects, all hoping to document the rich legacy of private material held in private spaces during the First World War centenary. It is in many ways of no surprise that there are rich collections of family material: domestic spaces are precisely where family memories concentrate, crystallizing around material which is of great significance to individuals who do not perhaps think it is of interest to the world at large. Family memory and memorial items have been kept within families for the past century, and it was only in the centenary of the First World War that institutions took an interest in, or had the funding to support, these personal histories.

The two digital collection initiatives discussed over the next few pages, 'British Jews in the First World War: We Were There Too', a community-based project which grew into a national one, and the Imperial War Museum's 'Lives of the First World War', a national project, emphasize the ways that family memory has now turned digital. The 'British Jews in the First World War' site is a cross-community project which began as an effort to capture and record the experience of Jewish communities in London during the First World War through a digital archive. The project has a 'history' area which focuses on the East End of London during the First World War, a collection of life stories about people affected by the war, and an online space to memorialize them. Although the 'history' section focuses on London, people affected by the war across Britain are recorded and remembered. There was genuine engagement with the project, and people who donated were excited about seeing their family history online. Interim project findings indicated that people who donated to the project were particularly relieved that '"their story" had now less chance of being lost'.[67]

'Lives of the First World War' was launched in May 2014 and was an online attempt to document the lives of those involved in the British war effort during the First World War. Members of the public could donate items and histories relating to individuals. The site was initially populated through record sets supplied by Findmypast, an online genealogical research company, and members of the public could add additional information to the individual

[65] London Jews in the First World War: We Were There Too, 'Evaluation Document, Initial Phase January 2016–January 2018' (London, 2018), 5.

[66] London Jews in the First World War, 'Evaluation Document', 12.

[67] London Jews in the First World War, 'Evaluation Document', 12.

records created through collaboration with the company, or suggest the names of people who were missing. Altogether, approximately 7.7 million individual histories were collected.[68] Sometimes these additions can reveal a memorial motive for adding information to a record. One man briefly told the story of his uncle, writing, 'I know my Dad cherished Charlie's memory. The older of my brothers has Charles as a middle name and Charlie's "Death Penny" was always displayed at our family home.'[69] On the whole, however, examples of family members providing the emotional reasons for donation are rare.

Significantly, both projects built permanent digital remembrance into their platforms. 'British Jews in the First World War' allowed people to digitally remember the dead through an online yahrzeit for the First World War dead. The 'Memorial Wall' displays the photographs of the individuals being remembered on the anniversary of their death, alongside their name. People could choose to remember someone already on the site through clicking the candle icon next to their entry, or could add a record before remembering the individual, if they were not already on the site. This site was intended to act as a long-term memorial, and in 2021, for a fee of £50, individuals could permanently memorialize their chosen person.[70] Following a slightly different model, the 'Lives of the First World War' site was live for people to add information to until 2019, and has now transitioned into a 'permanent digital memorial'.[71] As James Wallis argued at the beginning of the centenary, the emotionality of remembrance has the potential to transform a personal connection to a memorial presentation, translated into the digital realm through the online portal.[72] Visitors were able to click on the 'Remember' button on a 'Life Story' to commemorate that individual, although this function was frozen when the site changed from its active phase and became a memorial.

Both digital projects were designed as repositories of data and places of remembrance, which is a tricky combination to balance. Serge ter Braake has written about the tension within large-scale digital projects which try to provide a repository of 'factual information' while acting as a memorial for individuals and communities affected by the subject matter. He suggests that the two

[68] House of Commons DCMS 'Lessons from the First World War', 18.

[69] Imperial War Museum, 'Lives of the First World War: Charles Thomas Colbert' https://livesofthefirstworldwar.iwm.org.uk/story/33429 [Accessed 09.04.2021].

[70] British Jews in the First World War, 'What is a Yahrzeit?', https://www.jewsfww.uk/what-is-a-yahrzeit.php [Accessed 15.01.2021].

[71] IWM, 'Find out more about Lives of the First World War', https://livesofthefirstworldwar.iwm.org.uk/about [Accessed 20.01.2021].

[72] Wallis, '"Great-grandfather, what did *you* do in the Great War?"', 32.

goals can be difficult to reconcile, because they are doing different public work: the former appeals to people who study the past whilst the latter works for people wanting to remember the event in question, perhaps not in the complex way the data suggests.[73] Families donating their family history to these online collections were both trying to ensure that their family history is remembered globally, and, through the act of donating and remembering, commemorate the dead. One is an action for posterity, while the other is a call for recognition in the present.

These two digital memorials dedicated to people who served in the First World War have allowed distant family members to publicly commemorate their loved ancestors. Contemporary memorialization on the web is characterized by social spaces which bring together family, friends, colleagues, and others to remember the dead in ways they previously would not have interacted with.[74] What is significant about the 'Lives' Remember button and the 'British Jews in the First World War' yahrzeit page is that they use modern memorial techniques for people with whom those remembering have no living connection. This application of modern memorialization techniques to the long dead is an innovative way of bringing the dead into discussion with those alive today. Yet this treatment of the dead in a modern manner forces them out of their natural memorial pattern, when their memory fades from social groups after a hundred years.

There is a certain amount of emotional performativity in engaging with these sites. This 'doing' and showing of emotion is clearly important to the individuals using the Remember button to commemorate the dead.[75] They allow the families of the dead, and online community members, a chance to action their emotions in a digital and recognizable space. The reclamation of the dead through the internet allows families to continue their memorial trends, or to create new ones which surpass geographical boundaries.

What is particularly interesting about these sites is that not only do they provide for the long-term memorialization of the war dead, but do so with the understanding that objects and memories will remain important keepsakes within the home. The 'British Jews in the First World War' website contains pages filled with basic curatorial information about how to preserve different

[73] Serge ter Braake, 'Between History and Commemoration: The Digital Monument to the Jewish Community in the Netherlands', in Chiel van den Akker and Chiel Legêne (eds.), *Museums in a Digital Culture: How Art and Heritage Became Meaningful* (Amsterdam, 2016), 104–6.

[74] Tony Walter, 'Communication Media and the Dead: From the Stone Age to Facebook', *Mortality* 20:3 (2015), 226.

[75] Claire Langhammer, Lucy Noakes, and Claudia Siebrecht, 'Introduction', in Langhammer, Noakes, and Siebrecht, *Total War*, 10.

types of objects. It warns against people handling metal without gloves, of dip-tarnish removers, and against cleaning the items at all.[76] This kind of practical advice about how to care for a family archive is significant, as it is one of the few large family digitization projects that openly recognizes that these items are going to physically stay within family homes as valued objects. Instead of regarding the online site as a way of preserving the items through a digital reincarnation, 'British Jews in the First World War' instead recognizes the inherent value of these items as family objects, and helps to preserve them for future iterations of the family.

The family memory of the First World War is now almost exclusively captured through online spaces. 'Antiques roadshow' collection drives, which digitize family objects, have been popular since they were first run by the Oxford University Great War Archive in 2008.[77] The model was highly successful and has since been used by various institutions such as Europeana 1914–1918 and the People's Collection Wales, who also allow people to take photographs of their objects and upload them, without professional assistance. These sites have generally helped to cement understandings of war as white-male-based and pathos-laden.[78] In part, this might be because the accompanying information tends to be lost in these online sites. The ability to read the words of donors is essential to understanding how and why families want their histories to be preserved in museum collections. When that information is detached from objects, the meaning of the gesture, although it can often be inferred, is lost.

This has rather serious implications for the sites as digital repositories. On an individual level, families can tell narratives that go against received cultural understandings of war, but when asked by an institution to donate wartime items, pre-existing biases come to the fore. Addressing British cultural memory of the First World War, a 2014 report produced by the British Council highlighted that UK public knowledge of the war's international aspects and its aftermath was limited, recommending that the centenary offered 'an opportunity to share a fuller understanding of the war'.[79] A post-centenary

[76] British Jews in the First World War: We Were There Too, 'How to preserve your family treasures: a how to guide for the preservation of different types of artefact' https://www.jewsfww.uk/family-treasures-640.php [Accessed 11.01.2020].

[77] University of Oxford, 'The Great War Archive: Introduction', http://ww1lit.nsms.ox.ac.uk/ww1lit/gwa [Accessed 09.04.2021].

[78] Ann-Marie Foster and James Wallis, 'The Memorial Afterlives of Online Crowdsourcing: "Lives of the First World War" at Imperial War Museums', *Public History Review* 30 (2023), 89–104.

[79] British Council, 'Remember the World as Well as the War: Why the Global Reach and Enduring Legacy of the First World War Still Matter Today' (University of Exeter, Exeter, 2014), 3, 38.

report published in 2019 found that there was a rise in public knowledge about Indian troops participating in the war (rising from 44 per cent of the British public knowing of their involvement to 71 per cent in 2018), though there was still little public knowledge of Kenyan troops and their involvement (from 22 per cent in 2014 to 38 per cent of the British public being aware of this in 2018).[80] During the centenary there were a wealth of community projects which highlighted the involvement of global majorities in the war; however, general knowledge remains patchy, with the 2019 report recommending that awareness of the diverse backgrounds of soldiers needs to be increased in predominantly white areas.[81]

While these sites are undoubtedly of memorial significance for the donors, problems around the elevation of certain narratives appear pervasive within a number of First World War collection drives. 'The Welsh Experience of the First World War', a crowdsourcing project run by the National Library of Wales, determined that people tended to bring in information that largely focused on soldiers, despite their calls for information about the home front.[82] A focus on male soldiers, in particular, is another facet of the gendered understanding of war which continues to dominate British cultural history. This brings us back to gendered ideas about war memory, where older women are likely to describe male accounts of war when prompted about family experiences, obscuring the roles that women played in wartime.[83] The fact that the donation of items by families only corresponds to war narratives they are familiar with means that the collections as a whole are skewed. If people think of the First World War as white-male and Western Front focused, these are likely to be the family histories that will be offered to the site.

This bias is shown quite starkly in the data presented in the 'Lives of the First World War' site. Here, while the names of Black, South Asian, and East Asian men who served during the war are featured on the site, their 'stories' and 'additional evidence' sections are nowhere near as populated as their white-soldier counterparts. The majority of the histories collected in 'Lives' pertained to white soldiers who fought on the Western Front. Through this collection, whole swathes of combatants, support troops, auxiliary workers, and nursing personnel have had their role in history reduced. Working-class

[80] James Wallis, 'Capturing Commemoration: Reflections on the Centenary of the First World War' (University of Essex, 2019), 9.

[81] Wallis, 'Capturing Commemoration', 9.

[82] Lyn Lewis Dafis, Lorna M. Hughes, and Rhian James, '"What's Welsh for Crowdsourcing?" Citizen Science and Community Engagement at the National Library of Wales', in Mia Ridge (ed.), *Crowdsourcing our Cultural Heritage* (London, 2014), 149.

[83] Noakes, '"My husband is interested in war generally"', 617.

women's war experiences, of all ethnicities, are under-represented on these sites. In the Imperial War Museum's 'Lives of the First World War' digital collection only seventeen munitions workers have details of their lives recorded.[84] Due to a lack of formal memorial items, remembrances of people who have not been traditionally recognized as equal wartime actors are still hidden.

For those whose family member fits the 'classic' idea of war, these sites are clearly of memorial importance. Public engagement with the dead through online initiatives to detail their lives and remember their names allows individuals to claim their dead in a more public way than ever before. Through digital memorialization people can adopt ancestors, including people with whom they share no blood or matrimonial ties, and make them part of their future family narrative. These rediscoveries, or continuities, of remembrance mean that an individual who was on the cusp of falling out of family memory is resuscitated. With an online memorial, or site where discussion of their death can be returned to, how will they continue to be a part of family history? Will they simply be subsumed into cultural memory only or will the two forms of memorialization run alongside each other? These are not static images stored on a physical site, but can be accessed from around the globe, offering an unprecedented opportunity for family and cultural memory to engage with each other in a new way. In a generation or two it will be clear if these new-found digital ancestors are the first in a new wave of cultural and family memory joining to remember ancestors online. Presented en masse, they bolster national understandings of the war. Individually, they represent a way of sharing a known past, or reconnecting with the previously unknown. The modern memory of the First World War is one that is plural, digitally engaged, and publicly visible.

Conclusion

The cultural memory of the First World War and the memory of large disasters developed along strikingly different historical trajectories. By the early 1990s, the cultural memory of war was fixed and family memories of the individual dead became intertwined with popular understandings of the war which emphasized tragic narratives of soldiers on the Western Front.

[84] Imperial War Museum, 'Lives of the First World War', search for 'munitions' and 'munitionettes', https://livesofthefirstworldwar.iwm.org.uk/searchlives/munition/filter/type%3Dagent/?page=4; https://livesofthefirstworldwar.iwm.org.uk/searchlives/munitionette/filter [Accessed 02.02.2021].

The memory of mining disasters remained strong in public understandings of mining communities. While local communities and families remembered the disaster dead, only notable disasters had any effect on the public imagination. Official commemoration of the dead was absent, and memorials to disaster were prolific in the 1980s and 1990s, commemorating large losses of life that had not been recognized with stone monuments until that point. Yet war and disaster communities both have a digital presence. The internet has allowed families to publicly reconnect with their war and disaster dead while forming communities of transgenerational loss, although the institutionalization of war loss means that these are the memories that will likely stand the test of time, leading to an increasingly skewed understanding of British family memory cultures.

While family memories can and do push against these sweeping memories of tragic events, they are prey to cultural influences upon them. With the deaths of those who could give countercultural testimony, the cultural memory of war seeped into family consciousness. The advent of online communities of loss and digital collections of family material rearticulate these tragic narratives, taking them back through the family and into the public sphere once again. Family memory, which already shared a porous boundary with cultural memory, was both influenced by and began to influence cultural memory when presented as a homogenous mass of individual family histories. Over the course of the centenary, institutions privileged histories of certain family events and experiences, legitimizing some families' experiences while holding others at a distance. In time, this will likely dictate that family memories held within institutional settings, in any form, will outlast those that remain solely in the family.

The relationship between the emotionally freighted cultural memory of the war, the military-service-based national commemorations, and individual family histories is complex. What differences in memory highlight particularly well is that the memory of family loss is complicated and highly nuanced. It is changeable, adaptable, political, and alters with each successive generation. Its symbiotic relationship with cultural memory means that it is constantly in flux. Yet, for all that this is true, family members do weave events into their greater histories which occupy a fixed moment in time, and can tell us something about how people in the past were remembered by their relatives. Memories of individuals are kept within objects, and successive generations may lay claim to them in ways that their current owners may not imagine. This poses questions for future memory formation. If people can reclaim the experiences of their First World War relatives online, in what ways will technology continue to alter our relationship with the dead? Only time will tell. But this fusion of commemoration, family memory, and cultural memory is one which is only going to get greater with time, and will pose difficult questions for historians of the family for some years to come. Perhaps this is fitting. In life people are not easily slotted into neat categories, so why should their memorial afterlives be any different?

Family Mourning After War and Disaster in Twentieth-Century Britain. Ann-Marie Foster, Oxford University Press.
 DOI: 10.1093/9780191968129.003.0007

Conclusion

After sudden death in war or disaster, parents, siblings, spouses, lovers, children, and more distant relations and friends had to work out how to grieve. They did so by drawing on a rich variety of existent death practices, but theirs were tinged with otherness. The families of the dead were often denied access to a corpse, and to choices over burial rights, while dealing with an increased amount of death-based bureaucracy. The memorials that they created were imbued with additional meaning because of this lack of agency elsewhere. The choice of whether to use a photograph, the memorial verse selected, and who these items were sent to all formed part of an intimate network of mourning, which respected the traditional dissemination of news about the dead. Families were denied their domesticated understanding of death, and by re-domesticating it they managed the emotions attached to these 'abnormal' and highly traumatic deaths.

Throughout the early twentieth century the state slowly assumed the family's responsibilities for dealing with death. Antemortem measures to identify the dead were rapidly developed in the first two decades of the century. This ran in tandem with the increased regulation and bureaucratization of death. After disaster, deaths were registered by local authorities, who also organized mass burials on behalf of the families of the dead. In wartime, the War Office and various military bureaucrats assumed this role. The regulation of the corpse was, in the overwhelming majority of cases, undertaken by those outside of the family. The families of the mining disaster dead might be lucky to receive the body of their dead back into the home—this was denied to them in particularly destructive disasters, and increasingly so over the course of the twentieth century as mortuaries became more common. Very few families of the war dead received their bodies, or had any sort of influence over their grave. Instead, servicepeople were buried and reburied by the state, who allowed families a scant sixty-six characters to personalize their grave (although families did attempt to personalize the graves in other ways well into the interwar period).

Public expressions of grief by the family after disaster deaths helped set the tone for how the dead of the First World War were to be publicly grieved. These families married traditional memorial practices, such as the creation of memorial ephemera, with the recognition that theirs was an unusual and highly tragic death. This positioning of the dead as different was in use before the First World War, and helped families to understand how they might frame their dead in socially accepted ways after loss in wartime. All family members could be involved in this activity. Primary mourners were often parents and spouses, but all family members, and even friends, were involved in the production of memorial items. Different communities of people helped shape commemorative items, from a niece who collected letters from the friends of her aunt to the friends who posted In Memoriam notices. In wartime, sweethearts gained extra visibility, and these women, either part of the family or not depending on the attitudes of their never-to-be parents-in-law, also mourned through objects. Mourning was supported by the state through sweetheart brooches, and items sent home, although reminiscence with friends and family remained of paramount importance to the bereaved.

Families of all classes engaged with the creation of personal memorials immediately after the loss of a loved one. This ranged from poor families, who might only have a single photograph to offer a memorial pamphlet, to wealthy ones who might commission a memorial book. Household shrines, which featured pictures and objects, formed focal points of domestic memorialization, and were married with personal rituals which allowed the bereaved to mourn their dead. From handcrafted memorial plates, which merged print and paint, to the display of photographs with poppies attached to the frames, the interwar period showed a rich and long-lasting memorial culture, which allowed families to display their grief within the home.

This was a porous activity, and print culture, ephemera, and domestic memorialization enmeshed to create remembrances which ranged from the extremely private to the quasi-public. Working-class families posted death notices and In Memoriams to local newspapers, while upper-middle and upper-class families could do this on a national stage. People invited others into their homes, and decided on the level of grief they wanted on display, from a working-class family's hand-sewn Next of Kin Memorial Plaque pouch to an upper-class family's cleverly designed shuttered frame for the same mass-produced memorial item. Itinerant workers engraved memorial glasses to the disaster dead in Northumberland and families created memorial plates in South Wales. These household items were elevated into memorial objects in inventive and personal ways, turning commonplace domestic items into objects of memory.

Wary that the scale of loss meant that families needed a personal yet national memorial item, the state attempted to influence domestic memorialization in wartime through the creation of the Next of Kin Memorial Plaque.

This proved popular, with the mass manufacture of frames springing up to support this memorial form. For all that some families highly valued their plaque, others did not engage with it in any meaningful way, and people domesticated or ignored this memorial object accordingly. What were intended as non-religious memorials, which drew on loose ideas of sacrifice in wartime, were woven into domestic memorial practices, and, due to the materials they were made from, survive in many family collections to the present day.

In part, the history of memorial items is a history of collections and their role in mass memory formation. Many items owned by poorer mining families were destroyed in the 1930s and 1940s and leave a legacy of loss, not just of the deceased but of the items crafted in their memory. However, running alongside stories of material loss is also a history of the creation of collections. The First World War was an outlier in public donations of mourning material to the Imperial War Museum. This nationally crowdsourced collection was remarkable in its scope, even more so for the agency it reveals in bereaved wartime families. People from all classes donated memorial items to the museum. Working-class families were initially discouraged from donating items relating to dead men, which makes their efforts all the more poignant. They claimed equity with those the museum was more happy to represent, creating a community of the dead which the working class were as entitled to as any other family. However, this parity of treatment was not shared across gendered lines, and the Women's Work collection struggled to achieve equal recognition with the men's collections.

Generational shifts in the composition of the family members involved in the care of the dead meant that those who had lost a family member in the first four decades of the twentieth century grappled with radically different memory cultures. The Imperial War Museum, a prominent cultural memory institution, quickly set the tone for what was to be nationally remembered. Women's deaths were largely written out of the war narrative, despite attempts to recognize their loss. Memory-building initiatives, such as the collection of family mourning material, taken alongside national commemorative acts, meant that the memory of the First World War became culturally fixed in a way that the memory of disaster was not. Disaster deaths were instead commemorated locally, many with only a monument created in the late twentieth century. During the centenary families of the disaster dead stepped forward to pay tribute to their ancestors through social media sites, but were not given access to the types of mass memory-building platforms that the families of the war dead were.

Above all, families were resilient in the face of sudden death. Bereaved families negotiated state, official, and social conventions, amidst a backdrop of public interest, to carve out a space to remember their dead. Although there were general trends in mourning and commemoration which were followed, the families of the war and disaster dead were not a homogenous group. Every loss was a blow to individual families, and, as their attempts to individualize the dead show, each loss left the memory of a person, with their own personality, habits, and name. Although these individualizing traits were largely erased through a lack of control over bodies and burial rights, they were accessible in the home. In the case of the First World War they were re-nationalized through engagement with external memorial activities in museums. People domesticated their loved one's deaths, constructing legacies of family loss which emphasized the individuality of the dead. Families left a trail of memorial material that shaped individual, family, and cultural memories of mass death events in the twentieth century, leaving legacies of loss that bore witness to the inventive ways families chose to communicate their grief.

Family Mourning After War and Disaster in Twentieth-Century Britain. Ann-Marie Foster, Oxford University Press.
 DOI: 10.1093/9780191968129.003.0008

APPENDIX

List of Disasters Mentioned in this Book[1]

Wales

1901 Senghenydd mining disaster, South Wales. 81 men died when there was an explosion in the mine.

1913 Senghenydd mining disaster, South Wales. 440 workers died (including one rescuer) from an explosion of gas (firedamp), which set fire to loose coal dust.

1927 Marine Colliery mining disaster, South Wales. 52 workers died in a gas (firedamp) and coal explosion.

1934 Gresford mining disaster, North Wales. 266 workers died after an explosion ignited a fire.

England

1908 Washington Glebe mining disaster, North-East England. 14 workers were killed when coal dust and gas (firedamp) caught alight.

1909 West Stanley mining disaster, North-East England. 168 workers died when gas (firedamp) caught fire and exploded.

1910 Wellington mining disaster, North-West England. 137 workers died due to an explosion and fire caused by the ignition of gas (firedamp).

1910 Pretoria mining disaster, North-West England. 344 workers died in an explosion of gas (firedamp) and coal dust.

1917 Silvertown munitions explosion, London. 73 people died during an accidental explosion of TNT.

1918 Chilwell munitions explosion, Midlands. 134 workers were killed during an accidental explosion of TNT.

1931 Bentley Colliery disaster, South Yorkshire. 45 workers died in a gas explosion (firedamp).

Scotland

1915 Quintinshill railway disaster, South-West Scotland. 226 people died when three trains rapidly crashed into each other.

1918 Stanrigg mining disaster, Central Scotland. 19 men died when moss and water broke into the mine.

[1] Please note this is not an exhaustive list of the disasters that occurred in Britain in the early 1900s.

Bibliography

Archival, Museum, and Unpublished Sources

Beamish Museum: GS 20.2.92, GS 04.08.2010, 1982-192.2, L.141, F.245, 2006-58.13.
Big Pit National Coal Museum: 2003.189.
British Library: Tab.1174.aa.2.
Brunel University London Archives and Special Collections, Burnett Archive of Working Class Autobiographies: J. H. Armitage, 'Twenty Three Years or The Late Wary of Life and Living by "The Exile" '; Lottie Barker, 'My Life as I Remember It'; Miss M. Collisson, 'Memories of a Country Rectory'; Jean Nettleton, 'Autobiographical Letter'.
Commonwealth War Graves Commission: efiles, WG 783 Pt. 1.
Dumfries and Galloway Archives: D37524.
Durham Light Infantry Collection: 4090, 2567/2, 2149/1, 2013.10.1+2.
Glamorgan Archives: DWAW33, Elizabeth Saunders.
Gwent Archives: D3335.5.
Imperial War Museum: 'Lives of the First World War' digital collection, Eph.C. INMEM K.3100-K.08., EN1/3/DEA/(003-3), EN1/1/PHO/(27-47), K,98/1562, Q31113, HU 82199.
John Johnson Collection of Ephemera: Funerary Box 3.
Mass Observation: Mantelpiece Directive 1937; MO Autumn 2014.
National Maritime Museum: AGC/S/27, HIS/8.
National Coal Mining Museum: YKSMM:1999.88, YKSMM:1999.90; YKSMM:1992.1404, SR59.
National Museum of Ireland: HE:EW.4147.
National Railway Museum: 1976–7973.
Newham Archives: Silvertown Box 1.
Oxford University: First World War Poetry Digital Archive.
Public Record Office Northern Ireland: D1618/15/15, D3019/1/5.
Richard Burton Archives: SC177/1.
South Wales Coalfield Collection: MNA/PP/35/53(12), VID/18.
St Fagans National Museum of History: 46.316.12, 58.418.15.
British Jews in the First World War: We Were There Too: digitized collections.
Whitehaven Archive: TCNB 6-71.
Women's Archive Wales: WaW0355.

Private Collections

Courtesy of Harry Taylor and Alastair Fraser.

Newspapers and Periodicals

Acton Gazette, The Auckland Times, Birmingham Gazette, The Carlisle Journal, Chronicle Live, Consett Chronicle, Cumberland News, Daily Mail, The Daily News, Daily Sketch, Doncaster Chronicle, Dumfries and Galloway Standard & Advertiser, Durham Chronicle, Durham Chronicle & Chester-le-Street Chronicle, Durham Chronicle & Seaham Weekly, Durham County Advertiser, East London Observer, Evening Chronicle, The Evening Standard, Farlam Hall Journal, Illustrated Chronicle, Northern Echo, Perthshire Advertiser, The Railway Gazette, Thomson's Weekly News, The Times, West Cumberland Times, Western Mail, Whitehaven News, The Woman's Dreadnought.

Acts and Regulations

Births and Deaths Registration Act 1836.

Births and Deaths Registration Act 1874.

Registration of Births, Deaths and Marriages (Army), 1879.

Coal Mines Act 1911.

HMSO 'Field Service Regulations Pt. II Organisation and Administration 1909, Reprinted with Amendments 1913' (London, 1913).

HMSO, 'The King's Regulations and Order for the Army 1912 Reprinted with Amendments Published in Army Orders up to 1st August 1914' (London, 1914).

HMSO, 'Summary of Accidents and Casualties Reported to the Board of Trade by the Several Railway Companies in the United Kingdom, During the Three Months ending 30th June, 1915' (London, 1915).

HMSO, 'Various Amendments and Reprints of Amendments to the King's Regulations Published Between 1916 and 1921', (London, 1920).

House of Commons Digital, Culture, Media and Sport Committee 'Lessons from the First World War Centenary: Thirteenth Report of Session 2017–19' (2019).

Published Sources

[Anonymous], 'Wellington Pit Explosion, May 11, 1910: Portraits of Entombed Men', (Whitehaven, [1910]).

[Anonymous], *Memoir and Letters of T.I.W. Wilson, M.C. Captain Manchester Regiment* (London, 1917).

Bishop, Alan, and Bostridge, Alan (eds.), *Letters from a Lost Generation* (London, 2004).

Braine, Sheila E., *'That's for Remembrance': A Collection of Quotations for Present-Day Use, Suitable for Monuments, Mural Tablets, Memorial Wreaths and Cards, &c.* (London, 1918).

Brittain, Vera, *Chronicle of Youth* (London, 1981).

Bullock, Jim, *Bowers Row: Recollections of a Mining Village* (Wakefield, 1976).

Church, John, *'It's like old wine to see you again, lass': An Account of the 1931 Bentley Colliery Disaster* (Doncaster, 1991).

Dalton, Lilian, *Harry: Schoolboy and Soldier* (London, 1919).

Geare, William Duncan, *Letters of an Army Chaplain* (London, 1918).

Hill, Susan, *Strange Meeting* (Harlow, 1989).

Jones, Lewis, *Cwmardy* (Cardigan, 1937).

Kenyon, Frederic, *War Graves: How the Cemeteries Abroad will be Designed* (London, 1918).
Kerry, Ann, *Connie's War: a young girl's life in the munitions factory at Gretna in the Great War of 1914–18 told in letters home to her family with additions by her daughter Ann Kerry* (Gwynedd, 2005).
Kipling, Rudyard, *The Graves of the Fallen* (London, [1919]).
[Leighton, Marie Connor], *Boy of My Heart* (London, [1916]).
McCallum, A., 'In Memoriam Verses, Texts, &c.' (Newcastle, [1914]).
Mineworkers' Federation of Great Britain, 'Gresford Disaster: Report of the speech by Sir Stafford Cripps, K.C. at the government inquiry into the causes of the disaster, April 15th, 16th and 17th, 1936' (London, 1936).
Muller, Nadine, and McDaid, Ailbhe, *War Widows' Stories: A Collection of Oral History Interviews* ([Liverpool], 2017).
Neasham, Eleanor, 'Consett Chronicle Art Memento' (Consett, 1909).
Parkinson, George, *True Stories of Durham Pit Life* (London, 1912).
Peel, C. S., *How we Lived then 1914–1918: A Sketch of Social and Domestic Life in England during the War* (London, 1929).
Redmayne, R. A. S., *Men, Mines and Memories* (London, 1942).
Stewart, H. F., *Francis Jenkinson, Fellow of Trinity College Cambridge and University Librarian: A Memoir* (Cambridge, 1926).
Tinson, Beverley, *The Gresford Letters: Aftermath of a Disaster* (Gwespyr, 2009).

Select Secondary Literature

Acton, Carol, *Grief in Wartime: Private Pain, Public Discourse* (Basingstoke, 2007).
Allan, Graham, and Crow, Graham (eds.), *Home and Family: Creating the Domestic Sphere* (Basingstoke, 1989).
Ashbridge, Sarah I., and Verdegem, Simon, 'Identity Discs: The Recovery and Identification of First World War Soldiers Located during Archaeological Works on the Former Western Front', *Forensic Science International* (2020), 1–14.
Assmann, Aleida, 'Transformations between History and Memory', *Social Research* 75:1 (2008), 49–72.
Assmann, Aleida, *Cultural Memory and Western Civilisation: Arts of Memory* (Cambridge, 2011).
Assmann, Jan, *Religion and Cultural Memory: Ten Studies*, translated by Rodney Livingstone (Stanford, 2006).
Basil Phillips, J., *Senghenydd: A Brave Community* (Gwent, 2002).
Batten, Sonia, 'Memorial Text Narratives in Britain, c.1890–1930' (Unpublished PhD, University of Birmingham, 2011).
Bourke, Joanna, *Dismembering the Male: Men's Bodies, Britain and the Great War* (London, 2009).
Brooks, John, and Cowan, William, *An Alarming Accident: Or Every Glass Tells a Story* (Newcastle upon Tyne, 2008).
Cannadine, David, 'War and Death, Grief and Mourning in Modern Britain', in Joachim Whaley (ed.), *Mirrors of Mortality: Social Studies in the History of Death* (London, 1981), 187–242.
Chamberlain, Mary, and Richardson, Ruth, 'Life and Death', *Oral History* 11:1 (1983), 31–43.
Church, Roy, *The History of the British Coal Industry, Vol. 3* (Oxford, 1986).

Cowan, William, 'Look Back in Wonder: Disaster Glasses Revisited: A Catalogue of Known Engravings within the "Northeastern Disaster Glass" Genre' ([Beamish], 2013).

Damousi, Joy, *The Labour of Loss: Mourning, Memory and Wartime Bereavement in Australia* (Cambridge, 1999).

Davies, Douglas, *Mors Britannica* (Oxford, 2015).

Dixon, Thomas, *Weeping Britannia: Portrait of a Nation in Tears* (Oxford, 2015).

Dutton, Philip, '"The Dead Man's Penny": A History of the Next of Kin Memorial Plaque', *Imperial War Museum Review* 3 (1988), 60–8.

Erll, Astrid, 'Locating Family in Cultural Memory Studies', *Journal of Comparative Cultural Memory Studies* 42:3 (2011), 303–18.

Fathi, Romain, '"We refused to work until we had better means for handling the bodies": Discipline and the Australian Graves Detachment', *First World War Studies* 9:1 (2018), 35–56.

Fell, Alison S., *Women as Veterans in Britain and France after the First World War* (Cambridge, 2018).

Forster, Eric, *Death Pit* (Newcastle upon Tyne, [1969]).

Frances, Hywel, *Miners against Fascism: Wales and the Spanish Civil War* (London, 2012).

Frawley, Oona (ed.), *Women and the Decade of Commemorations* (Bloomington, 2021).

Gitelman, Lisa, *Paper Knowledge: Towards a Media History of Documents* (Durham, 2014).

Grayzel, Susan, *At Home and Under Fire: Air Raids and Culture in Britain from the Great War to the Blitz* (Cambridge, 2011).

Green, Anna, and Luscombe, Kayleigh, 'Family Memory, "Things" and Counterfactual Thinking', *Memory Studies* 12:6 (2019), 646–59.

Green, Anna, 'Grandparents, Communicative Memory and Narrative Identity', *Oral History* 49:1 (2019), 81–91.

Green, Anna, 'Intergenerational Family Stories: Private, Parochial, Pathological?', *Journal of Family History* 38:4 (2013), 387–402.

Gregory, Adrian, *The Last Great War: British Society and the First World War* (Cambridge, 2014).

Gregory, Adrian, *The Silence of Memory: Armistice Day 1919–1946* (Oxford, 1994).

Hallam, Elizabeth, and Hockey, Jenny, *Death, Memory and Material Culture* (London, 2001).

Hallett, Christine E., *Containing Trauma: Nursing Work in the First World War* (Manchester, 2009).

Hamlett, Jane, *Material Relations: Domestic Interiors and Middle-Class Families in England, 1850–1910* (Manchester, 2010).

Hamilton, J. A. B., *Britain's Greatest Rail Disaster: The Quintinshill Blaze of 1915* (London, 1969).

Hetherington, Andrea, *British Widows of the First World War: The Forgotten Legion* (Barnsley, 2018).

Hill, Kate, *Women and Museums 1850–1914* (Manchester, 2016).

Hirsch, Marianne, *Family Frames: Photography, Narrative, and Postmemory* (Cambridge, 2002).

Horne, John, and Madigan, Edward (eds.), *Towards Commemoration: Ireland in War and Revolution 1912–1923* (Dublin, 2013).

Horne, John (ed.), *Our War: Ireland and the Great War* (Dublin, 2008).

Howarth, Glennys, *Death & Dying: A Sociological Introduction* (Cambridge, 2007).

Hughes, Anne-Marie, 'Death, Service and Citizenship in Britain in the First World War' (Unpublished PhD, University of Manchester, 2009).

Hurdley, Rachel, *Home, Materiality, Memory and Belonging* (Houndmills, 2013).

Jalland, Pat, *Death in War and Peace: Loss and Grief in England 1914–1970* (Oxford, 2012).

Jalland, Pat, *Death in the Victorian Family* (Oxford, 1996).
Jeffery, Keith, *Ireland and the Great War* (Cambridge, 2000).
Jupp, Peter C., and Gittings, Claire, *Death in England* (Manchester, 1999).
Jupp, Peter C., and Howarth, Glennys, *The Changing Face of Death: Historical Accounts of Death and Disposal* (Houndmills, 1997).
Kafka, Ben, *The Demon of Writing: Powers and Failures of Paperwork* (New York, 2012).
Kavanagh, Gaynor, *Museums and the First World War: A Social History* (London, 1994).
King, Laura, 'Remembering Deceased Children in Family Life: The School Case of Poor Harold (1920–31)', *History Workshop* Journal 93:1 (2022), 225–44.
King, Laura, *Family Men: Fatherhood and Masculinity in Britain, c.1914–1960* (Oxford, 2015).
Kramer, Anne-Marie, 'Kinship, Affinity and Connectedness: Exploring the Role of Genealogy in Personal Lives', *Sociology* 45:3 (2011), 379–95.
Kuhlman, Erika, *Of Little Comfort: War Widows, Fallen Soldiers, and the Remaking of the Nation after the Great War* (New York, 2012).
Laidlaw, Roger, 'The Gresford Disaster in Popular Memory', *Llafur* 6 (1995), 123–46.
Laqueur, Thomas, *The Work of the Dead: A Cultural History of Mortal Remains* (Princeton, 2018).
Lieven, Michael, *The Universal Pit Village 1890–1930* (Llandysul, 1994).
Lloyd, David, *Battlefield Tourism: Pilgrimage and the Commemoration of the Great War in Britain, Australia and Canada, 1919–1939* (Oxford, 1998).
Loez, André, 'Tears in the Trenches: A History of Emotions and the Experience of War', in Jenny Macleod and Pierre Purseigle (eds.), *Uncovered Fields: Perspectives in First World War Studies* (Leiden, 2004), 211–26.
Longworth, Philip, *The Unending Vigil* (Southampton, 1967).
McCartney, Helen B., 'The First World War Soldier and his Contemporary Image in Britain', *International Affairs* 90:2 (2014), 299–315.
McCartney, Helen B., *Citizen Soldiers: The Liverpool Territorials in the First World War* (Cambridge, 2005).
Macdonald, Charlotte, and Leniham, Rebecca, 'Paper Soldiers: The Life, Death and Reincarnation of Nineteenth-Century Military Files across the British Empire', *Rethinking History* 22:3 (2018), 375–402.
Maynard, Linda, *Brothers in the Great War: Siblings, Masculinity and Emotions* (Manchester, 2020).
Moriarty, Catherine, '"Though in a picture only": Photographs and Commemoration', in Gail Braybon (ed.), *Evidence, History and the Great War* (New York, 2008), 30–47.
Noakes, Lucy, *Dying for the Nation: Death, Grief, and Bereavement in Second World War Britain* (Manchester, 2020).
Noakes, Lucy, '"My husband is interested in war generally": Gender, Family History and the Emotional Legacies of Total War', *Women's History Review* 27:4 (2018), 610–28.
Noakes, Lucy, Langhammer, Claire, and Siebrecht, Claudia, *Total War: An Emotional History* (Oxford, 2020).
Pedersen, Susan, 'Gender, Welfare, and Citizenship in Britain during the Great War', *American Historical Review* 95:4 (October 1990), 983–1006.
Pollard, Michael, *The Hardest Work Under Heaven: The Life and Death of the British Coal Miner* (London, 1984).
Reeve, Michael, *Bombardment, Public Safety and Resilience in English Coastal Communities during the First World War* (London, 2021).
Rickards, Maurice, *The Encyclopaedia of Ephemera* (London, 2000).
Roberts, Elizabeth, 'The Lancashire Way of Death', in Ralph Houlbrooke (ed.), *Death, Ritual, and Bereavement* (London, 1989), 188–207.

Roper, Michael, *The Secret Battle: Emotional Survival in the Great War* (Manchester, 2009).

Roper, Michael, and Duffett, Rachel, 'Family Legacies in the Centenary: Motives for First World War Commemoration among British and German Descendants', *History & Memory* 30:1 (2018), 76–115.

Routledge, Gordon L., *Black Wednesday: An Account of the Wellington Pit Disaster, Whitehaven, in the Year 1910* (Carlisle, 2011).

Routledge, Gordon L., *The Sorrows of Quintinshill* (Wigton, 2002).

Russell, Gillian, *The Ephemeral Eighteenth Century: Print, Sociability, and the Cultures of Collecting* (Cambridge, 2020).

Saunders, Nicholas J., and Cornish, Paul (eds.), *Contested Objects: Material Memories of the Great War* (Abingdon: Routledge, 2009).

Selway, David, 'Death Underground: Mining Accidents and Memory in South Wales, 1913–74', *Labour History Review* 81:3 (2016), 187–209.

Silk, Natasha, 'Witnesses to Death: Soldiers on the Western Front', in Martin Kerby, Margaret Baguley, and Janet McDonald (eds.), *The Palgrave Handbook of Artistic and Cultural Responses to War Since 1914: The British Isles, the United States and Australasia* (London, 2019), 147–61.

Smyth, Hanna, 'The Material Culture of Remembrance and Identity: South Africa, India, Canada & Australia's Imperial War Graves Commission Sites on the First World War's Western Front' (Unpublished PhD, University of Oxford, 2019).

Strange, Julie Marie, *Death, Grief and Poverty in Britain, 1870–1914* (Cambridge, 2005).

Streeter, Penny, 'Symbolic Jewels: The Military Sweetheart Brooch in Wartime Britain' (Unpublished PhD, University of Sussex, 2018).

Stuart, Natalie Ann, 'The Memory of the Spanish Civil War and the Families of British International Brigadiers' (Unpublished PhD, De Montfort University, 2001).

Tarlow, Sarah, *Bereavement and Commemoration: An Archaeology of Mortality* (Oxford, 1999).

Thom, Deborah, 'Making Spectaculars: Museums and how we Remember Gender in Wartime', in Gail Braybon (ed.), *Evidence, History and the Great War* (New York, 2008), 48–66.

Todman, Dan, *The Great War: Myth and Memory* (London, 2005).

Toulson, Ruth E., and Newby, Zahra (eds.), *The Materiality of Mourning: Cross-Disciplinary Perspectives* (Milton, 2018).

Tradii, Laura, '"Their dear remains belong to us alone": Soldiers' Bodies, Commemoration, and Cultural Responses to Exhumations after the Great War', *First World War Studies* 10:2–3 (2019), 245–61.

Wallis, James, '"Great-grandfather, what did *you* do in the Great War?" The Phenomenon of Conducting First World War Family History Research', in Bart Ziino (ed.), *Remembering the First World War* (Abingdon, 2015), 21–38.

Walter, Tony, *On Bereavement: The Culture of Grief* (Buckingham, 1999).

Wellington, Jennifer, *Exhibiting War: The Great War, Museums, and Memory in Britain, Canada, and Australia* (Cambridge, 2017).

Whitmore, Lucie, '"A matter of individual opinion and feeling": The Changing Culture of Mourning Dress in the First World War', *Women's History Review* 27:4 (2018), 579–94.

Williamson, Bill, *Class, Culture and Community: A Biographical Study of Social Change in Mining* (London, 1982).

Williamson, Stanley, *Gresford: The Anatomy of a Disaster* (Liverpool, 1999).

Wilson, Ross, 'The Burial of the Dead: The British Army on the Western Front, 1914–1918', *War & Society* 31:1 (2012), 22–41.

Winter, Jay, *Sites of Memory, Sites of Mourning* (Cambridge, 1995).

Winter, Jay, *The Great War and the British People* (Houndmills, 2003).

Woodham, Anna, King, Laura, Gloyn, Liz, and Crewe, Vicky, 'We Are What We Keep: The "Family Archive", Identity and Public/Private Heritage', *Heritage & Society* 10:3 (2017), 203–20.

Woodhead, John, *The Bentley Pit Disaster: Friday 20th November 1931* (Doncaster, 1991).

Woodhead, John, 'Essay in Oral History: The Bentley Colliery Disaster', *Labour History Review* 31 (1975), 66–92.

Woollacott, Angela, *On Her Their Lives Depend: Munitions Workers in the Great War* (Berkeley, 1994).

Index

Since the index has been created to work across multiple formats, indexed terms for which a page range is given (e.g., 52–53, 66–70, etc.) may occasionally appear only on some, but not all of the pages within the range.